# PERSUASIVE BUSINESS PROPOSALS

## Writing to Win More Customers, Clients, and Contracts

### THIRD EDITION

## TOM SANT

**AMACOM**

AMERICAN MANAGEMENT ASSOCIATION
New York · Atlanta · Brussels · Chicago · Mexico City · San Francisco
Shanghai · Tokyo · Toronto · Washington, D. C.

This publication is designed to provide accurate and authoritative information in regard to the subject matter covered. It is sold with the understanding that the publisher is not engaged in rendering legal, accounting, or other professional service. If legal advice or other expert assistance is required, the services of a competent professional person should be sought.

LIBRARY OF CONGRESS CATALOGING -IN-PUBLICATION DATA

Sant, Tom.
   Persuasive business proposals : writing to win more customers, clients, and
   contracts / Tom Sant — 3rd ed.
      p. cm.
   Includes index.
   ISBN 978–0–8144–1785–0
1. Proposal writing in business. 2. Persuasion (Rhetoric) I. Title.
   HF5718.5.S26   2012
   658.15′224—dc23                                                        2011052025

**About AMA**

American Management Association (www.amanet.org) is a world leader in talent development, advancing the skills of individuals to drive business success. Our mission is to support the goals of individuals and organizations through a complete range of products and services, including classroom and virtual seminars, webcasts, webinars, podcasts, conferences, corporate and government solutions, business books, and research. AMA's approach to improving performance combines experiential learning—learning through doing—with opportunities for ongoing professional growth at every step of one's career journey.

Printing number

10 9 8 7 6 5 4 3 2 1

# For Susan...

*who accepted the most important proposal of my life*

# Contents

# SECTION THREE:
## The Art of the Part: Where to Put Your Effort

# SECTION FOUR:
## How to Manage the Process Without Losing Your Sanity

# Preface

THIS EDITION OF *PERSUASIVE BUSINESS PROPOSALS* has been thoroughly revised to reflect changes in the world of work that affect proposal writing and, more important, to incorporate lessons I have learned from working with some wonderful clients.

The basic principles of persuasion have remained consistent from the first edition onward, but thanks to insightful client feedback I have developed more effective ways to explain those principles. For example, the NOSE pattern that I present in Chapter 5 is an important instance of finding a simpler, more memorable way to communicate the key concept of persuasive structure. Likewise, the characterization of bad writing into the four categories of Fluff, Guff, Geek, and Weasel—an idea that I first presented in *The Language of Success*—has proved so popular in workshops and speeches that I decided to bring it to *Persuasive Business Proposals*, too.

The use of technology has exploded, moving us from the local area network to the cloud, and by collaborating with clients who are themselves at the forefront of information management I have learned how to use that technology to make the proposal writing task easier. I feel extremely fortunate to have the opportunity to work with proposal experts at Microsoft, Cisco, CIBER, Booz Allen, Thomson Reuters, Qvidian, and other leading high-tech firms. Technology can transform the way we work, as evidenced by the rise of virtual proposal operations on a global scale in recent years. But technology can also exert new pressures on the bidding process and the proposal writer, too. I have tried to address these new realities in this edition.

Other clients have been wonderful partners in exploring new ways to maximize the effectiveness of their proposals in a business environment in which the proposal is critical. Among those clients I am particularly grateful to are Kaiser Permanente, ISS, Wells Fargo, BNP Paribas Real Estate, and Rabobank.

One of the best things that can happen in business is the experience of having a client become a friend. I feel honored that many of my clients and colleagues are also now valued friends: Pat Coburn, Martin Doyle, Bill Geddy, Tom Graver, Michael Fedynyshyn, Marci Glennon, Brian Vass, Peter Ankerstjerne, Sandy Pullinger, and many others.

My wife, Susan Hirsch, and my son, Chris Sant, have provided intelligent, smart, yet kind feedback on the manuscript. Thank you for making the book better than it would have been without you. That said, its shortcomings are mine alone.

# Section I

## Seven Deadly Sins

# 1 A Good Proposal Is Hard to Find . . . But It's Worth Looking

I ONCE POSED WHAT I THOUGHT WAS A RHETORI-cal question to a group of sales and marketing people at a large engineering firm: "What's a good proposal?" From the back of the room came an answer: "One that's done!"

He was kidding, of course. Most of us recognize that just because a proposal is finished doesn't mean it's any good. Or that it will do the job.

**So . . . what is a good proposal?**

That seems like an easy question, but many businesspeople find it difficult to answer.

For one thing, they tend to confuse proposals with other kinds of documents or they want the proposal to do double duty. They want it to function simultaneously as a contract, a work order, or a bill of materials. Or they fail to understand the proposal's purpose. They think it's about giving the customer a ton of information. Or they lose sight of their audience and start writing to themselves. They forget that the jargon and acronyms and assumptions that they use around the office with their colleagues are incomprehensible to a prospect. Finally, some salespeople, even sales managers, treat the proposal as a checkbox item on the overall sales process diagram. Did demo? Check! Submitted proposal? Check!

Unfortunately, unless you have a clear understanding of what a good proposal is, the document you deliver may end up doing more harm than good. Although a great proposal by itself seldom wins a deal, a bad proposal can definitely lose one. Treating the proposal as a nuisance or a pro forma submission that doesn't really matter can raise doubts in the customer's mind about your commitment and competence. It can throw obstacles in your path and prolong the sales cycle.

So before we define what a proposal is, let's make sure we know what it's *not:*

**It's not a price quote.** If all you tell the decision maker is the amount to be paid for what you've offered, you've reduced what you're selling to the level of a commodity. You've said, in effect, "All products or services of this type are basically the same. We have nothing unique to offer. Choose based on cost." Unless you are always the lowest-priced vendor, that's not a strong position to take. Even if you are the lowest-priced vendor, it's still not a strong position, since four out of five large-scale deals go to a vendor other than the one offering the lowest price.

**It's not a bill of materials, project plan, or scope of work.** In technical and engineering environments, people sometimes take the attitude that if they just explain all the details of the proposed solution very clearly and accurately, the customer will buy. Actually, giving the customer a detailed bill of materials or project plan may have exactly the opposite effect. You've just given them a shopping list so detailed they may decide to do the job without your help. Ouch!

**It's not your company history, either.** Oddly enough, a sizable number of the proposals we see—more than 30 percent!—start with a company history. There seldom is a good reason to do this. Most company histories are not very interesting.

(However, I do remember one that was pretty intriguing. A regional telephone company used the same executive summary in every proposal, no matter what they were selling, and the opening line of that executive summary was a showstopper: "Founded in 1874, two full years before Alexander Graham Bell invented the telephone, we have a long history of service to the community." I don't know about you, but every time I saw that sentence, I immediately started wondering what they were doing for those two years. Were they sitting around in an office above the post office, waiting for Alexander to write? "Hey, guys, it works! Start selling!")

Several years ago I was contacted by a top-level executive at a major manufacturer of industrial systems. He said, "Some of our engineers attended a course you gave on proposal writing and said you have some unusual ideas. Would you like to come in and talk?"

His company produced proposals worth millions and millions of dollars every quarter, competing to win business from corporations worldwide in markets such as aerospace, automotive, and heavy equipment manufacturing, among others. It was justifiably famous as a technology leader, but its win ratio had been declining rapidly. By the time the company contacted me, it was winning fewer than one in ten of the deals it went after. Some members of management complained that they were the victims of cheap, knockoff products produced in countries where labor costs were significantly lower. Others, however, thought they needed to sell the total value of the company's products and services more effectively. Part of that job would be done by their proposals. And that was where I was supposed to help.

My concern was that the company seemed to have real difficulty in bringing about meaningful change. In spite of the red ink splashing over the company's books, senior management continued to cling tightly to traditional ways of doing business. That's not unusual, of course, and I don't want to minimize how difficult it is to change standard practice. "We've always done it this way" is often offered up as the ultimate argument as to why changes are not necessary. But in the business world, as in the natural world, the inability to adapt to cope with an evolving environment is a Darwinian recipe for extinction.

After talking with my contact, the vice president of sales and marketing, I agreed to lead a two-week task force on proposals. Specifically, I was to help them define a new process that would cut the time it took to produce a proposal from weeks down to days. Second, I was to help them figure out a way to make their proposals more persuasive so their anemic win ratio would go up.

The following week I entered a conference room to meet for the first time with a half-dozen handpicked engineers, project managers, account managers, and other professionals. The vice president of engineering, the executive who owned the proposal process, introduced me by saying, "This is Tom Sant, who's going to show us where to put the fancy words and pretty pictures."

*Hmmm,* I thought. *I think I see where part of the problem comes from.*

"Actually, I'm not very interested in fancy words or pretty pictures," I said. "I'm interested in showing customers that what you're offering is what they ought to buy. So let's get started by agreeing on some basic terminology. First of all, from your perspective, how would you define a proposal?"

That seemed like a harmless enough question at the time. But to my surprise we spent a long time wrestling with it. What became increasingly clear was that these people—all of whom had written numerous proposals—couldn't define one.

Eventually, we agreed that a proposal is a sales document. If it doesn't lead to an agreement to do work together, the proposal has failed. The proposal's job is to move the sales process toward closure.

That's it. It's not complicated.

A good proposal helps you win. It helps your company make money by convincing people to choose you to provide the products and services they need. The proposal positions what you have as a solution to a business problem, and helps you justify your price, even if it's slightly higher than your competitor, by showing that you will provide superior value.

To do the proposal-writing job well, you need to make sure that your proposal is persuasive, accurate, and complete. Unfortunately, lots of proposal writers invert the order of those qualities, producing proposals that are bloated with detail and scarcely persuasive at all.

## The Value of Your Proposals to Your Clients

Most of us have had the experience of presenting to a client and hearing the decision maker say, "Wow, that sounds great! It looks like it's exactly what we need."

(At this point our hearts start soaring.)

"Why don't you put together a proposal for us and we'll take a look?"

(That sound you hear is our dashed hopes crashing to the floor.)

Why do customers ask for a proposal when the recommendations we have made in person so obviously make sense? Because the proposal has value for them. A proposal helps the decision maker:

- ✦ Compare vendors, offers, or prices in order to make an informed decision
- ✦ Clarify complex information
- ✦ Make the buying process more "objective"
- ✦ Slow down the sales process
- ✦ Solicit creative ideas, become educated, or get free consulting

Buying products or services can be tough, especially when the decision maker must deal with an array of options, lots of conflicting claims, and little practical knowledge of the area under consideration. "Getting it in writing" is the traditional way to deal with this problem.

*Comparing vendors, offers, or prices.* Are you the only vendor this prospect is talking to? It's also possible you are being asked for a proposal so that your recommendations, pricing, and evidence can be compared to a competitor's.

*Clarifying complex information.* Do you sell something so complex that it would take you more than ten minutes to explain it to your mother? If so, it's possible some of your prospects don't understand it, either. A proposal gives the nontechnical customer a chance to read, analyze, ponder, get help, and eventually understand.

*Adding objectivity to the buying process.* It seems odd, but some people don't want to buy from people they like. They're afraid that if they really like the salesperson, they will somehow make a bad decision based on rapport or friendship.

As a result, these individuals often issue detailed RFPs (an RFP is a request for a proposal) and establish elaborate scoring tables. They weight various parts of the proposal, and then assign points to each of your answers. To add a further element of "objectivity," they may divide the price you are quoting by the number of points you receive to determine which vendor has the best dollar/point ratio. It can get pretty complicated.

You are also likely to see this approach when a company hires a consultant to prepare the request for proposal and evaluate all the submissions. Consultants often use point systems to score and eliminate candidates. These complicated scoring systems reassure the client that the consultant's recommendations are made without prejudice. (They also suggest how wise the client was to hire an expert to handle such a difficult process.)

*Slowing down the sales process.* Sales is a little bit like dating. The very word "proposal" applies to the final stages of both activities. In the early stages of both, the process can take on a momentum of its own. We get excited, we become enchanted with new possibilities, and we rush forward.

Asking for a written proposal slows down the sales process. The buyer figures that it will take several days, maybe even a couple of weeks, for the salesperson to put together a proposal, which gives the buyer time to think about this decision calmly, to weigh the options, to determine whether this opportunity will look as good the morning after as it does right now.

*Soliciting creative ideas, becoming educated, or getting free consulting.* One way busy decision makers can establish the base of information they need is to ask for proposals. By asking a potential vendor for a proposal, they find out what's available. They learn whether this vendor is somebody they want to work with. A quality proposal suggests that the vendor is likely to do a quality job.

What about companies who issue RFPs or who request proposals with no intention of buying anything? They may be looking for free consulting, and to the extent you answer all of their questions, you may be giving away the solution or providing a template that the company can use to solicit bids from your competitors. Or the company may solicit bids in an effort to "beat up" the existing vendor or in hopes that someone will submit a crazy, lowball price that it can use to extract concessions from the incumbent. Does this happen? Yes. Is it ethical? No. This doesn't happen frequently, but it happens often enough that you should be careful. Sometimes people really don't know any better. They may not realize that the proposal you submit is a valuable piece of intellectual property. On the other hand, some of the people who pull these stunts will do anything they can get away with. (In Chapter 12, we'll discuss how you can protect your proprietary interests.)

The important point is that you should always do some prudent qualifying before committing yourself to the time and effort of writing a quality proposal. There is no use submitting your offer to someone who has no budget, no authority, or no real interest in working with you. And there is even less point in submitting to someone who may take your material and share it with your competitors.

## The Value of Your Proposals to You

Look at your proposals broadly as part of your overall sales and marketing activities, rather than narrowly as the formal means of responding to a specific request. Seen that way, a proposal can help you build your business in ways that extend far beyond winning the immediate opportunity to which you are responding.

**The proposal as a sales tool.** The proposal's most important job is to help you sell something, such as specific applications, products, projects, or services. (In the nonprofit realm, it should help you obtain funding in support of your mission and objectives.) To go a little further, though, a high-quality, carefully constructed proposal can help you:

+ *Sell on value instead of price*
    Use your proposal to move the decision maker's focus away from price and toward such measures of value as lower total cost of ownership, higher reliability, superior customer support, documented technical superiority, or some other message that separates you from your competitors.

+ *Compete successfully without having personal contact with every member of the decision team*
    In larger opportunities you are likely to find that a team makes the buying decision. You may never have the opportunity to meet every member of the team in person. A good proposal can speak to each member of the team on your behalf, helping make your case.

+ *Demonstrate your competence and professionalism*
    It's probably not fair and it's definitely not logical, but almost

everybody does it: we judge a vendor's ability to deliver goods or services from the quality of the proposal they submit. Our conscious, rational mind tells us that spelling and grammar have nothing to do with the ability to provide help desk support for our PC users, yet we find those misspellings and grammar mistakes raising doubt and uncertainty in our mind.

✦  *Offer a bundled solution*
The customer may ask you for a proposal for basic bookkeeping services. In your proposal, though, you can add a brief description of your tax preparation services, too, as part of a total solution. That may differentiate you from other bookkeepers who submit a proposal, or it may just make the customer aware that you also do taxes. Both of those are good things.

✦  *Sell the "smarter" buyer*
Smart buyers want to gain as much as possible while spending as little as possible. If you don't show them how much they gain by choosing your recommendations, they will inevitably focus on the other half of the equation: spending very little. A good proposal always contains a compelling value proposition to show the smarter buyer why you are the right choice.

✦  *Sell a complex, technical product to nontechnical buyers*
Speaking the buyer's language is an important part of winning that person's trust. A flexible proposal process can help you communicate effectively even if the customer lacks in-depth knowledge of what you're offering.

**The proposal as a marketing tool.** Try this exercise. Take a clean sheet of paper and list all of the characteristics, traits, or attributes that are typically associated with your company. List them all, positive and negative. Be honest, but be fair. (I find that people are often extremely hard on themselves and their companies, demanding a level of perfection that their own customers don't expect. Try to get out of your head and see things the way a customer or prospect probably does.)

A short list might look something like this:

Expensive
High-quality, experienced vendor
Significant local presence
Not interested in small jobs or small clients

This list is mixed. The question is how to use your proposals to capitalize on the positives and to minimize or overcome the negatives. One of the negatives on the list is the fact that clients perceive your company to be expensive. Why not counteract that impression by issuing an unsolicited letter proposal every time you have a price reduction? In particular, you would want to target current customers whose costs can be reduced if they adopt the recommendations you're proposing.

One of the positives on the list is that your company has a significant local presence in your market. Why not play that up in each proposal you submit to local customers? Remind the decision maker that he or she will be dealing with a vendor who can respond to problems or concerns immediately, in person, rather than sending someone in from out of town in a day or two or providing support over the phone.

**The proposal as a means of influencing clients.** Each time you write a proposal, think in terms of your account plan for that client. Where do you want the relationship to be in six months? In a year? In five years? What intermediate steps are necessary to get the relationship there? Perhaps you're currently providing system software to the client, but you'd also like to take on developmental projects. Or perhaps you are currently providing call center operations on an outsourced basis, but you'd eventually like to expand that to include outbound telemarketing and help desk functions, too. Rather than seeing proposals as a kind of test that's been set up by clients to exclude you, start looking at them as tools and opportunities to help you accomplish your objectives. That's the real challenge you face—not merely getting the proposal done on time so you can check it off your list of sales "activities," but making sure that when it is done, it accomplishes exactly what you want.

Of course, it's one thing to recognize the challenge. It's quite another to know what to do about it. For that, keep reading!

# 2  Recognizing Reality

THE BEST WAY TO RECOGNIZE WHAT WORKS IN A sales proposal and what doesn't is to put yourself in the position of a buyer. Unfortunately, many salespeople and full-time proposal writers never have the chance to review proposals and make business decisions based on them.

So let's try it. Read the following executive summary—don't spend more than a few minutes on it—and answer one question: *Does it go on the "keeper" pile or does it go on the "discard" pile?* That's the first question your prospects are probably going to ask, because it's likely that the reviewers are staring at a pile of submissions much larger than they can reasonably handle. So let's put you in the role of a buyer, too. Let's say you own a small business called "ACES," a regional chain catering to golfers and tennis players consisting of seven stores located in three states. The local bank you were doing business with for years was recently acquired by a big international bank. Fees have gone up; service seems to have gone down. As a result, you're open to changing banks. It's just that it has to be worth it to you, because you're not naive about the hassle involved in changing banks.

---

### • EXECUTIVE SUMMARY

We at Mainstay National Bank are pleased to respond to the request for proposal issued by ACES (hereinafter "Customer"). We recognize that a strong banking relationship is a fundamental perquisite for success in today's economy for all types of businesses, governmental institutions and agencies, healthcare facilities, educational institutions and nonprofits, as well as high net worth individuals and others. We acknowledge that the process of identifying a new financial institution is a complex undertaking and we believe that our enclosed response demonstrates Mainstay's commitment and ability to satisfy all of Customer's requirements for cash handling, treasury management, payroll, and investment services.

Mainstay National Bank has achieved a well-deserved reputation for meeting the needs of a diverse range of customers with global business requirements and for providing a caliber of service and quality of people that make us a leader in the industry. Our comprehensive portfolio of financial products and innovative approach to delivering accurate and reliable service is one way we are different from our competitors.

Mainstay believes that we have the capabilities and experience to provide the level of service Customer requires. Mainstay occupies a strong position in the financial industry and corporate banking market in particular with particular strengths in lending, clearing, and electronic banking services. Our head office, located in New York City, is a major player on the global foreign exchange and money markets, which means we are well suited to meet the demands of international business. We can provide accounts in more than 30 different currencies and can initiative ACH credits to 20 foreign countries via the SWIFT network.

Mainstay prides itself on delivering a consistent quality of service and this commitment has been recognized with a rating of Outstanding by the prestigious American Banking Council. To support our ability to deliver quality service, even during periods of unusual stress, we have established two fully certified disaster recovery centers, located in Denver, Colorado, and Wheeling, West Virginia, respectively, with fully redundant systems and a fail-safe mechanism for cut-over in the event of natural disaster or other disruption to service.

Mainstay National Bank is a well-managed and financially sound institution that has shown growth in profitability year over year for more than a decade. We are well positioned to offer best-of-breed treasury management solutions to meet your needs. We will provide you with a professional Account Management Team that will handle your day-to-day contacts with Mainstay. The Team consists of well-seasoned professionals who have dozens of years of banking experience meeting the needs of customers like you.

In the following sections, a response is provided to each question Bountiful Healthcare has asked. Mainstay has answered each question to the best of its ability and we believe we have interpreted the meaning of each question in the sense intended by Customer. If we have misinterpreted any questions, we apologize in advance for any misunderstanding. Please note that this proposal is preliminary and does not constitute a binding offer to deliver services nor a final statement of pricing. We look forward to partnering with you.

What do you think? Was that a keeper or does it get stuffed in that round filing cabinet under your desk?

An overwhelming majority of people—more than 95 percent—say they would toss it in the trash. And they offer some very compelling reasons:

✦ There is absolutely no evidence that this is anything other than a generic piece of boilerplate. It mentions the prospect's name only once (compared to referring to themselves either by name or by pronoun more than twenty times) and then uses the rather insulting term "Customer" from that point forward. What's worse, they actually call us by the wrong name in the last paragraph. They refer to "Bountiful Healthcare," which must have been the last prospect to get this jewel of an executive summary.

✦ The first five paragraphs all start with "Mainstay" or "Mainstay National Bank." That creates a self-centered tone that communicates volumes about the bank's real attitude toward "partnering" with customers.

✦ The executive summary never addresses our business issues. In fact, it doesn't appear that they even know what kind of business we're in.

✦ There is no value proposition and there are no meaningful differentiators. What do we gain from choosing Mainstay? Are their rates lower? Do they have specific products that will help us tie our stores together? They don't offer any relevant differentiators, either. They do mention that they have an excellent disaster recovery program and that they are successful in doing business internationally, but neither of those strengths matters to us.

✦ This is not easy to read. There are some overly long sentences: the second one is 40 words long, and the third is 42. It also includes a couple of acronyms—ACH and SWIFT—that we don't recognize right away.

✦ It contains a typo in the second sentence—"perquisite" instead of "pre-requisite"—and says they will "initiative ACH credits" rather than "initiate."

✦ The executive summary is an odd combination of chest thumping ("Mainstay prides itself . . ." and "well managed and financially sound . . ." among other bits of marketing fluff) and equivocation ("Mainstay believes that . . ." and "we apologize in advance . . ."). Yuck.

✦ In spite of vague, general claims of excellence, Mainstay provides very little evidence of their success. And their clichés sound silly: "well-seasoned professionals" (sprinkled with salt and a little oregano, maybe?) and "best-of-breed treasury management solutions" (which sounds like something you'd find at a dog show).

There are other reasons to reject this executive summary, but that's more than enough to justify tossing it on the discard pile. And here's the saddest observation of all—it's pretty typical of what people submit. On the bell curve of executive summary quality, from total embarrassment to brilliance, this one is hunkered right in the middle.

When we read an executive summary or watch a sales presentation in the role of buyer, we quickly recognize whether the message is working. That's because we read or listen with specific intentionality: as a buyer, we want to hear or see the right content in the right order so that we can make a decision. We want the proposal to address our business issues or problems right away, so that we're confident the recommendations will be relevant. Then we want to see that solving the problems will actually be worthwhile. We look for a clear, specific solution that is tied back to solving the problem and delivering the results, and finally we look for evidence that the vendor can deliver on time and on budget.

We instinctively look for these things when we read with the intention of making a choice, yet most people don't put them into their proposals when they write with the intention of selling. For some reason we seem to know what we like in a persuasive message when we're buying, but we become utterly clueless when we're trying to sell. One problem is lack of training. Very few colleges show students how to write an effective business proposal. English composition classes may include an assignment or two on "the persuasive argument," but that typically has no relation whatever to the kind of writing people do in the real world. Sometimes technical writing classes will include a few perfunctory comments about proposal writing, but technical writing is not a particularly good base for learning how to write persuasively. In technical writing, a student is taught to focus clearly and accurately on the subject, but proposal writing requires focusing on the customer.

Once they are in the workforce, people are often thrust into situations where they must perform quickly. There's no time to study or learn. Just get it done!

In short, many proposals are fatally damaged by one or more of the "seven deadly sins" of proposal writing. When you look at this list of "sins" you probably agree that nobody would choose to write proposals containing mistakes like these. And yet people do it time and time again. In the next chapter we'll briefly discuss why they commit these sins.

### The Seven Deadly Sins of Proposal Writing

1. No focus on the client's business problems and payoffs.

2. No persuasive structure—the proposal is an "information dump."

3. No clear differentiation of this vendor compared to others.

4. No compelling value proposition.

5. No impact, no highlighting—key points are buried.

6. No orientation to the audience—overuse of jargon, too long, or too technical.

7. No credibility—misspellings, grammar and punctuation errors, use of the wrong client's name, inconsistent formats, and similar mistakes.

# 3 Rushing to the Exits

RECENTLY I WAS SPEAKING AT AN INTERNAtional conference sponsored by Microsoft. The attendees were integrators, developers, and resellers from all over the world. More than 800 people attended, so I asked them a question I've asked many other groups over the years:

"How many of you honestly enjoy writing proposals?"

Fewer than 20 hands went up. And that response is fairly typical. Most people do not like writing proposals.

## Four Exit Strategies You May Have Seen

Because they dread writing proposals and perhaps because they know they don't do them very well, people have found creative ways of avoiding the job. These are "exits" toward which they rush to avoid the hard work of writing a client-centered, persuasive proposal. You may recognize methods that some of your colleagues use. Maybe you have used them, too. Please stop—they don't work.

### Cutting and Pasting for Fun and Profit

The most popular way to avoid writing a good proposal involves cloning. Proposal cloning. Have you ever seen a salesperson stride impatiently into the office and demand, "Who has a proposal I can use?" He or she grabs an electronic copy of somebody else's proposal, does a global find/replace to change the former client's name to that of the new prospect, and then fires it off. The fact that the original proposal was to the Southern Regional Medical Center and the new proposal is to Oscar's Cigar Shop shouldn't matter, right? Of course, Oscar is probably a little confused when he sees his business referred to as the region's leading cancer center. But that's a minor detail, right?

We both know what happens when you cut and paste old boilerplate together. The proposal doesn't flow. The tone, and sometimes the formatting, jump around randomly. It doesn't address what the customer cares about. It sounds generic because it *is* generic. It may even contain embarrassing errors—such as calling the prospect by the wrong name— which can lose the deal. Delivering big slabs of boilerplate may actually be worse than delivering no message at all because the boilerplate will sound "canned" and will undercut the rapport you've created with customers.

Effective proposals, on the other hand, are built from a combination of content and insight. You must have something worthwhile to say and you must say it in a way that shows customers that it's relevant to them. That's not as hard as it sounds, and if you make the effort you will differentiate yourself from your competitors in a way that creates a dramatic and positive impression on the customer.

Effective salespeople do not deliver one message over and over. They do not treat customers as demographic units. They engage in conversations, they listen, and they view customers as individuals. They create proposals that communicate clearly and specifically to those individuals.

### Diving in the Data Dump

Another escape method that people sometimes use is the "data dump" approach to proposal writing. The author gathers up all the internal marketing documentation, product slicks, case studies, white papers, technical specifications, and anything else not clearly labeled "proprietary," forms it into a neat stack, drills three holes along the left-hand margin, and puts it all into a binder.

For obvious reasons that approach yields very little in terms of positive impact. Customers don't want bulk. They don't want irrelevant detail. And they don't want to do more work than is strictly necessary to understand your proposal.

Working with an IT integration firm, one that responds to complex RFPs for enterprise resource planning (ERP) systems, I urged them to cut their documents down. "Nobody has time to read this much," I told them, riffling the edges of an 800-page proposal. "Besides, the important part of your message is getting lost in a sea of verbiage. Make it shorter so the good parts are easier to find."

It took a bit of convincing, but they finally tried it. They wrote a proposal to implement an ERP system for a large city government that was much more concise and focused than anything they had done before. They submitted their proposal in person and felt humiliated when they saw that their proposal was dwarfed by the submissions of the leading professional services firms, who were also bidding. The competitors' bids were actually well over a thousand pages each, while theirs was less than 400. Well, as you probably guessed . . . their proposal *won*. Not only did it win, but when they attended the conference where the award was formally made, the city manager told them confidentially that theirs was the only proposal anybody could get through. "We just got lost in those others," he said. "They were like reading *War and Peace*. In the original Russian."

### Talking About What We Know and Love the Most

When people are under pressure, they tend to revert to what they know they do well. In the case of writing a proposal, what they know is their own stuff—their products, their services, their company history. And what they do well is to describe it. They write informatively, not persuasively.

Some years ago I was asked to evaluate the standard proposal used by a company that provided account management software tools. When I opened the file containing their executive summary, I found that the first word was their company's name. But it was actually worse than that. They had created an interesting logo in which their company name was written in a cursive script in a kind of arching pattern, the kind of design that might appear on an old fashioned baseball uniform. So in their executive summary, they had not merely started with their name, they had embedded their actual logo at the start of the paragraph. It was large, it was bold, it was eye-catching. And then they started the second paragraph the exact same way. And the third. And the fourth. It went on this way for three solid pages! And the content of the paragraphs was equally self-centered. They covered the background of the company, its revolutionary new web-based data handling model, interesting product features, and a list of the awards and accolades its technology had won. It contained full-color graphics showing the technical architecture of the company's product. The summary even contained brief bios of the three founders. The only thing it didn't have was any focus on the client.

If you submit a proposal that is filled with boilerplate text that focuses on yourself, you are giving the customer an *impersonal* experience. You are delivering a document that fails to acknowledge the customer's unique needs, values, or interests. Ultimately, you are undercutting the notion that you are offering a solution. Instead, you are providing the customer with a generic experience that suggests what you have to offer is a commodity—it's the exact same thing for everyone.

### Burying the Deal

While doing a consulting engagement with one of the most successful sales-training organizations in the United States, I had the opportunity to interview several of the firm's star producers. Think for a moment about who these people are. These are the best of the best—the top salespeople representing a top sales-training organization. All of them had stellar careers in selling professional services against tough competition. So I asked them how they handled proposals and RFP responses. Noses wrinkled. Lips lifted in sneers.

"I avoid them," one woman said. "Trying to get anybody to help on a big RFP is impossible. Announcing you have to respond to an RFP is like turning on the lights in a dark room and watching the cockroaches scatter."

They all preferred to sell a lot of small deals rather than a single million-dollar deal that involved a complex RFP response. One of them admitted that he hadn't bothered to go after a seven-figure contract with a major high-tech firm because the RFP was too complicated.

If you can close business without writing a proposal, you should do so. The fact is that writing a proposal can be a lot of work, sometimes involving tons of annoying detail. However, burying deals just to avoid writing a proposal is never acceptable. Besides, proposal writing can be extremely rewarding, both professionally and financially.

## Reaping the Rewards

Learning how to write a great proposal can be one of the most important business skills you ever acquire. It will enable you to communicate your solutions effectively and persuasively to your customers, your colleagues, and your own management. In doing so, you'll meet their needs for information and insight while achieving your own goals.

How much will it help? A survey of several hundred companies found that their win ratio increased by an average of 39 percent when they implemented the methodology I will show you in the remaining chapters. In some cases the improvements were even more dramatic: An international bank increased its win rate from 19 percent to 67 percent in one year just by changing the way the message in its proposals was presented. Other results have been equally dramatic: An international property management firm saw its win rate double. A training company won 11 out of 12 major opportunities using these techniques. A satellite communications firm lifted its win rate from just below 25 percent to just over 75 percent in the space of a year. And one of the world's largest IT consulting firms has won every deal they've gone after with the U.S. federal government for which we helped them create the right message the right way.

If results like these interest you, just keep reading!

# Section II

## A Primer on Persuasion

# 4    Understanding Persuasion

Persuasion is simply a form of communication that enables people to make decisions confidently. That's really all it is. Persuasion, in fact, is the flip side of decision making. When we are trying to persuade someone, that person most likely is trying to decide something. So if we can present the right content in the right order so that decision makers see we have the right solution, we will win and so will they.

## The Four Maxims of Success

The brilliant philosopher of language, Paul Grice, pointed out that all human communication must observe what he called four "maxims" in order to work. These maxims are particularly important when the purpose of our communication is to persuade.

**The maxim of quality.** When we communicate, we tell the truth. We do not say things for which we lack adequate evidence. This is the foundation of trust.

**The maxim of quantity.** We provide the audience with only as much detail as it needs. This can be a difficult maxim to adhere to, because we sometimes misjudge what and how much the audience needs to know. In regard to quantity, however, I urge you to live by the principle that less is better than more.

**The maxim of relation.** The statements we make are relevant to our audience. Observing the maxim of relation is often a matter of getting out of your own head and trying to get into the head of your audience.

**The maxim of manner.** Be clear. Avoid using obscure language, jargon, technical terms, and acronyms that the audience won't recognize. Avoid ambiguity. Be concise. Use words correctly and proofread carefully. The maxim of manner is so important that I wrote a whole book about it—*The Language of Success*—and have devoted Chapter 9 to the principles of clarity in this one.

Few people would argue with Grice's maxims. They represent a commonsense description of the fundamental principles that make it possible for human beings to communicate with each other. Are they enough, though?

In the following chapters, I will answer that question, based in part on empirical studies that range from neurolinguistics to economic behavior. We'll explore the essential best practices— the techniques that are critical to anyone's success.

# 5 Winning by a NOSE:

## *The Structure of Persuasion*

In an organizational setting, people write for one of three reasons—to inform, to evaluate, or to persuade. For each of these purposes, there is a structural pattern that will produce the best results. You can think of these structural patterns as templates for delivering content in the right order. Keep in mind, however, that these are not templates created by English teachers or document designers. Rather, they arise from the brain of the reader. They are part of our innate mental apparatus.

The human brain is hard-wired to look for content in a specific order, depending on what purpose we will make of the message. If you use the wrong pattern in organizing your content, you will get the wrong results. It's like trying to drive a nail with a screwdriver—you might eventually get the job done, but it's going to be a lot harder than it has to be. In Chapter 2, I asked you to read an executive summary and make one simple decision: is it worth keeping or not? By asking you to make a decision, I established intentionality in your reading process. You were approaching the task with the goal of making a decision, so you were looking for certain kinds of content in a very predictable order. If I had given you a different challenge, such as reading the executive summary to determine how many factual statements the bank made about itself, you would have looked for a different pattern. And you would have approached the task differently.

Information doesn't create momentum toward a decision. Persuasion does. Unfortunately, people are often most comfortable providing information, particularly when they are speaking or writing to an audience that knows almost as much about their topic as they do. (See Figure 5-1.) That doesn't work. We have to move out of our comfort zone and into the persuasion zone—a different structural pattern and a less-expert audience.

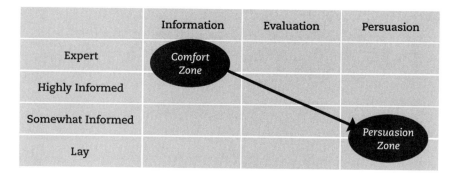

Figure 5-1. Move out of the Comfort Zone to Persuade Effectively

The purposes that govern informing, evaluating, and persuading are so different that using one mode when your purpose calls for the other will condemn your efforts to failure. So let's distinguish among the primary reasons people write in a business setting and look at how those different purposes require different approaches.

# Information

The first and most common reason people write is to inform. They're writing to share content with somebody who needs it. The ideals of informative writing are clarity and conciseness, and the focus is on transferring the information quickly and easily.

The best way to communicate informatively is to use the pattern taught in journalism classes: the funnel. (See Figure 5-2.) Start with the fact or set of facts most important to the reader. In journalism, that's often *who, what, when, where, why,* and *how*? Then go to the next most important fact. Then the third level of importance, the fourth, the fifth, and so on, until there is nothing left to say. By structuring your document this way, you allow your readers to stop reading as soon as they have seen enough.

The challenge in writing informatively is to figure out which fact is most important to the reader. Too often we assume that everybody will have the same orientation to the material that we have. But that can be a big mistake. Even a single reader is likely to have different interests in the same story. If you pick up a copy of the *Wall Street Journal*, you'll look for a different set of facts in the lead paragraph of an article than you would if you picked up a copy of *People* that contained an article about the same story. From one publication we expect a financial orientation, while the other will give us the human interest angle.

The most common mistakes in presenting information are writing chronologically, which usually leads to wordiness, or starting with facts that matter to the writer but not to the reader, which usually leads to confusion or false emphasis. Another error is to place important content at the end of an informational piece of writing. People tend to scan this kind of writing from the top down, so they bail out of the process when they think they have gist of it. They won't see the content you put at the end unless you work hard to highlight it.

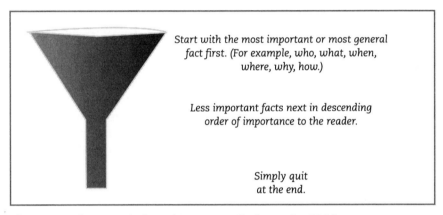

Start with the most important or most general fact first. (For example, who, what, when, where, why, how.)

Less important facts next in descending order of importance to the reader.

Simply quit at the end.

**Figure 5-2.** The Funnel-Shaped Structure of Informative Writing.

We use informative writing in proposals when we answer the simple, pro forma kinds of questions that often appear in RFPs—your headquarters location, names of top managers, or how many offices you have. Most of the time, these are just facts, not tactical differentiators that are going to help you win the business. When you believe the question being asked is simply a checkbox item, use informative structure to answer it.

## Evaluation

The second reason businesspeople write is to evaluate something or somebody. A performance appraisal, a competitive analysis, an appraisal of an asset—in all of these cases, simply presenting the facts is not enough. What people want to know is what you think, what your opinion or value judgment is.

When they are offering a professional opinion, people are trying to interpret what the facts *mean*. This is particularly true when the information being offered is being compared to another set of related facts. For example, consider what happens in a court case when one side calls in an expert witness. Such a witness isn't asked to establish facts about the case—"Where was the defendant on the night of July 15?" Instead, the expert witness is asked to offer an opinion about what a certain body of facts indicates: "On the basis of these facts, do you think the defendant is mentally competent?" "Do these actions match the accepted standard of care?"

The pattern for evaluative writing is depicted in Figure 5-3, in which an evaluation is compared to a hamburger. The point of the illustration is that you need a top bun (the introduction), a bottom bun (the conclusion), and lots of meat in the middle. By contrast, informative writing doesn't need an introduction to set the scene and it really doesn't require a formal conclusion. To write an effective evaluation, however, you must begin with an introduction, in order to define your subject—what (or who) you are evaluating—and the criteria on which you are basing your evaluation. Then you need to present your observations and evidence. Finally you need to offer your opinion. If you follow that structural pattern, your opinion will sound logical and your evaluation will be easy to follow.

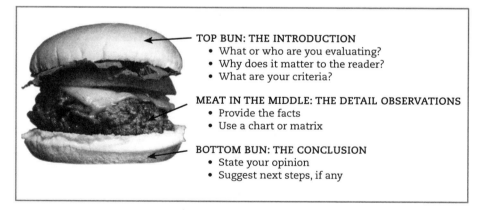

**TOP BUN: THE INTRODUCTION**
- What or who are you evaluating?
- Why does it matter to the reader?
- What are your criteria?

**MEAT IN THE MIDDLE: THE DETAIL OBSERVATIONS**
- Provide the facts
- Use a chart or matrix

**BOTTOM BUN: THE CONCLUSION**
- State your opinion
- Suggest next steps, if any

**Figure 5-3.** The Three-Part Structure of Evaluation.

Good examples of evaluative writing can be found in *Consumer Reports*. If you were thinking about buying a new camera or a refrigerator or snow tires, you could find articles there that would evaluate the various brands and models available. Because we trust the source, we usually skip the opening and middle and go right to the end of the article, which tells us which brand is the "best buy."

Sometimes, though, you get an evaluative report in which the opinion is shocking or doesn't make any sense. Suppose you are looking for an appraisal of a piece of real estate you own, perhaps to use it as collateral on a loan. Typically, a bank will want to get two appraisals of that property. You probably have a pretty good idea of what the property is worth, so if one of the two appraisals comes in at half the value of the other one, you'll immediately turn to the body of the report to find out why they are so different.

We use evaluative writing in proposals when we are asked questions that involve comparing two or more approaches. Sometimes the question will be worded to ask for "strengths and weaknesses in your opinion" of a particular approach, technology, or other element of the solution. I have even seen RFPs that ask you to indicate what differentiates you from your competitors. Using the evaluative structure enables you to set up the terms of comparison so that you offer a reasonably objective opinion based on rational assumptions.

## Persuasion

The third reason people write is to persuade. In this kind of writing you are trying to influence the audience so they are motivated to take action. Effective persuasion requires more than delivering a bunch of facts, and opinion alone isn't going to persuade a customer to buy. Instead, you have to structure the message so that what you write or say influences the audience.

Fortunately, the most effective pattern for persuasion is easy to understand and use. It consists of four steps. It's a straightforward process:

+ State the customer's needs, issues, or concerns.
+ Identify the outcomes the customer seeks.
+ Recommend a solution that solves the problem and delivers the right results.
+ Present evidence that you can deliver the solution on time and on budget.

That's it.

My clients began calling this the NOSE pattern because the four elements of persuasive structure—Needs, Outcomes, Solution, Evidence—create the acronym NOSE. So now I tell people that they can win by a NOSE if they use effective persuasive structure.

The four steps to persuasion embodied in the NOSE pattern are summarized in Figure 5-4.

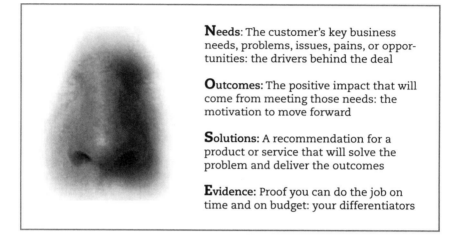

**Needs:** The customer's key business needs, problems, issues, pains, or opportunities: the drivers behind the deal

**Outcomes:** The positive impact that will come from meeting those needs: the motivation to move forward

**Solutions:** A recommendation for a product or service that will solve the problem and deliver the outcomes

**Evidence:** Proof you can do the job on time and on budget: your differentiators

**Figure 5-4.** The NOSE Pattern of Persuasive Structure.

Let's take a closer look at each element.

**First: the customer's Needs.** The initial step in persuading is to restate your understanding of the customer's needs, issues, or problem. Summarize their business situation briefly, focusing on the gap to be closed or the competency to be acquired or the problem to be solved.

By focusing on customers' pains, you gain their attention. In fact, they will probably be surprised that a vendor has actually listened to them closely. They will also be less anxious about moving forward, because they will see that you have defined the problem correctly. As a result, the solution you propose is likely to be sound. People approach the buying process with a lot of anxiety. *Will I waste my money? Will I waste my time? Will I damage my career by making a bad choice?* If your proposal starts with your company history, the buyer's anxiety level shoots up. But if you start with the customer's needs, immediately the buyer feels calmer and more confident about looking at your recommendations.

Research into the psychology of judgment and economic behavior by Daniel Kahneman and Amos Tversky led to what they called "prospect theory," an explanation of how people make decisions under uncertainty—or, in other words, in the real world. This work is the foundation of what is frequently called *behavioral economics* and resulted in Kahneman receiving the Nobel Prize in Economics in 2002. At the risk of oversimplification, we can say that prospect theory describes how people choose among alternative courses of action according to a reliable heuristic. In making a buying decision, customers typically follow a heuristic that poses three questions:

1. Are we getting what we need?
2. Is it worth it?
3. Can the vendor actually do it?

The first question grounds the decision in relevance. Does each alternative address something that the buyer thinks is important? The second question then poses the issue of utility: Is this the best way to spend our money, our time, our energy? Note that in asking this question, customers are not assessing the features and benefits of the various solutions. Instead, they're asking whether the problem itself is worth addressing. Will solving it pay enough dividends that the investment will yield a positive return? Finally, the last question addresses the issue of the probability of a successful outcome. How likely is it that this vendor will be able to deliver the solution? By answering these three questions in that order, you deliver a message that motivates the customer to say Yes.

The traditional view of human decision making, certainly since the rise of rationalism, is that human beings make decisions by following logical pathways. Some people do make decisions that way—Charles Darwin describes how he created a list of pros and cons for getting married and when the pros outweighed the cons decided to ask his cousin, Emma Wedgewood, to be his wife. (On the pro side he wrote that a wife would be "better than a dog anyhow.") But research done by Antonio Damasio, head of the University of Southern California Brain and Creativity Institute, has shown that emotions underpin decision making. In his book *Descartes' Error: Emotion, Reason and the Human Brain*, which is based on his studies of brain-damaged patients, Damasio shows that without the ability to generate emotions, we have no ability to make decisions. Accordingly, by first addressing Needs and Outcomes, you are flipping the emotional switch that will lead your customer to make a decision in your favor.

Sometimes people with a strong technical orientation—the kind of people who have been trained using materials that are rigorously informative in structure and who are most comfortable themselves writing informatively—are very suspicious of persuasion. They just want to get right to the solution. They think that's all that matters. However, by showing customers that you "get" it, that you listened to them and understood what they told you, you raise the level of the customers' confidence. You help them feel confident that what you propose will be appropriate for them.

**Second: the desired Outcomes.** This part of the persuasive structural pattern is probably a bit counterintuitive. After all, wouldn't it be logical to state the problem and then give the solution? The point to remember is that your goal is motivation. If you don't create a sense of urgency in the decision maker to go forward with your recommendation, you have not been successful. Most businesses are faced with dozens and dozens of problems or needs, most of which will never get solved. You don't want your solution to fall into this category. You want to create a strong motivation to move forward by showing your customers that the problems you are addressing are the ones that really should be fixed because of potential yield. You want them to see that the Outcomes, the return on investment or improvement in productivity or whatever, is so big that they can't afford to wait. And you need to do that right away, as soon as you have identified those Outcomes.

This is a key principle of Kahneman and Tversky's prospect theory: we see options that yield lesser outcomes as net losses and options that yield greater outcomes as gains. We pursue those courses of action that are most likely to yield the highest rate of return or the most value (what Kahneman and Tversky call "utility") and reject those that offer less. This is particularly true when we are making decisions on behalf of a group to which we belong. (We will discuss the relationship between decision heuristics and value in more detail in Chapter 7.)

Focus on their pain to get their attention; focus on their gain to get their commitment.

**Third: the Solution.** The heart of your proposal is, of course, your Solution. If you have first whetted the client's appetite for it by focusing on Needs and potential Outcomes, your client will be eager to hear your Solution. But many proposals stumble at this point.

The problem is that the presentation of the Solution often lapses into technical details and jargon, focuses on details rather than impacts, and comes across as self-centered because it never connects back to either the Needs or the Outcomes. The client still wants to know why you're recommending this approach or that product. What makes this the right way to go? How does it solve the key problems? Why is it the best way to deliver the results the client seeks?

Another problem is that most proposals don't actually recommend anything. They lapse into informative writing and merely describe products or services in flat, factual ways. To be a Solution, the products and services you are recommending must be linked to the customer's specific situation. "You indicated that one of the problems you are facing is declining value in your e-commerce transactions. To help increase transaction value we recommend . . ."

Also, when you recommend a solution, sound like you believe in it.

Say the words: *"We recommend* the immediate installation of LeadPoint asset management software." *"We urge you . . . " "We are confident . . . "* Don't be wishy-washy. Don't depend on telepathy to get your point across.

To solve the puzzle of the solution, write from the top down. In your first sentence focus on a general statement of what you are recommending as a means for solving the client's problem. The next sentence or two should explain the recommendation in functional terms. What will your solution do for the client? How will it work? Then make sure you have shown the linkage with the client's specific needs. To do that, explain which component(s) of your solution are intended to address each need, what positive impact each aspect of the solution will deliver, and finally cite a brief bit of proof—a reference, an award, test data, or some other form of objective validation—that substantiates your claim.

The following solution statement, which was written in the format outlined in the previous paragraph, will help you understand how to put these principles into practice.

---

To address your need for improved physical security in the office environment at your corporate headquarters in Pittsburgh we recommend an electronic security system that limits access to authorized personnel only. The access system will prevent anyone from entering your offices unless he or she first swipes an electronic ID badge through an automated card reader. We recommend the InVicta IronClad model 2100 Access Control system, which includes all the hardware and software necessary. At the heart of the system, the InVicta uses a comprehensive control panel, known as the "head end" hardware, and a software package that controls all access points, reads the ID cards, checks the database, and provides constant monitoring around the clock. We recommend this system because it matches your specific needs:

- *Budgetary compliance:* The total price for the InVicta system is more than $20,000 below the budget you have established. Other systems that use biometric data rather than card readers are much more costly without providing any more security. The InVicta's lower price will free up funds to cover installation and training, assuring a smooth roll-out. For example, when we installed an InVicta system for a large automobile dealership, the entire package cost, including all support services, was less than the hardware costs alone for competitive models.

- *Minimal disruption to workflow:* Your employees will find the ID card system easy to use and intuitive to learn. The benefit for you is that they will quickly accept the new system and will make very few mistakes in using it. As a result, your normal pattern of working will not be disrupted and there will be no impact on productivity. To indicate how easy this system is to learn, consider this: we installed a new access control system at a major Pittsburgh bank over a three-day weekend. When people arrived at work on Tuesday morning, management greeted them in the lobby, gave them their new ID cards, and showed them how to swipe the card reader for entry. From that day forward, the bank experienced only two access control problems out of more than 250,000 uses of the system!

**Fourth: the Evidence that you can do it.** The last step in persuasion is to provide Evidence that you can do the job. Basically, you are trying to show that you can and will keep your promises. You are providing proof that you can deliver the solution you have proposed on time and on budget. You want to convince the decision maker that this is your area of expertise. Sometimes your Evidence is intended to establish that your firm is financially stable, properly managed, and well prepared.

Providing Evidence is usually the part of the persuasive job that most proposals handle pretty well. But there are a couple of ways you can do the job better. First, you can be thoughtful in selecting your evidence, choosing items that are most likely to appeal to the specific decision maker and are most relevant to the opportunity. Second, you can present your evidence in the most effective way possible.

In Chapter 7 we'll deal with selecting the right evidence to support your value proposition, and in Chapter 16 we will cover the best ways to write typical kinds of evidence, such as team member resumes, case studies, company histories, and so forth. For now I just want to discuss briefly the "rules of evidence."

The first is that just because you have a particular bit of evidence you don't have to use it. Even though you have a snazzy, full-color map of North America showing all 78 of your company's office locations, don't use it unless it's relevant. If you're trying to sell to a company that also has numerous locations in the United States, Canada, and Mexico, and they closely match your locations, then it's relevant and helpful. If you're selling to a prospect who only has one location, forget it.

The second rule about choosing evidence is to consider the source.

There are three kinds of evidence—things you say about yourself, things your clients say about you, and things independent third parties say—and each has a different level of credibility.

Among the things you can say about yourself, you might include information about product features, about the members of your team, about your project management methodology, or about your quality control philosophy. Those things are relatively noncontroversial, and a prospective client could check for accuracy if he or she really wanted to. These forms of evidence help establish your competence, which is why the questions in an RFP often focus on eliciting this kind of information. They answer a key question in the decision maker's mind, namely, "Can these people really do what they claim?"

Another form of evidence you can offer about yourself—a type of evidence that helps minimize the client's sense of risk or enhances their perception of the value of your offering—focuses on measurable performance indicators and special financial terms. For example, you might provide information relating to unique contractual terms that you are offering. Or you might outline a "gain sharing" or "risk sharing" program based on specific performance guarantees or service level agreements.

The second source of evidence is your previous clients. What they're willing to say about you is often more convincing than what you say about yourself for the obvious reason that they presumably have nothing to gain from it. (Whether they do gain anything is a different issue, and many companies provide tradeoffs and concessions for clients who give them strong endorsements. All the same, no client has to say anything, so the fact that one is willing to, even if it involves inducements, is still significant.)

You can provide evidence to a new prospect from prior clients by including references in your proposal. Just make sure you check to make certain those clients are still happy with you. Sometimes yesterday's glowing reference becomes tomorrow's flaming lawsuit and you aren't even aware that there's a problem. You might also include testimonials, including images of letters of praise from previous clients.

One of the most convincing forms of evidence coming from a client is the case study. As long as your case study is from a client similar in nature to your prospect, who had a similar problem that was alleviated by a solution similar to the one you're proposing, and who achieved measurable positive results from your work—then you're in great shape. However, if your case study just rehashes the history of some project in chronological fashion, forget it. That's boring.

Case studies are usually the single most compelling form of evidence that a decision maker encounters. They have a lot going for them. For one thing, they appeal to what Robert Cialdini in his classic book, *Influence,* calls the "social proof" principle—other people have used this solution and benefited from it, so why not us? If the case study involves a well-known client, it may also benefit from what Cialdini calls the "appeal to authority." A big company or a huge government agency chose this vendor, so it must be good.

Finally, third-party evidence comes in the form of awards, rankings, recognition, articles, analyst reports, and so on. Although that form of evidence used to be the most convincing of all, the fact that so many analyst firms are willing to sell their "approval" to the highest bidder has made this form of recognition somewhat suspect in recent years. All the same, if you were named the "best place to work" or an "industry innovator" or "Five Star Quality Award Winner" or some such thing, take advantage of it when you can. That's still good stuff.

## The NOSE in Action

Let's take a look at what happens when we use our structure to create a persuasive message. First, here is an e-mail written to an internal audience. The author brought it to me in frustration. "This is really important," he said. "We need to do something. But when I make a recommendation it just gets ignored. What do you suggest?"

The following is his internal proposal.

---

*SAMPLE PROPOSAL*

---

**To:**     Bill Henderson
**From:**   Woolie Crofft
**Subject:** Data Base Software

Today Mike Hinger stopper to explain the software available from his company which could give our executives personal access to the corporate data base in a way that would provide information to facilitate the decision-making process.

There are all kinds of things wrong with this message, so many that it's difficult to begin to enumerate them. There's the vague subject line, the typo that transforms the verb into something that sounds like a Swedish surname ("Hinger-stopper"), the incredible sentence length, the use of nonspecific language ("personal access," "decision-making process"), and the fact that its chief organizing principle seems to be a loosely chronological stream of consciousness. But the most glaring problem, I think, is that it has no clear purpose to it. If you were Woolie's manager, Bill Henderson, your reaction to this e-mail would probably be a hearty "So what?" This message sounds like one of those worthless scraps headed "FYI," most of which end up being deleted from our inbox or tossed into the garbage. It certainly doesn't look or sound persuasive. It's not addressing a problem. It doesn't clearly recommend a solution.

Sadly, the author of this message told me how frustrated he was that "nothing had happened." "Management complains about these problems we have with the database," he said, "but then, when you make a recommendation on how to fix it, they just ignore you." He honestly did not perceive that his e-mail hadn't recommended anything, that it failed to propose a solution. He was surprised when I suggested that it could be clearer and more persuasive.

Proposals need to be organized in a way that clearly, effectively, *persuasively* communicates to the audience. They need to penetrate the noise and clutter surrounding the customer to make a strong point, which can appeal to the innate tendency people have to look for specific content in a specific order.

What happens if we restructure the writing using the NOSE pattern? Well, we immediately see some dramatic improvements.

## REVISED SAMPLE

**To:**     Bill Henderson
**From:**   Woolie Crofft
**Subject:** Improving Executive Access to the Database

Our executives need access to the corporate database. The information it contains will be invaluable in helping them develop strategies, make decisions, and respond quickly to changing market conditions. Unfortunately, they are currently blocked from obtaining that information by a number of system-related problems.

Software available from Hinger Associates will remedy the situation. It interfaces easily with our existing system, creating a user-friendly "shell" that allows even nontechnical people to select, format, and manipulate the data they need without affecting the database itself. I recommend we lease this software system for a six-month trial with an option to buy.

Mike Hinger, the developer of the system, indicated that installation will take about four days. He will provide all the necessary documentation and support. A six-month lease runs $2,500 a month, with the full amount credited toward the purchase price of $30,000. If this software offers even a modest increase in executive productivity—saving each member of the executive team just two hours a month, for example—it will pay for itself well before the trial period is completed.

Shall we proceed?

You can see the difference immediately. Notice how it gets right to the point in the subject line: Improving executive access to data. This is reinforced in the Need statement in the first two sentences: our executives need access to the database to make good decisions. Anyone who glances at this message will see immediately why it's important and what kind of problem it's trying to solve. Also, the solution is now clearly stated in the form of a recommendation: "I recommend we lease this software system . . . " No ambiguity there.

The final paragraph adds an extra fillip by providing a value proposition of sorts. It would be better if we had a bit more development in this area, perhaps, but at least the recipient's thinking has been turned toward impact.

# 6 Seven Magic Questions:
## *How To Develop a Client-Centered Message*

People Buy From People They Trust. And They tend to trust people who demonstrate specific qualities. To demonstrate how these qualities interact, we can express trust as a quasi-equation:

$$\text{Trust} = \frac{\textbf{Credibility x Rapport}}{\textbf{Risk}}$$

What this means is that for someone to trust us, we must demonstrate a high degree of expertise in our own field while also demonstrating good knowledge of the customer's business and industry. It's one thing to be recognized as an expert on social media. It's something else to be able to apply that knowledge to help customers achieve their goals, whether we're dealing with a consumer product, a healthcare organization, or a small college.

Most proposals (and sales presentations, too) focus first on establishing credibility. Unfortunately, that's the wrong move. We will get better results if we first pay attention to establishing or maintaining rapport and to minimizing the customer's perception of risk in doing business with us.

At the same time, we must be someone the customer likes doing business with. Dale Carnegie was right when he said that the more people like us, the more our influence grows. In terms of sales skills, we need to show up on time, return calls and e-mails promptly, pay attention, listen closely, smile, and show interest in the other person as a person, not just as a customer. In our proposals, we need to use the customer's name, personalize the message, focus on their needs, use their jargon, avoid the typical business clichés, and write in a natural, friendly tone. If they give us permission, we can also use their logo on the title page of our proposal and in the header or footer.

Finally, we need to minimize the other person's sense of risk in dealing with us. Risk in a business setting arises, among other causes, when we perceive that the other party is engaged in self-serving behavior. For example, suppose your doctor recommends a course of treatment and you later find out that (a) it is not the standard form of treatment for your condition, and (b) the doctor gets paid 400 percent more by the insurance company for that treatment than he or she would for using a more conventional approach. Do you still trust your doctor's judgment? Do you think this is someone who has only your best interests in mind? Or is the doctor prescribing a treatment regimen that primarily is effective in making the doctor's bank account healthier?

A similar problem arises when management insists on throwing extra products into a proposal, even though they have nothing to do with what the customer wants. "They need to know we offer these things," the manager will say. Really? Why? And what makes the proposal the right time to tell the buyer about these other product lines and services?

## The Primacy Principle and Cognitive Dissonance

All of us live by the *primacy principle*, the principle of first impressions. We assume that what we experience first is a good predictor of what will happen in the future. If you've ever taken a course in statistics, you know that this is not a methodologically sound approach to predicting the future. A sample of one is not statistically significant. All the same, we all do it. The impact of our firsthand experience is so vivid and convincing, it overrules logic.

The primacy principle also works in documents. A manufacturer of material handling systems developed a standard proposal, the first twenty pages of which consisted of a history of the company. Why did they do this? It's a Fortune 500 company, so it certainly didn't need to work that hard to introduce itself. What's worse, the history was boring. It was a litany of mergers and acquisitions, financial maneuvers, and so forth. It wasn't too hard to imagine potential clients leafing through all that verbiage, trying to find something—anything!—that addressed their own concerns.

How often have you abandoned a book after the first few pages failed to grab your interest? A notable research laboratory typically wrote proposals for grants that read like articles for technical journals. Each one plunged right in to discuss obscure technical issues. Never did the research being proposed connect to the granting foundation's mission or interests. As a result, the lab's success rate was unpredictable.

Such proposals address what the writer is interested in long before the proposals discuss the prospective client's needs and objectives, if they ever do. This is a big problem because people tend to notice the differences between themselves and others before they notice the similarities. If you are trying to sell me something, I do not notice that we are both middle-aged men, that we both have two children, that we both love to play golf, and that we both love golden retrievers. Yet I will have noticed that we work for different companies and that your job is different from mine. The differences make someone distrustful.

This is a variation on the psychological phenomenon known as *cognitive dissonance*. When Leon Festinger, a Stanford research psychologist, first articulated his theory of cognitive dissonance in 1956, he focused on what happens when people are confronted with information that contradicts closely held values. He found that people will ignore or even deny reality in order to hold on to political, religious, artistic, or other beliefs.

In the context of making a buying decision, therefore, people tend to assume that those who work for other companies cannot be trusted even though there may be significant evidence to the contrary. It's a big challenge for us as salespeople—and as proposal writers—to overcome that distrust. One effective way to do it is to show customers that we think the way they do and that our priorities are the same as theirs. Self-centered content does not achieve that goal. The whole proposal should be oriented toward the client, but it's particularly important in the executive summary.

One simple way to check whether your executive summary is client centered or not is to count how many times your company's name appears compared to the customer's name. If you're client centered, the customer's name should appear two or three times more often than that of the writer's company. Focus on the proposed client's business situation, the client's needs, their desired outcomes, and how your solution will match up against their expectations. If it's all about you, it's a bad executive summary. It will also help if you answer the following seven questions before you write.

## Seven Questions to Keep You Client Focused

To create a client-centered message, we need to demonstrate that we know the client. Answering the questions that follow in this section will help you to achieve this goal.

> ## Seven Questions for a Client-Centered Proposal
>
> 1. What is the client's problem or need?
>
> 2. Why is this problem worth solving?
>
> 3. What results does the customer seek?
>
> 4. Which specific result is the most important?
>
> 5. What products or services can I offer that will solve the problem and deliver the right results?
>
> 6. Of the solutions I can offer, which one is the best fit for this client?
>
> 7. Why are we the right choice?

If you are a proposal writer who supports a field sales organization, ask these questions of your colleagues in sales when they submit an RFP they want you to work on. Without knowing the answers, you can't give them the best possible support. If you meet resistance, point out that you don't want to undercut the work they've done during the sales process by delivering a boilerplate proposal. If they still aren't helping, maybe they haven't actually done any work during the sales process and don't know the answers. In that case, you should question whether or not the opportunity is "real."

Let's look at each of these questions in detail. Answering them effectively takes a bit of thought but it makes a huge difference to the success of your proposals.

### 1. What is the client's problem or need?

Sometimes the client issues a request for proposal that specifically states what they want:

*The FAA needs a course that will teach customer service and total quality principles to its management staff and hourly employees.*

*Smith, Goldblatt, and Wong, attorneys at law, are hereby soliciting bids for an office telecommunications system to be installed in the firm's new quarters no later than May 15 of this year. The system must provide the following features: . . .*

*The trustees of the Kallaher Group of Homes for the Aged solicit bids for an audit of all of the properties for the fiscal years 2002 and 2003.*

*Tom's Auto Parts seeks a system to manage the inventory of parts and equipment at all thirteen store locations. The desired system will use bar code data to maintain a current inventory of parts and will integrate with our existing MAS 90 accounting system to automatically update inventory as parts are sold.*

These are all pretty clear. The temptation is to immediately start responding in proposal form. That's not a good idea.

In the first place, the RFP almost never states the actual problem. Each of the preceding samples describes the general category of solution the client is seeking, but does not tell why they need it. As the late Tom Amrhein, one of the most successful proposal writers in the world, used to say, "You can be 100 percent compliant to the RFP and 100 percent wrong because you don't know the real reasons it was issued."

Amrhein was right. Most companies, government agencies, and other organizations prefer to keep their shortcomings to themselves. After all, an RFP can quickly get into the hands of a competitor. In addition, bear in mind that the client isn't always right. Use the RFP as a springboard for understanding the client's situation, but don't stop there. See if you can figure out why the stated need would be important to a customer. Here are some examples. Why do you think the customers would be willing to spend the time and money necessary to address these issues?

✦ ***The client needs a detailed inspection of all cabling and wiring in the Blue River Nuclear Generating Station.***

*The business driver that makes this need important:* The utility company faces potential liability issues if they are found to have defective or noncompliant cabling in their nuclear power plant. Compliance is a volatile and potentially costly issue in the utility industry. Failure to comply can result in significant financial penalties including total shutdown.

✦ ***The client requests proposals for nondestructive evaluation or other advanced testing processes that can be used to guide life management practices in the maintenance and repair of turbine blades.***

*The reason this problem or issue is important:* The entire aviation industry is under tremendous financial pressure. Reducing maintenance costs on engine turbine blades will lower overall operating costs, easing some of the pressure on airlines and other operators. That will make this vendor's engines more competitive from a total cost of ownership standpoint.

In many sales situations, there is no RFP. You are working with a client who has expressed interest and has uncovered a need as part of the sales process. The client agrees that it's worth looking at the issue in detail, and requests that you address it in a proactive proposal. This is actually a great situation for you, because you now have the opportunity to offer an unsolicited proposal without facing any direct competition. But you still need to probe carefully to make sure you understand its implications and consequences.

Try to state for yourself the client's problem or need (or opportunity) as succinctly and clearly as you can. If possible, write it out in a sentence or two. Sometimes the client is very clear about the need, problem, or issue that must be addressed, but sometimes they are rather vague. You might hear, "We're not happy with our employees' ability to use spreadsheets to develop pricing models." Why? What does that lack of skill lead to? Or in an RFP you might see that the client has described the kind of solution they want as though it were a need: "Network Intrusion Detection, the world's premier provider of online security systems, seeks a vendor who can provide mid-level managers with effective training in sound leadership practices." Okay. But why? What's going on at the IT security company that they think can be improved or fixed by providing that kind of training to middle management?

*Common Mistakes in Defining the Needs*

Besides assuming that the RFP spells out the client's need in detail, there are three other mistakes that proposal writers regularly make. These errors undercut the persuasiveness of your message, so avoid them:

**1. *Defining the customer's need as being identical with your solution.*** This happens all the time. Some people have a hard time getting outside their own head and thinking like the customer. Any time your description of the client's need contains the name of your product or service, you have totally missed the point.

While working on a major proposal with a national bank, I asked the sales team, "What is the customer's key need?" After some thought the account manager said, "Well, they need real-time verification of credit cards on their Web site."

"Hmmm. Really?" I said. Somehow that seemed a little narrow to be driving such a large opportunity, so I asked, "If that's their need, what's your solution for them?"

"Well, we're going to provide them with the ability to verify credit cards online in real time."

"Sounds like a perfect fit!" I said. "But I'm curious—why do they need to verify credit cards online?"

The account manager rolled his eyes and gave a look to the other members of the team, obviously more than a little impatient at my obvious lack of insight, but he finally explained, "So they can sell stuff on the Web."

"Oh, of course. So this is an e-commerce strategy."

"Exactly," he said.

"And why do they want to do that?" I asked.

"Do what?"

"Sell stuff on the Web. They have stores in every mall in North America. Why are they so concerned about having an Internet presence?"

Now he was getting visibly agitated. "Because," he said, "their two biggest competitors have e-commerce sites and are selling products over the Web!"

"Okay," I said. "But from what I know of this company, they're bigger than their two main competitors put together. So why do they want to copy what those guys are doing?"

He was totally exasperated now. He practically exploded at me, "Because they've lost over 20 percent of their market share over the past year, that's why!"

Ding! Ding! Now that sounds like a need statement, doesn't it?

I guess the moral of this anecdote is that sometimes it pays to act like a four-year-old. Or to put it another way, adapt the Six Sigma technique of asking "why" five times. Keep probing until you get to the root cause of the opportunity.

**2. *Failing to push your analysis far enough*.** Try to trace the "chain of pain" as far into the customer's organization as you can. Ask to interview other key managers. Look beyond the obvious to see what results are being affected or impeded at the client organization. By taking a larger view, you can see the breadth of the problem and can then present it in your proposal as having organizational implications. That will increase the sense of urgency associated with solving the issue, and will also make it easier for you to establish a compelling value proposition.

**3. *Not talking to enough of the management team in the client's organization*.** The HR and operations departments are likely to have ideas regarding the company's problems that are very different from those of finance or sales. Go beyond a single contact or a single department to get a well-rounded view of the issues or problems the company faces.

*Talk with the Client to Discover Needs*

Here are three options to understand a client's needs:

1. Ask the customer questions.
2. Do some research.
3. Think about comparable customers and what they needed.

Each of these methods is useful, and we would be smart to use all three, but talking to the customer is best.

**Ask questions.** When you speak with the client, ask open-ended questions such as the following:

+ What problems or gaps in capability are impeding the organization's success?
+ Who is experiencing pain from this problem?
+ What makes this problem worth solving?
+ Have you tried anything before to solve the problem? How did that work for you?
+ What are your key objectives or initiatives? How are you doing in achieving them so far?
+ How have you responded to economic conditions?
+ If the problems aren't solved, what happens? Who is affected?

Of course, the key to success in asking the customer questions is to listen carefully to the answers. Too often salespeople prepare a list of questions for the customer, which they dutifully ask one at a time. Unfortunately, they become so absorbed in making sure they get through the questions, they don't really pay attention to what the client is saying.

**Do your research.** Before you make your first sales call, spend half an hour on the Internet. What can you find out about the client's organization?

During a survey conducted by the University of North Carolina's Kenan-Flagler Business School, more than 400 senior executives were asked, "What does it take for you to be willing to listen to a sales person?" The overwhelming answer was that the salesperson must demonstrate knowledge of the executive's business. A generic sales pitch that was focused on the vendor turned them off instantly.

The same thing is true of your sales proposal. If your content sounds generic, if it focuses almost entirely on your own company or products, or if you get the basic facts about the client's business or industry wrong, you lose credibility and kill rapport.

By spending 30 minutes on a search engine, you can uncover a lot about a company or a public sector entity. Here are some ideas of where to look:

+ Check the company's Web site. What do they say about themselves? What are their key themes? What kinds of products or services do they provide? Who are their customers?

+ If they are publicly traded, look at their recent financial documents. What achievements are highlighted in their annual report? For an American company, what risks are highlighted in the 10K? Have there been changes in organization or leadership? Have they made any acquisitions or spun off any divisions?

+ What are the basic public facts about the company? Check Reuters.com or Hoovers.com to learn more—how the company ranks in its industry, who the top executives are, and who its main competitors are.

+ Once you've identified the key executives, enter their names into your search engine. What pops up? A useful search technique is to put the executive's name in quotation marks and then add +PPT. This will pull up any PowerPoint presentations the executive has given or in which he or she has been mentioned that are available via the Internet.

+ Take a quick glance at the Web sites of the company's key competitors. What are the main differences?

***Consider the comparables.*** When an appraiser attempts to determine the fair market value of a building or a portfolio of properties, that person gathers the basic facts about the property—size, condition, location, and so on. Then the appraiser will start combing through the records to find similar properties that have sold recently. These so-called comparables provide a strong indication of what the property in question might be worth.

We can use the same approach in writing the proposal. It's not as effective as actually talking to the managers in the customer's organization and isn't as specifically relevant as doing your research on them. But if your research and your conversations have not yielded much insight, this approach can be helpful. Ask yourself what customers your company has worked with that are similar to your prospective client. Look for customers that are in the same industry, in the same geographic area, or at least are the same size. If you are selling to a bank, it would be valuable to look at the needs of other banks with which your firm is already working. If you don't have banks, perhaps you have other customers who are involved in the financial industry, or who have a similar number of locations, or a similar number of employees.

When you use this approach, it's generally easiest to work backward from existing projects to uncover the business drivers that caused the client to seek help in the first place. Accordingly, once you have identified some customers who are similar to your prospect, ask yourself these questions:

- ✦ What solution did we sell or propose to provide in these analogous situations?
- ✦ Why did those customers need our services or expertise?
- ✦ What made the situation urgent for them? Why did they decide to seek help rather than wait?
- ✦ Why couldn't those customers solve the problem internally?
- ✦ Why wasn't the existing staff or existing provider able to do the job?

Just like the appraiser who begins to get a sense of the value of a piece of property by looking at other buildings in the area that are similar, you'll begin to see a pattern of needs and problems. When you subsequently present to the prospective client, you can say, "Our firm has worked with a number of companies in your industry. Although your challenges may be somewhat different, the key challenges that we helped them deal with include . . . " Then you can show that you understand the client's industry and that you are focused on solving problems.

## 2. Why is this problem worth solving?

Try to look below the surface. Ask yourself, Why? Why now? Who in the organization is being affected by the problem? What corporate objectives are being blocked? What outside pressures are making this problem something that cannot be ignored?

As we noted earlier, every business confronts all kinds of problems and needs almost daily. Most of them will never get fixed, because they're just not important enough. So what makes this situation one that can't be ignored?

## 3. What results does the customer seek?

The second element of the NOSE structure is Outcomes, and that's what questions three and four will help you define. We are looking at the results the customer wants to achieve once you meet their needs.

Before you can figure out what to propose, you must know how the client will judge success. What is the client trying to accomplish? What is the company trying to avoid? Knowing the client's goals will help you shape the right solution. It will also give you important insights that will help you position your proposal so that you are linking your recommendations to outcomes that matter to the decision maker.

> *Delivering the right results through your solution is usually more important than quoting the lowest price.*
> *In fact, that's a definition of value.*

So, what are results? You can define them as the impact your services or solutions have on the customer's organization. Sometimes a desirable result is simply the elimination of a problem, but compelling value usually comes from a solution that goes beyond merely solving the problem to deliver important improvements.

The customer always gets to define value. Some helpful questions to uncover the client's thinking include these: How will you measure success? When you look back on this project, what do you hope to see as a consequence? How will the organization be better than it is now? What measures will you use to determine whether or not you got good value for the money?

As you question your customer about how the company will measure success—in other words, defining the results the customer seeks—look for outcomes that meet three criteria:

### ✦ *Measurable or quantifiable*
"Improved efficiency" is not an outcome or a meaningful goal, because you can't measure it. "Reducing system downtime by 20%" is a measurable result, assuming there are reliable baseline statistics available.

"Increased profitability" is not quantified; "reducing total cost of ownership for core generating hardware by $1,250,000 annually" can be measured.

### ✦ *Organizational in nature*
Personal goals are not the kinds of outcomes that can be quantified or used in a proposal. Results and outcomes are important and defensible if they benefit many people across the organization, not merely one decision maker.

✦ ***Directly linked to the solution you will provide***
The customer must see a link between what you are offering and what the company wants in terms of results. If you "own" the outcomes in the buyer's mind, you probably own the deal. In this regard you have three possible options:

1. You can *implement* a process or provide a capability that the customer does not have.
2. You can *fix* a process that isn't working.
3. You can *improve* a process that is already in place.

Always push for deeper insight into the goals. We will discuss this in more detail in the next chapter, but you should look into four overlapping areas of performance: *strategic, tactical, social/ political,* and *individual.* (See Figure 6-1.)

Examples of **strategic** goals include the traditional financial metrics that businesses use to track how they're doing—profit margin, cost of goods sold, cost of operations, market share, shareholder value, and so on. Strategic value is often measured in monetary terms, but not exclusively. If you are proposing to a government agency, replace the concept of business goals with mission objectives. Most government agencies or departments have a clearly defined mission, and your recommendations should be focused on helping them achieve that mission faster, safer, more completely, or more economically.

Here are a few more examples of strategic outcomes your client might seek:

✦ Accelerating the rate of growth
✦ Penetrating a new market
✦ Responding effectively to a new competitive threat
✦ Reducing critical risks
✦ Successfully completing a merger or acquisition
✦ Improving clinical outcomes in a healthcare setting
✦ Achieving budgetary compliance (particularly important for government agencies and departments)
✦ Providing more service to constituents within the available budget

**Tactical** goals address improvements in operational performance or enhancements to the infrastructure. For example, a customer's goal might be to reduce the amount of manual effort required to complete a task, to gather more data about visitors to the company's Web site, or to reduce downtime. The client might track tactical goals in terms of reduced headcount, improved quality metrics, enhanced compliance with regulatory or other standards, or enhanced productivity (as measured by throughput or volume).

An IT manager who wants the solution to be Microsoft compatible is looking for a technical outcome. It's possible, of course, that a "technical" goal may have nothing to do with technology. Instead, it might involve the implementation of quality management methodologies or achieving standards of compliance. For example, a factory might need to reduce emissions of volatile nitrous oxides in order to meet regulatory standards. How they achieve compliance may not matter to them, so long as they can avoid having their plant shut down and fined.

Here are some other examples of tactical outcomes a client might desire:

✦ Introducing best practices
✦ Adding flexibility to current processes
✦ Automating a labor-intensive process
✦ Reducing losses due to shrink or theft
✦ Achieving improved measures of workplace safety
✦ Reducing liability

**Social** or **political** goals are primarily associated with improving relationships. They can be directed either internally or externally. Internal social goals involve employees and might address improving morale, reducing turnover, increasing the professionalism of the company's sales representatives, raising awareness among all employees on issues of diversity, and so forth. External social or political goals focus on relationships outside the company, such as those with customers or suppliers. A client might desire an enhanced corporate reputation, a higher level of customer satisfaction, an increased percentage of return business from current customers, reduced employee absenteeism, or a reduced carbon footprint. Social goals involving suppliers might include supplier certification, integration of data systems, or development of long-term contracts.

Measuring social value is often more challenging than measuring strategic or even tactical value. The key question to ask our customers who are seeking a social value—a "soft" measure such as improved employee morale—is this: What behaviors or other forms of evidence will tell you that you are getting the results you want? Of course, you will want to phrase this question as specifically as possible. In the case of improved employee morale you could ask the client, What behaviors or phenomena are telling you now that morale is not very good? What will tell you that it's getting better? The decision maker might say that results would be seen in better survey scores, less employee turnover, or higher productivity rates. Everything is measurable, but some things require a bit more creativity to measure than others. Feelings are usually harder to quantify than finances, but that doesn't mean we can't do it. Other examples of social value include:

+ Public approval for a major initiative
+ Higher trust scores
+ Recognition as a market leader
+ Attractiveness as a desirable place to work

There is a fourth area of outcomes that a client might seek in addition to strategic, tactical and social/political results: **individual** gain. This area includes all the outcomes that affect the decision maker's own career, income, or prestige. Here we are asking what the individual decision maker wants to achieve on a personal level, such as a promotion, a bonus, or increased responsibility. Naturally, human beings sometimes have their own personal interests in mind when they make buying decisions on behalf of their companies. Usually there's nothing wrong with that. In fact, in well-run organizations, senior managers try to align the company's goals with those of the individual employees so no one feels that he or she is working at cross-purposes to their own interests. However, personal value usually needs to be addressed outside the realm of a formal proposal. If our proposal is explicit about the individual reward a decision maker or recommender gains, others in the organization may question that person's objectivity and judgment.

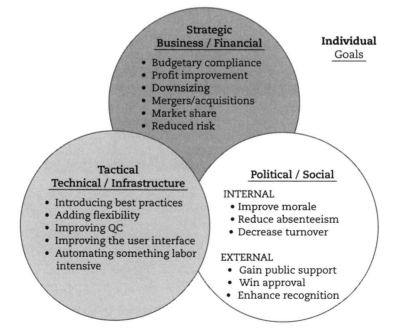

Figure 6-1. Types of Outcomes Clients Typically Seek.

Note that in Figure 6-1, I have left out a circle to represent individual goals. That's because they can fit into the diagram any number of ways. Individual goals may stand completely apart from the strategic, tactical, and social/political goals as a separate set of issues in the decision maker's mind. In other cases, individual goals can overlap all three goal categories, or may be contained entirely within one of the other three goal categories. Finally, personal goals may cancel out if you are selling to a team.

## 4. Which specific result is the most important?

You've identified the client's desired outcomes. Now which one matters the most? You need to know what's most important to the decision maker for two reasons.

First, you want to present your ideas in the same order that they matter to the reader, because seeing them presented from most important to least important will create the impression that you think the way the reader does. This is the primacy principle again. The customer will assume that what you mention first is what you think is most important. If that matches what the customer thinks matters the most, you have just reduced cognitive dissonance and increased rapport.

Second, you want to know which goal is most important so that you can use it as the starting point for developing a value proposition. Presenting your value proposition based on improving quality in a production environment may be easy—for example, given the features and functions of the nondestructive test system you sell—but if the customer is actually looking for a way to increase market share, it may not be very convincing. The customer always defines the terms of the value proposition.

## 5. What products or services can I offer that will solve the problem and deliver the right results?

Brainstorm. Look at all of the approaches to solving a problem with an open mind. For example, you might be able to meet the needs of a client who is seeking a training program by offering a one-day seminar at the client's site. Or you might be able to do it via a Webinar delivered live and then archived for future reference. Or you might propose developing a computer simulation that can be downloaded and reused throughout the organization. Maybe you can just give the trainees a book to read, followed by a test.

The more creative you can be in combining what you know about the client's needs and goals and what you have to offer, the more likely you are to separate yourself from the pack and develop a truly client-centered solution.

### 6. Of the solutions I can offer, which one is the best fit for this client?

Make an educated guess, perhaps based on prior experience with other customers. Will the probable results lead to the client's most important goal? Will they provide competitive advantage? What will they cost? How long will they take? Are cost and timing important issues? Will they require the client to commit employees to the task?

Even though it can be tough sometimes, try to resist the temptation of recommending the solution that offers you the highest profit margin or the biggest commission check. Manage your proposals and your business for the long term.

### 7. Why is my company the right choice?

What makes you the right choice? What differentiates your company from your competition? Select differentiators that will help the client see that choosing you is the best option. If the client is trying to save money, mention those aspects of your product or service that make it cost effective. If the client is trying to eliminate errors and improve quality, focus on that.

## Redefining the Customer's Need

Sometimes the client tells you the company's need explicitly, either by explaining it in conversation during your sales process or by defining it in the statement of work in an RFP. And sometimes the client is wrong. For example, suppose the manager of a telemarketing operation contacts you because she's unhappy with the sales volume her group is producing. "We need a course on closing techniques," she tells you. "Can you do that for us?"

Well, you can do it, but after observing the company's salespeople in action, you realize that what they really need is a course on telephone courtesy. These people are so aggressive they cross the line into rudeness. The question is, what do you propose?

Or perhaps your CPA firm wants to bid on that job to audit the Kallaher Group of Homes for the Aged, but finds out that the firm is in receivership. You can do the audit, but you know the trustees favor one of the big firms. In addition, it's clear that a mere audit, as requested in the RFP, is not going to be of much help. What the group really needs is a full-blown analysis of Medicaid reimbursements, accounts payable, and operating expenses, plus a plan to come out of bankruptcy. How do you respond?

These are tough choices. You may find yourself torn between wanting to propose the very best, most effective solution you can and wanting to submit the most competitive proposal possible. Clearly, if you deviate too far from what the client has requested, you may look nonresponsive. On the other hand, if you don't amend the request somewhat, you may win the job and find yourself in the uncomfortable situation of doing work you really don't think ought to be done or that you know won't deliver the desired results.

The best course is to communicate with the potential client, discuss your concerns or your observations, and try to educate and inform the decision makers before you write your proposal. Sometimes, however, you can't do those things. Sometimes, when you're dealing with a formal RFP released in quantity to many potential vendors, or when you're dealing with a consultant who has written the RFP, or when ego or politics or governmentally mandated procurement rules get in the way, you have to respond to the client's need as it's stated, even if that's not appropriate. And sometimes you must be sensitive to the client's or consultant's need to save face.

You have three basic options in this situation:

**1.** *Accept the need as defined in the RFP and study the various ways in which you or your company can satisfy that need, select the best among them, and propose a solution in terms of that approach.* In the short term, this is the safest approach to take. Bid on the job as it's been described, try to win it, and then hope you can convince the client to alter the statement of work after you have the contract in your pocket. Unfortunately, what's safe in the short term is risky in the long. You're basing the business relationship from the outset on less than full honesty, and a tough customer who is looking for performance guarantees or service-level commitments may not be willing to approve change documents or authorize additional funding to get a solution that works.

**2.** *Study the client's situation as accurately as you can, independent of what the proposal may tell you, and redefine the client's need based on your analysis.* Use your own definition of the client's need as the basis for the proposal you submit.

Redefining the need is a high-risk approach, particularly when the client has provided the original analysis or has paid a consultant to develop it. Sometimes, though, you really have nothing to lose. For instance, when the analysis has been provided by an outside consultant or a competitor, redefinition may be necessary in order to position your company more competitively. If your competition has written the RFP, you can assume that there will be nothing in it that favors you. This approach only has a chance if you can demonstrate a startling superiority in value or an unbelievable cost advantage while still solving the essential problem.

**3.** *Do both of the above.* Respond to the client's definition of the need, but also offer an alternative perspective. You could discuss the situation frankly in the executive summary as a way of introducing your proposal. State that while you're fully prepared to respond to the statement of work as written in the original RFP, and have included a response that proves you can do exactly what the client has asked for, your analysis has led you to develop another approach to solve the client's problem. In addition, because this alternative approach will be less costly or more effective (or both), you feel obliged to at least present it as an option.

A variation of this approach is to offer a phased approach to solving the total problem. This is reasonably safe to do, particularly when the client hasn't misdefined the need but simply hasn't requested the total solution that the company needs. By structuring your proposed solution in terms of phases, with each phase priced separately and each requiring a joint review of progress and commitment to the next phase, you provide a structure in which the client can change direction without scrambling the budget or being embarrassed.

Bear in mind that redefining the need usually works only if the client can be persuaded that your redefinition is accurate. Rethinking the situation along the lines you propose must be explained as highly beneficial to the client, not just to your chances of writing a good proposal. This is much easier to do if your redefinition of the need produces the same outcomes the client is looking for, but does it in a less costly, less time-consuming, or less complex way. Finally, the degree of trust and credibility you and your company have established with the client during the pre-proposal process is vital to the client accepting your redefinition of need.

# 7 Why the Inuit Hunt Whales and Other Secrets of Customer Behavior

$T$HE DEFINING MOMENT IN ANY SALES PROCESS is the customer's decision. From the moment we first find a lead and qualify it as a real opportunity, through all the meetings, presentations, conversations, and communications between salesperson and prospect, our focus is on getting the customer to make a decision in our favor.

Understanding how people make that decision helps us sell more effectively. With insight into the customer's decision process, we can deliver the right message in the right way at the right time. Surprisingly, though, sales methods have generally ignored this crucial element of the sales process.

## How People Really Make Decisions

When we and our customers must make a decision, we usually find ourselves dealing with huge amounts of complex, confusing, often conflicting information. We are often under tremendous time pressure. We need to make the "right" decision because the consequences of a bad one could be catastrophic for our business or careers. So how do we do it?

Recent research has documented for the first time how people actually make decisions. An interdisciplinary team, based at the Max Planck Institute for Human Development (Berlin and Munich) and the University of Chicago, has published results of extensive inquiries into the methods people use in all kinds of situations. This study, *Simple Heuristics That Make Us Smart* (Oxford University Press, 2000), documents the specific techniques people use for making decisions quickly based on a minimal amount of information.

It turns out that people use a limited set of decision making strategies or techniques. We use them from the time we're children (kids who are taking "multiple-guess" tests in school resort to these techniques for narrowing their choices), in college, in our personal lives, and of course in our business activities.

The researchers speculate that these techniques, or "fast and frugal heuristics" as the authors of *Simple Heuristics* call them, are hard-wired into our brains, part of our evolutionary survival package. Our ancestors didn't have the biggest teeth or the sharpest claws, so they needed to make good decisions. These heuristics helped them survive and they help us function today.

A decision heuristic is simply a means of gathering a subset of the available information, processing that information, and then stopping the process to make a decision. The less information required, the faster the processing and the more efficient the individual is. But do these heuristics, with their emphasis on speed and minimal data, actually produce good decisions? The researchers found that in some cases, using less information actually produced better decisions than relying on thorough analysis of all available information. Anyway, common sense tells us that if fast and frugal heuristics didn't work, we probably wouldn't be here as a species.

So what are the techniques? And what do they tell us about how to write proposals effectively?

In *Simple Heuristics* the authors describe seven heuristics of choice, but three of those are particularly important for making business decisions.

## Recognition

The basic principle of the simplest technique is that if one of two objects is recognized and the other is not, we infer that the recognized object has higher value. This is a very simple process.

Recognition is fundamentally binary: yes, I recognize that person; no, I do not. We assume that the one we recognize is the "better" choice. End of story. End of decision process. If you recognize both objects, you need to move on to a different kind of heuristic to make your decision. Degrees of recognition don't matter much, because recognition is not the same as recall or experience.

Here's an example: Suppose your laptop computer suddenly died. You go to your IT manager and tell her that you need a new one. She says, "Well, you're in luck, because I happen to have two brand-new laptops with all the software installed. You can have either this Dell XPS or this Kretzenheimer Millennial. Which one do you want?"

Chances are you'll take the Dell. Why? Because you've never heard of the other one.

What does this mean for our proposal efforts?

First, it suggests how important pre-proposal activities are. If the evaluator has never heard of us and our proposal lands on his or her desk, chances are we won't get much more than a cursory glance. (Conversely, if you work for a Fortune 500 company, you may get passed along to the next stage of evaluation based on recognition alone. This can lead to an overestimation of how effective your proposals are.)

The recognition heuristic indicates the importance of repeated exposure, in the form of advertising and branding activities at the corporate level and repeated contacts, in the form of phone calls, e-mails, and other forms of what the marketing guru Jim Cecil calls "nurturing" the account. Our pre-proposal activities lay the foundation for choice by establishing recognition.

I used to think that corporate sponsorship of sports stadiums and golf tournaments and so forth were exercises in executive vanity rather than a good investment of marketing dollars. However, as this heuristic indicates, there is an important value in working to establish instant recognition. Advertising, marketing, and branding activities will have significant value for our sales efforts downstream.

How much value? This has been notoriously difficult to calculate. Perhaps this gives us a hint: More than 1,800 firms compete for more than $7 billion worth of federal business based on GSA Schedule 70 (which allows federal offices and agencies to purchase equipment and services directly, bypassing the formal RFP and solicitation process). The bulk of this business is going to just a few vendors: the top 50 companies won over 70% of all the business and the top five companies won 20%. (The number one and number two companies respectively were Dell and IBM, by the way.) Now, when you look at the ten companies that sold the most under GSA Schedule 70 you will find that the exact same ten companies were also the most aggressive in marketing themselves as measured by advertising in government trade publications, direct mail campaigns to government employees, participation in trade events, and a consistent look, feel, and message in all of their advertising, collateral material, Web sites, and proposals. Top-of-mind awareness results in top-of-the-list sales figures.

What else does the recognition heuristic tell us? Well, it certainly suggests that if we represent a small or new company and our prospects have never heard of us, we may have a difficult time winning deals. Conversely, if we receive an RFP from a potential client we have never heard of and with whom we have absolutely no relationship, we probably ought to "no bid" it. Our chances of winning are minimal.

Finally, it means that if you are a sales professional, you can't depend solely on the corporation to handle recognition-building activities. You should make the effort to communicate with your prospects, leads, and customers on a regular basis to maintain recognition. Send the prospect a clipping, drop them an e-mail with an interesting Web link, leave a voice mail, and make other efforts to communicate something of interest or value every six weeks or so. That way, when the customer is ready to buy, you won't be relegated to the discard pile because the decision maker doesn't recognize you.

## Single-Factor Decision Making

But how do customers decide if they recognize both us and our competitors? Or if they have never heard of any of us?

Typically, at that point they move to a slightly more complex heuristic and choose among the options based on a single criterion or factor. This single factor is assumed by the decision maker to be a useful indicator to sort among the options. (Sometimes there are as many as two or three criteria, but seldom more than that.)

For example, suppose a company issues a Request for Proposal and receives 20 proposals in response. Someone at that company has to sort through those submissions quickly to eliminate most of them. At this stage of the evaluation, there is not much in the way of careful analysis, no real weighing of the evidence. An initial set of "no names" will be discarded. That's the recognition heuristic in action. Then the evaluator will begin to apply a decision factor or two. Some of the proposals will simply be eliminated because they did not follow the RFP instructions. Some will be cut because they didn't answer all of the questions or indicated by their answer that they were noncompliant with a key requirement. The decision process will move very quickly until the evaluator has the pile down to something more manageable.

Even if your customer has not issued an RFP, he or she will probably evaluate competitive offers on the basis of a key criterion. It might be price. It might be timeline. It might be references or relevant experience or the "business fit" of your solution.

There are three varieties of single-factor decision making that your customer may use. At the simplest level, he or she may use what the experts call "minimalist" criteria, but which we might call arbitrary. The decision maker uses a single factor, selected more or less at random, to make a choice. The programmers who work at my company provided a rather amusing example of this kind of decision making when it comes to choosing a lunch destination. They used to waste a sizable portion of their lunch period arguing and debating about where to go. Finally, they resolved it as only programmers would—they wrote a piece of software that makes the decision for them. At first, it was a random lunch generator, but then they got a bit more sophisticated. Now they enter a single factor, such as proximity or price, and click the mouse. The system generates a lunch destination based on that factor. And off they go, content with the choice.

A slightly more sophisticated version of single-factor decision making involves asking ourselves what criterion we used the last time we made the same or a similar decision and whether that produced a good outcome. This is called "using the last." Some examples might be:

+ "The last time I entered the office pool, I chose teams by flipping a coin and I won $20. I'll do the same thing again."
+ "When we bought our annuals for planting last spring, we chose specimens with dark green leaves and they did really well in the garden."
+ "Whenever we've hired a vendor who has done the same kind of project before, things have turned out pretty well."

Finally, decision makers sometimes go a step further and develop a limited set of criteria by thinking back over several situations in which similar decisions were made. Which criteria produced the best results? Which didn't work? This heuristic, called "taking the best," assumes that some criteria will produce better results than others. For example, most people who have bought cars before will enter a showroom already knowing the limited set of criteria that matter to them. Further, market research indicates that most female car buyers regard safety as the number one criterion and they will look at any potential car purchase in terms of its safety ratings first.

What does this mean for our sales efforts?

First, it suggests that during our sales contacts with a prospect, we should probe to find out what factors they will use to make a decision. We can uncover their decision criteria rather simply. We just have to ask:

+ "When you compare different vendors, what is the most important factor for you in choosing one?"
+ "The last time you made this kind of decision, what factors did you use to guide your decision? What did you look for? Did that work for you?"
+ "Looking back over the last several times you have made a buying decision like this, what characteristics or components of the offer would you say were the most useful in making a decision that worked out well?"

Second, this technique opens up opportunities for us to help the decision maker during the sales process. A naive or inexperienced customer may take a simplistic approach, looking only at price. By using the sales process to educate the buyer, we can introduce other factors beyond price that may be more helpful to them in making a good decision and that may give us more of a competitive position.

Third, we need to differentiate between opportunities where we are reacting to the customer's request for a proposal and opportunities where we are offering a solution proactively. When we submit a proposal in response to an RFP, we must recognize that our first job is to avoid elimination based on some arbitrary or trivial issue. That means following directions carefully, answering all of the questions and requirements, and making our compliance to the bid as obvious as possible. An effective tool in this area is the compliance matrix, a table in which you list each of the customer's requirements, your level of compliance with that requirement, and possibly offer a brief comment or explanation. (An evaluator who works for the U.S. Postal Service told me that he looks at all the proposals and sets the ones that do not include a compliance matrix on the floor. That leaves him with a manageable few.) It's also a good idea to highlight your proposal so that the customer can quickly find the high-value content that directly addresses the factors he or she thinks are important.

For proactive opportunities, customers tend to search on their own key criteria until they find a differentiator. Then they stop and make a decision. This implies that it's vital that we organize our sales presentations and proposals to focus right away on the criteria that the customer thinks are most important. Not surprisingly, these factors will address such key issues as:

+ Are we getting what we need? Does this solve a significant business problem? Will the proposed solution work in our environment?
+ Does this represent good value for money? Is the proposed pricing fair? What kind of return on our investment will we receive?
+ Can this vendor really do it? Do they have the experience and resources to perform on time and on budget? Are they competent?

### Estimating the Rate of Return

For thousands of years, the Inuit people of Alaska and Canada have hunted whales as their primary source of food. They go out into the freezing ocean in open boats made of wood frames covered with animal skins. Surrounding a pod of whales, the hunters pound on drums and the sides of their boats to drive the whales toward shore (whales have very sensitive hearing, you know). Then, when one of the whales is in shallow water, they attack and kill it. Now they use harpoon guns and more advanced weapons, but they used to do it with wooden spears.

Now why on earth would they do that? There are much less danger-ous game animals they could hunt—geese, rabbits, seals, walruses even. They could fish. They could have developed a tribal economy based on herding, the way Laplanders did with reindeer. Why go after the largest, most powerful mammal on earth?

The experts who contributed to *Simple Heuristics* have come up with an answer. Their research suggests that one of the built-in decision heu-ristics people use is an innate capacity to calculate the "rate of return" for their efforts, particularly as they pertain to the group as a whole. In other words, hunting a whale has a bigger ROI for the tribe than hunt-ing a rabbit does. These researchers even went so far as to calculate the calories required to kill a whale compared to the calories the community will get from that animal, then calculated the calories expended vs. the calories obtained for other prey. The result: the whale was by far the best investment of the tribe's energies.

Apparently, all of us have hard-wired into our brains the capability to make a quick but accurate estimate of the rate of return to be derived from one course of action vs. another. In evolutionary terms, it probably helped our ancestors survive.

What does this "estimation heuristic" mean for us as we attempt to sell ERP software systems or healthcare programs or broadband telecom-munications services or executive jet leasing programs or whatever it is we have to offer? Simply this: if we don't help the decision makers figure out the rate of return from our recommended solution, they will resort to one of the simpler heuristics, such as recognition or single-factor deci-sion making, and that may not be to our advantage, particularly if a competitor is showing a strong value proposition.

The fact is that when people are making decisions on behalf of a group to which they belong, they instinctively want to make a decision that gives their organization the best possible return on investment. They'll even buy something more expensive and complex if they're con-vinced it's the best choice for their company.

How can we help them use the estimation heuristic to our advantage?

First, every proposal should include calculations and graphic displays of ROI, total cost of ownership, payback period, productivity improve-ments, speed of delivery, or other measures of gain.

Second, provide your decision maker with case studies that show how other customers got big rewards from selecting your products or services. Quantify the impact your solutions had for those customers whenever pos-sible.

Third, find out what kind of outcome the key decision maker thinks is most important for his or her company. Is it increased revenue? Regu-latory compliance? Greater customer loyalty? Extended useful life for critical equipment? Elimination of downtime? Whatever the customer thinks is important defines the value proposition.

Finally, emphasize your differentiators and explain how they add value for the customer. Customers want to know what makes us different from our competitors. They also want to know why those differences will matter to them and their companies.

If we provide the right information in the right way, one that corresponds to the processes our customers use to make decisions, our chances of winning business will soar. And, after all, winning business is what writing proposals is all about.

## Creating a Compelling Value Proposition

We need to include a value proposition in every proposal so the decision maker can use the estimation heuristic to see that ours is the best possible option. Unfortunately, most so-called value propositions are little more than marketing fluff:

"We are a true one-stop shop for all your financial needs."

"We enable the people-ready business with leading-edge technology and world-class service."

"We offer a full range of enterprise-strength, integrated solutions."

Do any of those so-called value propositions make you want to reach for your wallet? No, I didn't think so.

Marketing fluff consists of vague generalities, grandiose promises, and undefined, unsubstantiated claims that may not even be relevant to our interests. It simply does not work as an effective value proposition.

A value proposition is essentially a promise. It's our promise to deliver the kind of value the customer wants and needs, value far in excess of what we are charging. By demonstrating that we offer more positive value than any other company does, we maximize our chance of winning.

As they think about buying products or services, smart buyers typically weigh the expected cost of acquisition against the expected return on investment. In other words, smart buyers want to see positive impact in an area of performance that matters to the business. For example, they might seek to improve the company's bottom line by reducing the cost of operations or by increasing operational efficiency. Other areas where smart buyers often look for impact include:

✦ Generating more revenue
✦ Increasing the reliability of mission-critical operations
✦ Improving the quality of deliverables or execution

+ Enhancing the sustainability of the operation or reducing its carbon footprint
+ Increasing worker productivity

Of course, these are only a few examples of the extremely wide range of positive outcomes that buyers hope to achieve.

As an article in the *Harvard Business Review* pointed out, the basic value proposition can be expressed very simply:

$$\textbf{(Values – Costs) > (Value}_a \textbf{ – Cost}_a\textbf{)}$$

where:

**Value**$_s$ = the value of your solution
**Cost**$_s$ = the cost of your solution
**Value**$_a$ = the value of the next best alternative
**Cost**$_a$ = the cost of the next best alternative

As you can see, you don't have to have the lowest price to have the greatest value. What matters is the difference between value obtained and price paid. If you can convince your buyer that your solution offers the biggest delta between value and cost, you have a very good chance of winning. You are appealing to them based on the estimation heuristic.

**The Four Principles of Effective Value.** How do we make sure our value message is as effective as possible? We have to pay attention to four principles:

1. The value we offer must be value the customer wants.
2. The value will be more compelling if we quantify it.
3. If we can quantify the value, we can present it graphically.
4. To prevent a competitor from claiming that they will offer the same value, we must link our value proposition to our differentiators.

Let's discuss each principle in more depth:

*1. The value we offer must be value the customer wants.* This statement probably seems obvious. Of course the customer has to want the value we are offering! That's common sense, right? But many proposals and sales presentations offer a generic value proposition—one that goes out to every customer regardless of industry, role, or recent experience. Some companies have a standard page labeled "Our Value

Proposition" containing ten bullet points. That page gets inserted in every proposal, regardless of who the client is or what they seek in terms of outcomes. That means the value offered in those proposals and presentations is often irrelevant to the decision-maker's interests.

Remember: the customer always defines the value. Just as in playing chess, in which white always gets the first move, in the game of compelling value propositions, the customer gets the first move in defining what the most important area of impact will be. Find out what specific results this specific customer seeks and then make the strongest possible case that your recommendations will deliver more of that value than any other option. That's the best way to win the customer's approval.

**2. The value will be more compelling if we quantify it.** Numbers bring greater credibility to our value proposition, both because they suggest we have calculated the impact and because they give the customer a way to measure our performance against our promise.

Without quantification, value propositions can sound like marketing fluff: "improved productivity," "increased employee morale," "lower cost of operations." These are wonderful sentiments, but they leave open the key question: *How much?* How much will productivity improve and what is that worth to the client? How much will morale increase and how can that be measured in tangible terms? How much will costs drop for normal operations?

Sometimes people hang back from quantifying value because they're worried that the numbers have to be precise. All financial projections are estimations, so precision or pinpoint accuracy isn't relevant. In his book *How to Measure Anything: Finding the Value of Intangibles in Business,* Douglas Hubbard shows how to develop quick estimations of value with a high degree of confidence, and his techniques can be used easily to develop quantifiable value propositions for most businesses.

The place to start is with the client's current performance data. If you have established trust, they will usually share this information with you. However, sometimes they won't and sometimes they don't have it. They literally do not know how their performance stacks up. In that case, use available benchmark data. Compare your prospect's level of performance in a critical, quantifiable area with industry standard performance and with the performance of a key regional competitor. If you choose to compare your prospect to a competitor, do not mention the competitor by name.

**3. If we can quantify the value, we can present it graphically.** Other than making our proposal or presentation a little more attractive, is there any value for us in communicating the impact of our recommendations graphically? The answer is an emphatic "Yes!" times two:

✦ First, a chart or diagram is an effective way of stopping the decision maker from merely skimming through your proposal. When you add a data-rich visual, you cause your readers to focus on your message. They want to know what the graphic is telling them. They pause on the page and attempt to figure out what the illustration means. That means we have broken through and gained focused attention from a busy decision maker who is otherwise just scanning our proposal or half-listening to our sales presentation.

✦ Second, according to research done at the University of Minnesota, adding a chart or diagram increases the persuasiveness of your message by 47 percent compared to the words alone. This is a very important fact—after all, is there any part of your proposal or presentation that's more important than the value proposition?

Following is an example of a simple graphic representation of benchmark data (Figure 7-1), comparing our performance in terms of total cost of ownership to what the prospect is currently paying and to what they will pay if they switch to one of our competitors:

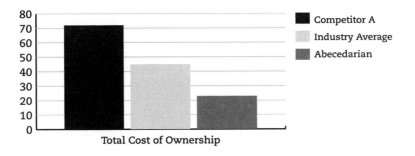

**Figure 7-1.** Benchmarking the Total Cost of Ownership.

**4. To prevent a competitor from claiming that they will offer the same value, we must link our value proposition to our differentiators.** A differentiator is something that sets you apart from others in the industry. If you can show that your differentiators combine to give you a unique ability to deliver the right results, you have made your value proposition impregnable. No competitor can swoop in and say, "Me, too!" because they cannot back up their claims the way you can.

This is a challenging step. Figuring out which differentiators make the strongest case in support of your value proposition can be difficult, but it is well worth the effort. Later in this chapter we'll look at a way to make the process a lot easier.

## Creating a Winning Value Proposition

Your value proposition needs to combine three elements into a clear argument:

1. The client's desired outcomes
2. Your business strengths or differentiators
3. Proof that you can deliver

Combining these three elements enables us to offer a compelling, unique value proposition to each prospect.

### Varieties of Value:
### Understanding Which Outcomes Matter to the Client

Earlier we identified three types of value that decision makers typically seek: *strategic value*, which focuses on the core measures of business performance; *tactical value*, which focuses on operational efficiency and effectiveness; and *social value*, which focuses on relationships with other people and institutions—employees, customers, vendors, the community. Focus on the kind of value that matters the most to your decision maker.

In framing the value position for your proposal, you can take either a positive or negative approach. Positive strategies are based on *gain*. Your goal is to persuade the client that what you are recommending offers him or her the greatest amount of gain of all the available options. Negative strategies are based on *fear* or *avoidance*. In that case, your goal is to alert the client to the risks (even disasters) that are possible unless certain measures are taken. You strengthen your competitive position by pointing out that your firm is uniquely qualified to take those measures. In fact, a well-thought-out risk register with appropriate mitigation strategies can be integral to your value proposition when the value is based on avoiding negative consequences.

Either approach works and both are ethical, as long as they are based on an honest assessment of the client's situation. Trying to alarm the decision maker by raising fears that are really phantasms is just another form of lying. In the long run, it'll ruin your reputation and make it impossible to sell into the same account again. Also, bear in mind that it can be difficult to convince a customer that a risk is genuine if they've never experienced a loss.

## Differentiate Yourself in Ways that Matter

Ask yourself: What is it that you do that no one else in your industry does? What is there that everyone does, but you do in a way that is clearly different, and that difference adds value for your clients?

Your differentiators don't have to be unique, but they should at least be rare. What you want to do is select a handful of differentiators and create a "stack" of evidence from them that no other firm can offer. It's that stack that will be unique, even if there are one or two competitors who could claim some of the same strengths that you are highlighting.

A few years ago I was asked to deliver a workshop on effective proposal writing for a company in Stockholm. As I was talking with the manager who was sponsoring the program about what aspects of it he wanted customized, I was surprised when he asked me to leave out the whole subject of identifying and using differentiators.

"Well, we can do that if you want," I said, "but may I ask why?"

"Because we don't have any," he said.

The surprised me. "How do you know you don't have any?" I asked.

"Because we hired a consultant on a two-week engagement to identify them for us and at the end of the first week he came into my office and quit. He said he couldn't find any."

I don't know what that consultant was looking for or where he conducted his search, but I can tell you that by noon of the first day of the workshop we had identified 13 differentiators for that company. By the end of the day they had a list of more than 30. Every organization has differentiators, no matter how many competitors you have and no matter how mature the industry within which you compete. If nothing else, the people who work at your firm are a source of differentiation because they presumably don't work for any of your competitors. But there are many other places to find your strengths.

For example, you might start by looking at your products or services and identifying the features that set them apart. This is fairly easy to do, particularly if you have kept an eye on your competitors' products and asked your customers what they perceive the differences to be. But bear in mind that product features are seldom the source for long-term competitive differentiation. Even patented features sometimes aren't enough. Slight advantages in speed for your machinery, for example, can be overcome quickly and may offer the customer little in terms of real value. Sustainable, meaningful differentiation is more likely to arise from your systems, processes, or methods of working.

The second approach to defining differentiators is to think about the cycle of activity involved in a typical customer engagement. From the early phases of the sales process all the way through post-installation and customer support activities, perhaps even to the decommissioning and removal of your products, think about the various moments when you interact with the customer. What do you do that's different? What do you provide as a deliverable that they don't get from anyone else? What processes or systems have you implemented that assure satisfactory outcomes?

If you sell services or some form of intellectual capital, either in conjunction with products or as a solution in themselves, there are four areas of differentiation that matter the most to your decision makers:

**1. *How you will do the work.*** In describing how you will perform the services you are proposing, explain how you will do the project, what is different or unique about your methods, and why your way is the best way. What special practices do you follow? What methodology underlies your approach?

**2. *How you will manage the work.*** Poor project management is the leading cause of failure in technical projects, and is a major fear for many buyers, even when the product or service isn't particularly technical. Present a detailed management plan, emphasizing the value-added components of your management approach, particularly in areas of measurement, tracking, and reporting. How will you handle change orders? What about cost overruns? If you are providing service-level agreements, how will you measure performance against the agreed-upon standards?

**3. *The people you will provide.*** Intellectual capital has to reside in somebody's intellect. Whose? Who are you providing and what makes them particularly well suited by training or experience to do the job right? In general, your customers want to see that the people you are providing have recent, relevant experience, specific training that prepares them for the task, general educational preparation, and a record of professional accomplishment, such as licensing, membership on committees or boards, speaking engagements, patents, and so forth.

**4. *Special facilities or equipment you have available.*** Are your gas analysis labs the best in the industry? Do you have a system developed in-house for handling Webcast auctions that is fully integrated into all back-office functions? If the project will benefit from special equipment or facilities that only you have, mention them.

### Provide the Proof that You Can Deliver the Value

You must support your value proposition by providing enough evidence to prove that what you claim is true. You will want to provide both top-level substantiation and incremental evidence.

Top-level substantiation consists of proof statements and factual evidence included specifically to make a point about your ability to deliver value. Examples include:

+ past performance reports
+ case studies
+ customer testimonials
+ project summaries
+ corporate capabilities

Incremental evidence consists of spots where you can mention or reinforce your overall value proposition with a phrase, a sentence, or a brief example. Look for opportunities to weave incremental evidence supporting the value proposition into these areas of your proposal:

+ cover letter
+ proposal title
+ executive summary
+ section summaries
+ headings and subheadings
+ product/service details
+ resumes
+ titles of figures and graphics

### Align Your Differentiators with the Customer's Values

Once you've taken the time to develop a comprehensive list of differentiators, you will want to use them quickly and efficiently to support the value propositions you offer. Some of your differentiators set you apart from a given competitor, so you only use them when you know you're going up against that competitor. Others might be specific to a certain product line or to particular services. Obviously, you only use them when those products or services form the core of your recommended solution.

Even allowing for all that, though, you're likely to have an unwieldy number of general-purpose differentiators. How do you choose which ones to emphasize in a given proposal? Let's assume that you have a list of differentiators that includes the following:

+ Standard code base
+ User-friendly tools for customizing the interface

+ True Web-based architecture
+ Awards for superior products
+ Lease or buy options
+ Financial stability with more than 25 years of profitable operation

Such a list is kind of a mixed bag. Some relate to your products, some to your policies for doing business, some to your corporate history, and so on. How do you choose the ones most likely to support your ability to deliver a specific kind of value?

Start by cross-indexing your differentiators to the various kinds of value you know your customers care about. Let's also suppose that many of the types of value we discussed earlier are of interest to some of your decision makers. Some are looking for a financial return, others for improved quality or risk minimization. And so on.

Create a table in which you list all of your differentiators in the first column and all of the value orientations across the top row. It will look something like the following.

|  | Financial | Technical | Quality | Social | Minimal risk | Industry trends | Competitive advantage |
|---|---|---|---|---|---|---|---|
| Standard code base | | | | | | | |
| Customization tools | | | | | | | |
| Web-based architecture | | | | | | | |
| Awards for products | | | | | | | |
| Lease or buy options | | | | | | | |
| Fastest loading time | | | | | | | |
| Smartphone access | | | | | | | |
| Open architecture | | | | | | | |
| First to market | | | | | | | |
| End-to-end provider | | | | | | | |
| ISO 9000 certified | | | | | | | |
| Six Sigma methodology | | | | | | | |
| Financially stable | | | | | | | |

Now for each item in the first column ask yourself: Does this specific differentiator support the value message that your client is seeking? If it's an excellent way of proving that you can deliver a particular kind of value, give it 5 points. If it's very weak, give it just 1 point. Something in the middle, assign a point value based on your gut instinct. Don't spend too much time on this. Your quick initial impressions are probably a good guideline. When you've completed this process, your table will contain point values, like this:

| | Financial | Technical | Quality | Social | Minimal risk | Industry trends | Competitive advantage |
|---|---|---|---|---|---|---|---|
| Standard code base | 4 | 5 | 4 | 1 | 4 | 5 | 3 |
| Customization tools | 5 | 4 | 3 | 3 | 2 | 3 | 2 |
| Web-based architecture | 2 | 5 | 2 | 4 | 1 | 5 | 3 |
| Awards for products | 1 | 5 | 4 | 2 | 4 | 1 | 4 |
| Lease or buy options | 5 | 1 | 1 | 2 | 4 | 3 | 3 |
| Fastest loading time | 3 | 5 | 4 | 4 | 1 | 1 | 3 |
| Smartphone access | 2 | 5 | 3 | 4 | 2 | 5 | 4 |
| Open architecture | 4 | 5 | 4 | 3 | 5 | 5 | 3 |
| First to market | 4 | 3 | 5 | 1 | 3 | 1 | 2 |
| End-to-end provider | 5 | 2 | 4 | 3 | 5 | 4 | 4 |
| ISO 9000 certified | 2 | 2 | 5 | 3 | 4 | 4 | 3 |
| Six Sigma methodology | 2 | 3 | 5 | 3 | 4 | 3 | 3 |
| Financially stable | 3 | 1 | 2 | 4 | 5 | 3 | 3 |

What does this chart tell you? If you add up the rows, you will see which differentiator has the highest overall value, regardless of the strategic positioning. In the case illustrated in the preceding table, your strongest overall differentiators are "open architecture" and "end-to-end provider." So if you had no idea what the client's value orientation was, you might want to include those two at least because they're fairly strong in general.

Similarly, if you add up the columns, you'll get an idea which value position is best for you, given the differentiators you currently have.

You'll also get an idea which kind of value position is weakest, suggesting that you may need to find some additional differentiators or you may need to focus on a different strategic value position. Referring to the preceding table, your best option is to base your value proposition on your technical superiority or your impact on quality.

However, the best way to use this chart is to figure out what value the client desires and then to choose the differentiators that reinforce your ability to deliver it. If you have a client whose focus is on minimizing risk, for example, your most important differentiators are those that scored a 5 or 4: open architecture, end-to-end provider, financial stability, standard code base, awards, and lease or buy options.

The worst mistake you can make with the differentiators in your proposal is not to include any at all. The second worst mistake is to just dump all of them into every proposal. Both mistakes lead to proposals that have no focus and make no point. State the value message clearly based on what the customer seeks, then identify the specific differentiators that prove you can deliver that kind of value in this opportunity.

## Final Thoughts on Value

It will help you and your colleagues compete more successfully if you develop standard approaches to quantifying impact. These may be ROI models or formulas to generate a payback analysis. Identify the questions salespeople should ask, what data they should collect, and what methods they can then use to transform the data into a meaningful calculation of ROI or other value. The result will be customer focused, since it will be based on numbers they provided.

Winning is a matter of chance if you don't show compelling value. Take the time to develop a clear value proposition for your proposals, even the renewals and the "sure things." Help your decision makers calculate the probable return from your solutions and you will have successfully shifted their attention away from price and on to value. That's a much better place to be.

# 8 The Cicero Principle:

## How to Avoid Talking to Yourself in Print

 THE ESSENCE OF CLIENT-BASED PERSUASION CAN be summarized in the words of the Roman orator and statesman Cicero:

*"If you wish to persuade me, you must think my thoughts, feel my feelings, and speak my words."*

This is great advice. When we break it down, phrase by phrase, we can see just how profound it is.

### If you wish to persuade me . . .

Why do you wish to persuade anybody of anything? Basically, you're hoping to influence their behavior, thinking, or attitude. If the context of the persuasion is sales, you're trying to motivate the audience to purchase your product or service. If the context is training, you're trying to motivate the audience to use certain techniques or procedures on the job. If the context is politics, you may be trying to win a vote.

### . . . you must . . .

Old Cicero doesn't cut us any slack here. This is mandatory. Not "it would be a good idea if" or "beneficial results may derive from . . . " No. *You must.* And he's right, because what he goes on to emphasize is the necessity of developing your persuasive arguments from the client's perspective.

### . . . think my thoughts . . .

One of the keys to thinking like the client is to try to see things from his or her point of view. In fact, that may be the fundamental key to all persuasion: getting outside your own head and away from your own interests and trying to get inside the decision maker's head.

To think the thoughts of your audience, you need to watch for clues regarding their preferences in terms of receiving and processing information. People arrive with certain predispositions wrapped up tightly in their DNA. Some people believe that decision making is a careful, analytical process that involves a lot of data gathering. Other decision makers, however, may find that approach frustrating or mechanical. For them, decisions should be made quickly based on an intuitive measure of bottom-line impact. Still others will take into account the feelings of those who will be affected by a decision, looking for consensus and an approach that yields the greatest good to the greatest number.

Not one of these approaches is inherently superior to the others. All are aspects of personality that result in a worldview and an approach to decision making that just feels "right" to each individual. The challenge you face as a proposal writer is twofold: you need to know what your own preferences are, since you will tend to write a proposal that you would like to receive; and you need to know what your customer's preferences for receiving and processing information are, since you want to adapt your own style to match his or hers more closely. We'll look at specific ways to do this shortly.

### . . . feel my feelings . . .

People tend to judge your proposal by using the same standards that are used to judge them. Factors that trigger a strong, positive emotional response in one person may produce no response, or even a negative one, in somebody else. To persuade somebody, you must pay attention to what counts most in that person's worldview.

I once heard the CEO of a data processing company, speaking to an audience of salespeople, who made this point very clearly:

"You all want to sell to me," he said. "I understand that. I used to be in sales myself, so I can sympathize with your situation. So let me make this process easier for both of us. If you want me to buy from you, you need to address the two things I wake up worrying about every morning. And I'll even tell you what they are. Every morning I wake up worrying about improving our net profitability and decreasing our processing cycle time. If you can help me with either of those problems, I *will* buy from you. And I don't particularly care what you're selling."

Most senior-level executives think this way. They are measured on certain key performance indicators and their compensation is often tied to those indicators as well. Help them achieve the right results, and they will buy.

### *. . . speak my words.*

The last element of Cicero's formula is vital. You need to use words that you are confident the customer will understand. And if there's a discrepancy between the language your audience uses and what you use, you should drop your own usage and mimic the audience. Your readers will understand more, feel more comfortable with your proposal, and be more likely to adopt your recommendations.

People get confused when they see more than two or three unfamiliar acronyms or pieces of jargon in a page of text. But they almost never tell you they're confused. They just wrinkle their forehead, shake their heads, and pull back. What they're thinking is, "This doesn't make sense. I don't understand this. These people are trying to snow me with a lot of techno-babble." And when customers think those kinds of thoughts, they become very reluctant to open their wallets.

Salespeople and proposal writers, in my experience, almost always overestimate the customer's level of understanding. We become so used to our own jargon that we find it easier to communicate that way than in everyday English. That's a big mistake and often results in delaying behavior. The customer wants one more demo, another presentation, needs another couple of weeks to consider the offers, and so on. What that often means is they don't understand.

## Analyzing the Audience

Cicero has given us the word: You must consider your audience when writing proposals. It's crucial. Ignoring or misunderstanding them dooms hundreds, probably thousands, of proposals to failure every year, proposals that otherwise answer the needs or solve the problems of the businesses soliciting them.

As Cicero has indicated, then, to write a winning proposal, you need to consider three key factors about the audience:

**1.** Personality type ("think my thoughts")

> Detail oriented
> Pragmatic
> Consensus-oriented
> Visionary

**2.** Level of expertise ("speak my words")

> Expert
> Informed

➤ Familiar
➤ Unfamiliar

   **3.**   Role in the decision process ("feel my feelings")

➤ Ultimate authority
➤ User
➤ Gatekeeper

To appeal to and hold the interest of this broad spectrum of readers, you must balance many presentation skills, providing enough technical data to please the highly informed, detail-oriented customer, but not so much that visionaries will be bored or the uninformed audience intimidated.

## Adjusting for Personality Type

The first factor about your decision maker is his or her personality type, by which I mean the individual's preferences regarding information gathering, information analysis, and communication styles. In fact, there are two questions to ask: what kind of personality type does my decision maker have? And what kind do I have? I guarantee you that if you don't consciously think about the customer's personality, you will inevitably create a proposal that is exactly the kind you would like to receive. Thus, if you're what I call a "pragmatic" and like things to be short, focused, and bottom-line oriented, you may get a rude awakening when you find out your reader is "analytical" and wants a lot of detail and thoroughness. You will definitely miss the mark unless you make a concerted effort to get out of your head and into the customer's.

Among the various tools available for analyzing and categorizing personalities, one of the most useful is the Myers-Briggs [Personality] Type Indicator. It is used by career counselors, family and marital therapists, educators, and many others to help people understand themselves and others better. The Myers-Briggs Type Indicator (MBTI) is a self-reporting test that indicates an individual's likely preferences on four pairs of opposing personality tendencies: introversion/extraversion; sensing/intuitive; thinking/feeling; and judging/perceiving.

The first pair has to do with the way people prefer to interact with the world. When you're on a plane, do you hope that no one sits next to you or do you welcome a bit of interaction? Would you rather read a proposal or watch a presentation?

The second pair indicates the two general ways people prefer to gather data. Some people, the sensors, are oriented toward facts by their nature. They tend to be very literal in their use of words. They need to look at all the details before reaching a conclusion. Their opposites, the "intuitives," find details boring and distracting. They prefer the big picture and appreciate the value of the generalist in an organization. Intuitives are often keen interpreters of nonverbal messages.

The third pairing, the thinking/feeling dichotomy, focuses on how people prefer to make decisions. Thinkers look at issues objectively, reach conclusions based on what is logical and fair rather than on what makes people happy. They find logic, facts, and technical detail more credible and appealing than emotion. Feelers, by contrast, consider a good decision to be one that builds consensus and harmony. They often make decisions by asking how any given course of action will affect the people involved. They would consider service and quality issues to be as important as price.

The final pairing, judging/perceiving, indicates how a person prefers to organize his or her time. Judgers prefer punctuality, structure, order, and closure. As a result, they are more likely to reach decisions quickly, to adhere to a schedule, and to be decisive. Perceivers prefer to "go with the flow." Spontaneity and flexibility are more important to them than organization or structure. They do not feel much inner pressure to reach closure or make decisions.

This brief summary of the Myers-Briggs approach does a disservice to a subtle, nonjudgmental, and extremely rich method of discussing personalities. Combining the various traits outlined in the preceding paragraphs yields sixteen different personality types. For a proposal writer, sixteen different types is a bit unwieldy, however, and it's pretty difficult to get your customer to take the Myers-Briggs test anyway. The point I want to make is that the various combinations of these tendencies do identify useful distinctions that we can use to help us modify the way we deliver our message. And we can reach conclusions about our customer's preferences without obtaining a detailed, clinical picture.

The kind of information you need is the kind you can garner from commonsense observation. What is the person's manner of speaking? Curt? Detailed? Emotional? Look at his or her office. How is it decorated? Are there schematics of jet engines on the wall or pictures of the kids? Golf and tennis trophies or Sierra Club posters? In your conversations, what really seems to matter to this person? If you had to list the ten things that your customer is most passionate about, could you do it? If not, start paying attention and asking. Learn about your decision maker as a person so that you can communicate with him or her as effectively and comfortably as possible.

The crucial personality characteristics that you need to consider when looking at your decision makers are (a) how they prefer to gather data and (b) how they prefer to make decisions. You might find it useful to set up a matrix based on those variables and position your key decision makers as accurately as you can within one of four quadrants. (See Figure 8-1.) For example, some decision makers prefer the information they receive to be factual, logical, empirical, or sensory in nature. Others are more prone to receiving information emotionally. In MBTI terms, this is a difference between thinkers and feelers. In terms of the second characteristic, how they prefer to make decisions, a useful distinction can be made between people who are prone to take action quickly and who want you to be brief (judgers), and people who are more passive and want you to be thorough (perceivers). When we combine these two characteristics, we get four types of decision maker: analytical, pragmatic, consensus-seeker, and visionary.

***Analytical or detail-oriented*** decision makers approach experience rationally and logically. They tend to dislike emotional terms and inexact language. They value accuracy and thoroughness. They want a lot of detail and substantiation. "How can I decide anything until I know everything?" they might ask. For them, truth resides in facts, procedures, evidence, or formulas, and they want to know how things work and how a decision can be logically justified. When they read your proposal (or watch your presentation), they constantly evaluate it even while they are in the act of perceiving it. If you are more of a bottom-line, pragmatic kind of decision maker, you may find their methodical approach frustrating, even irritating. That's a mistake. Be patient with their careful approach, demonstrate competence, back up everything you say with solid, factual evidence, avoid the use of hype or marketing fluff, base your persuasion on accuracy and logic, and to the extent possible, minimize their sense of risk by offering guarantees. Use words and phrases that are likely to trigger a quick, positive response from an analytical decision maker, such as *factual, proven, demonstrated, tested, experienced, detailed, criteria, objective, analysis, principles,* and *methodology.* Remember, though, that words alone won't cut it with this customer. They will want the words to be backed up with proof. Thus, merely saying that "we offer a wide selection of precise gas mixtures" may not be enough. Instead, get more specific: "We offer seven classes of calibration mixtures, ranging from EPA protocol certified mixes designed to meet the most stringent monitoring requirements to instrument calibration mixtures intended for the laboratory."

***Pragmatic*** types are results oriented. They focus on bottom-line issues. They want action. For them, the dominant issue isn't accuracy or thoroughness, it's impact. They want to know, "What have you got? What'll it do for me? How soon? At what price and at what payback?" They may become impatient with detail and want you to be concise, focused, and businesslike. (Can you see how a proposal written by an analytical person might alienate a pragmatic customer?) Like the analytical, they tend to be suspicious of emotional appeals. They want you to focus on facts, ideas, and evidence, not feelings or people. They admire precision, efficiency, and a well-organized delivery in both written and oral communications. Words and phrases that are likely to have positive connotations for the pragmatic decision maker include *planned, completed, mission, core competency, return on investment, competitive advantage, fixed, productive, total cost of ownership,* and *guaranteed,* among others.

**Consensus seekers** sincerely want to understand your message. They listen carefully, but in the process they are likely to focus on how everyone else is likely to feel about the decision rather than the details or facts. They value close working relationships, and want you to be dependable and reliable. They need to feel comfortable with you, your ideas, and the level of acceptance from the rest of the team before they will make a decision, and hate feeling pressured or rushed. Your personal interest and commitment to successful outcomes are an important part of your overall persuasive message, so back up your recommendations with your own assurances of support and follow through. Consensus seekers typically have a low tolerance for risk, so provide brief but compelling evidence and offer guarantees where possible. (Social proof is more likely to be convincing to this kind of decision maker than technical proof is, so great references and testimonials are important.) Consensus seekers often have flashes of insight into you as an individual and into your meaning, and they're likely to pick up inconsistencies between your apparent message and your hidden intentions. Unfortunately, they're also likely to garble technical or factual data, make erroneous assumptions, or introduce unwanted emotional messages. Trigger words and phrases for this type of decision maker include *reliable, flexible, consensus, adaptable, easy to use, widely accepted, loyal,* and *adaptable.*

**Visionaries** are the entrepreneurial types. They manage their lives, their responsibilities, and others on the basis of instinct and intuition. They tend to have strong egos and to believe that their ideas are fundamentally sound. They're the opposite of the detail-oriented types, in that they leap over logic and facts in quest of transformation and action. They're easily bored with technical data, but they love to be involved. On the down side, they have a hard time hearing or giving credence to any message that goes counter to their own assumptions or biases. They really aren't that interested in your product or service. What they're interested in is whether your product or service can help them accomplish their plans. They want you to be excited about their ideas, too, and to show that you are committed to them. Detail, routine, procedure, and process are not what they're about. Keep your proposal brief; make it interesting, colorful, and professional. Visionary decision makers want to know how your recommendations will move them closer to achieving their dreams. They also want to know who else is using your product or service, since they like to be associated with leaders, innovators, and winners. Visionaries fall into the category of customer that Geoffrey Moore in *Crossing the Chasm* has called the "early adopter," and they can be very helpful to you if you are going to market with something new, because they often will make a decision quickly even if there is little in the way of evidence that what you have actually works. Words and phrases that may work well in a proposal aimed at a visionary decision maker include *innovative, ingenious, creative, original, breakthrough, future, trend setting,* and even *cutting edge.*

These four broad personality types and their characteristics are summarized in Figure 8-1. Notice that the most difficult challenges will be between those personality types who are positioned on opposing corners of the diagram—a pragmatic selling to a consensus-seeker; a visionary selling to an analytical; and vice versa.

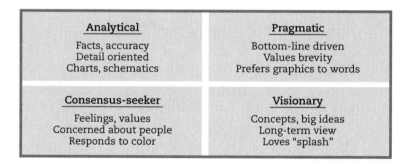

**Figure 8-1.** Four Personality Types and Their Preferences.

Sometimes a person's job requires him or her to act like a certain type of person even when that's not in alignment with their genuine personality. A high-level executive almost always has to think "pragmatically" and a person with technical responsibilities may have to adopt an "analytical" approach. Should you write to the "real" person or the "role" person? The answer depends on whether you're trying to inform or persuade. Information will be most acceptable if it's structured for the role; persuasion will be most successful if it's pitched to the real.

What about situations in which your proposal is going to a team or committee? What then? Write a different proposal for each member of the team? No, of course not. Instead, accommodate the different types of people who are likely to be on a team by structuring your proposal in two parts. The first part, which includes the cover letter, title page, table of contents, and executive summary, should be written for a pragmatic decision maker. Keep it short, focused on business issues, emphasize payback or ROI, and minimize the amount of jargon or technical detail. The second part, which consists of your substantiation, will contain technical details about your product or service, detailed timelines and project plans, and your "proof statements"—case studies, references, testimonials and awards, your answers to the RFP's questions, and other detailed content. This part should be written to appeal to the analytical decision maker. What about the other two types? Consensus seekers tend to get overrun in team processes by pragmatics, and visionaries are lousy team players by definition. So unless you have very strong evidence to the contrary, you don't need to worry much about those two when you are proposing to a team.

## Adjusting for Levels of Expertise

Another element of Cicero's formula has to do with the audience's level of expertise: "speak my words" means to use language or, more generally, content, that the audience understands. That applies to our use of jargon and acronyms, to the assumptions we explain and those we take for granted, and to the actual details we include.

In my experience, proposal writers almost always overestimate the level of understanding of their clients. One reason for this is that our own material—our products, our services, our technology, our methodology—becomes so familiar to us that it seems easy to understand. Another reason is that clients seldom tell us when they don't understand something. They may be worried that it's something they "should" understand, so they keep quiet. Or, in the context of a government bid, they may be forbidden by rules of procurement from asking for clarification.

Instead, when clients are not sure what you're talking about, they typically withdraw from the process and make noncommittal statements, such as, "We need to review this further internally." Or, "We may want to schedule another meeting before we reach a conclusion." Or, "We have some additional homework to do internally and then we'll get back to you." If you are hearing messages like these from prospects, it's possible they don't understand your proposal well enough to reach any kind of buying decision. And one thing you can count on is that when people feel confused, they don't buy.

Unfortunately, there's another reason why proposal writers communicate at a technical level that's over their clients' head: Laziness. Simplifying your content can be hard work. Once when I was working with a team at a major technology firm, I guess I began to annoy one of the technical sales specialists by my constant harping about simplifying. Finally, he turned to me and said, "Look, Tom, if the client doesn't understand this, he shouldn't be buying it."

"Don't worry," I said. "He won't."

One final comment before we look at specific guidelines for the four levels of readership: It's better to aim too low than too high. If the audience actually understands more than you thought they did, they may find your presentation a bit slow moving. As a result, they may skip over parts they already understand. But if the audience understands less than you thought, they're stuck. Your proposal content will go sailing over their heads and there isn't a thing they can do to make it more intelligible. So if you have to guess, err on the side of keeping things too simple, not too complex.

## Level One:
## The Uninformed Audience

As Will Rogers once said, "Everybody's ignorant, just on different stuff." The uninformed audience has virtually no background in your industry or area of expertise. For example, you might be dealing with a new hire, a subject matter expert from another discipline, or a general manager whose responsibilities are too broad to allow him or her to keep up with specific technical details. The CEO, to cite a fairly typical example, may have been an engineer at one point in his or her career, but today that person's responsibilities are unlikely to include nuts-and-bolts technology.

The level one audience is most likely to be a person who reads your cover letter and executive summary carefully, then skims the rest of your proposal, relying on colleagues or employees who are more familiar with the technical aspects to evaluate the details. For them, it's a good idea to try to keep your cover letter and executive summary short, businesslike, and focused on bottom-line issues.

Here are other guidelines to help you slant your writing toward level one audiences, people who are uninformed or unfamiliar with your field:

✦ *Provide only the information the reader truly needs to know.* Avoid digressions into technical details or options, no matter how interesting they may be to you. Keep your proposal focused on the specific functionality that will be of interest to this client.

Avoid giving the level one audience "extra" information—it is more likely to confuse than to impress.

✦ *Keep the presentation basic.* Short is better than long; simple is better than complex. Focus on what your solution will do for the customer, not on how it works.

✦ *Use clear, simple illustrations and lots of them.* There are two kinds of illustrations that can help the uninformed reader understand your message. *Visual illustrations* (bar and pie charts, uncomplicated graphs, simple flow charts, photos, maps, organization charts) communicate to many people more clearly than words. *Verbal illustrations* (comparisons, analogies, examples, metaphors, anecdotes) help the level one audience understand your point by making it more concrete.

✦ *Avoid using in-house jargon and keep acronyms to a minimum.* And don't forget that for this level of audience, your product and service names are jargon, too.

You may have been taught that the first time you use an acronym, you should present it in words and then put the acronym in parentheses immediately after the words. You might write something like this: "We have sales and support offices through Europe, the Middle East, and Africa (EMEA) to support clients of Abecedarian Avionics." But often that is not enough, because the words themselves may not make any sense to a level one reader. For example, one of the regional telephone companies was issuing letter proposals to small business owners for "ADSL service." When asked if the use of that acronym was appropriate for a level one audience, the proposal writers decided to make it clearer by spelling out the acronym the first time they used it. But ADSL stands for "asymmetric digital subscriber line," which isn't any clearer for a level one reader than the acronym itself. In fact, it might be worse. After some debate, they decided that a more effective way to communicate to their target audience was to start with the concept, explained in ordinary language:

*"You need high-speed access to the Internet. You can't afford to waste time while large file transfers crawl across your phone system to your computer. But you can't afford to replace your existing phone system or rewire your office, either. The answer? Our new Asymmetric Digital Subscriber Line, or ADSL service, which uses your existing phone lines but runs at speeds up to 125 times faster than traditional analog modems."*

Now the client understands the concept and the proposal writer can use the acronym in the rest of the proposal. Would it be necessary to define DSL service that thoroughly today? Probably not, since it has become a widely used application, but isn't it better to be too clear than too obscure?

✦ *Keep both the words and the sentences simple and short.* Use everyday language. Mainly choose words of one and two syllables. Try to keep your sentences to an average length of 15 to 18 words. For some reason, people often have a difficult time allowing themselves to write simply. Perhaps they fear that they won't be taken seriously if they don't use a complex vocabulary or long, convoluted syntax. But simplicity is a wonderful virtue in writing, particularly persuasive writing. In writing simply, you're not necessarily writing simplistically. By presenting information clearly, you're not guilty of patronizing the reader.

✦ *Avoid references to specialized reports, manuals, or sources.* This level of reader won't look for them, probably wouldn't understand them, and perhaps doesn't care. Your proposal needs to stand alone as a clear, self-contained document, particularly for the level one reader.

✦ *Describe procedures or processes in a simple, step-by-step fashion.* When describing a project plan or explaining how something works, you will communicate more successfully if you use a simple chronological structure rather than a series of complex options. Flow charts and similar diagrams can be a great help, too, as long as they're clear. A complex, multi-level Gantt chart would not be a useful tool for the level one reader.

## Level Two:
## The Acquainted Audience

An audience somewhat acquainted with your recommendations may have considerable education or experience, perhaps even in your general field (business management, electrical engineering, marketing, accounting, whatever), but still lacks detailed, in-depth knowledge of your specific area of expertise. Many of the decision makers to whom you write proposals will be at this level.

All of the guidelines for level one are appropriate for level two, because they enhance the simplicity and clarity of the writing. For the most part, you will make slightly different judgment calls regarding the jargon to be defined, the acronyms to be left unexplained, and the examples to be included. You won't offend anybody by producing a proposal that is too easy to understand, but for this audience you can make more assumptions and skip over the basics a little quicker.

Here are some guidelines to follow:

+ *Present your proposal in a larger context—a frame of reference within which your proposal can be positioned and categorized.* For example, if you are recommending an online inventory control system that provides remote access to real-time inventory data for field salespeople, start by discussing the client's current sales model, or the client's move to an e-commerce approach, or changes in the way supply chains are being managed. You could start with business objectives, regulatory changes, operational concerns, technological developments, or some other topic of broad concern. The point is to show that what you will describe (your product or service) is relevant to the reader's concerns and has a place within the reader's worldview. This positioning statement can be the springboard for your discussion of the client's problem, of course, but even in the more specifically technical sections of your proposal, you should move from general and familiar to specific and new.

+ *Use more complex graphics, tables, and figures.* This audience will look at and understand visual material that is more complicated and that contains more data. However, you should still avoid equations, programming statements, schematics, complex decision trees, and other specialized examples or illustrations. You should definitely resist the urge to include illustrations from user documentation or technical manuals.

+ *Include specialized content, such as technical reports, surveys, brief technical documentation, excerpts from manuals, product comparisons, and so forth, if it's really necessary.* But challenge yourself on this. Will it really help? Will it help them make a decision? Or are we succumbing to the tendency to build our proposals based on the "thud" factor—throwing in anything that adds bulk, even if it doesn't add much value? If you do decide to include this kind of specialized material, put it in an appendix and provide an introductory paragraph or two that explains its relevance.

+ *Use the accepted jargon of the field, but avoid in-house jargon.* If you are writing a proposal for telecommunications services to a level two audience, you could use terms such as "DSL," "VoIP" or "ISDN lines" without worry. (But remember that we all tend to overestimate the understanding of our audience, so if in doubt, clarify.)

*Level Three:*
*The Informed Audience*

This audience has extensive knowledge of your field, but less knowledge of the specialized project, product, or service you are proposing. For example, a longtime client may know a lot about your material handling systems, but may not possess any details about the new, photoelectric measurement tools you are introducing. An MIS or IT manager may be very knowledgeable about LANs, WANs, and corporate database administration, but may not be aware of the specific features of the software you provide to locate duplicate entries in a database.

The guidelines:

✦ *Establish immediate links between the familiar and the new.* Suppose you are proposing that your client outsource all facility management services to your firm. If you know that they already contract for cleaning and landscaping services, you can draw a parallel between those specific niches and the idea of turning over complete management of the property to your firm.

✦ *Focus on the new or unique aspects of what you are offering.* You can assume with a level three audience that they are familiar with the basics of your product or service. What they need to know is what differentiates your new offering from what they already have and how those differences will benefit their organization.

✦ *Stay client centered as you write your proposal.* The temptation when writing to a more knowledgeable audience is to lapse into informative writing, to use jargon, to focus on technology for its own sake. But that won't work. Even though this decision maker is very well informed, you must show how your recommendations help solve the prospect's problems or meet the organization's needs. No one buys a new product just to get cool new features. Instead, they buy products whose features will deliver important outcomes for their organizations that aren't otherwise available.

## Level Four:
### The Expert Audience

The expert audience knows as much (or more) about the products and services you are offering as you do. The expert has extensive knowledge not only of your field, but detailed familiarity with the latest work in that field, the various products and options offered by your company and your competitors, and the industry trends.

The good news is that it's very easy to communicate with the expert audience, because it's not much different from talking with your own colleagues. The bad news is that true experts in your customer base are extremely rare.

You will have some prospects or customers who think they are experts, of course. But in reality there are very few people inside your own firm who fit this description, much less somebody on the outside among your client and prospect base. Maybe that's a good thing. Even though it means you have to do a little more work in writing the proposal clearly, it also means that you are adding value to the relationship. If lots of people knew all about your products and your services, what role would you play?

If you do encounter a true expert among your prospects or customers, here are some guidelines to follow when you write your proposal:

✦ *Summarize technical background information or indicate where it can be obtained.* The expert decision maker is more likely to be an analytical personality type, so he or she will want to have access to as much detail as possible. If you provide it by reference or attachment, you will be presenting a "complete" proposal.

✦ *Use jargon (but be judicious).* Even for an expert, encountering a slew of acronyms and jargon makes for a distasteful reading experience.

✦ *Use math, equations, programming statements, or technical explanations if they're needed.* Almost without exception, this kind of technical content will appear in the body of a proposal, not in the executive summary.

✦ *Maintain your objectivity, use a professional tone, but remember that your most important job is to persuade.* Even for the expert audience, your proposal must constantly answer the question, "So what?" In providing details, link them to benefits the decision maker cares about.

## The Decision Maker's Role and Values

Ideally, every proposal you write will go directly into the hands of the final authority, the one person charged with responsibility for signing the contract or issuing the purchase order. But in this imperfect world of ours, you will probably have to deal with intermediaries, advisors, influencers, and others in the client organization, winning their approval as you inch your deal forward toward the final throne of power. Understanding how the concerns of a decision maker change depending on his or her role (as shown in Figure 8-2) can help you position your proposal as effectively as possible.

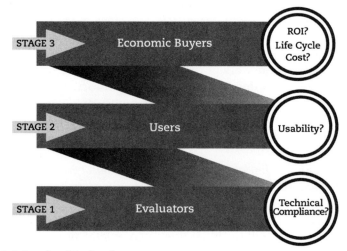

**Figure 8-2.** Levels of Evaluation.

Often a proposal must go through a series of evaluations. They may be sequential, with the number of candidate proposals decreasing as weak offerings are eliminated at each stage. Thus, the first-stage evaluator, who plays a gatekeeper's role, may initially review a dozen submissions, eliminating half of them very quickly on narrow grounds. The user community may then look at that half dozen, reducing the number of candidates to just two or three. From this crop of survivors, the economic decision maker will attempt to select the proposal that offers the best return on investment, the lowest total cost of ownership, or some other measure of payback.

In other cases, the evaluations may occur simultaneously, with the entire team offering critiques and comments. However, because the team members will come from different areas of the company where they perform different roles, their values will also be different.

## The Gatekeeper

A person who has the role of gatekeeper is there to winnow down the number of proposals to a manageable few. The gatekeeper's job is to filter out solutions that are inappropriate in terms of some set of clearly defined criteria. As a result, the gatekeeper is looking for a reason to reject rather than for a reason to recommend. In addition, gatekeepers may often feel that they're in a vulnerable position, since their recommendation could come back to haunt them if it proves to be a bad one. It's easier to justify rejecting what would have been a good choice than it is to explain why you recommended what proved to be a terrible one. Their tendency, therefore, is to be extremely critical and to assume the worst whenever they have doubts. Finally, gatekeepers are often drawn from that category of personalities who love details. As a result, you must provide the gatekeeper with clear, specific evidence that you meet the requirements of the RFP.

In an informal research study, we interviewed people who make their living doing the first pass at evaluating proposals—in other words, gatekeepers. We asked to them share their biggest complaints regarding the proposals they receive. Boy, did they vent! Their answers—and many have not been included in the Evaluators' Complaints sidebar—should give you an idea of what to avoid when submitting your proposal for review by a gatekeeper.

---

### Evaluators' Complaints

1. The author did not follow the "Instructions to Offeror."

2. The proposal contains no compliance matrix. As a result, evaluators spend a lot of time trying to figure out if the response is compliant or not.

3. Emphasis is placed on the "wrong" portions of the solicitation (failure to understand the award criteria).

4. Lack of meaningful proposal theme(s). No story is told to the evaluator.

5. Poorly structured response, illogical TOC, misuse of appendices.

6. Differentiators are not used at all or are not clear.

7. Many requirements are not addressed at all. (Silence on the requirements means the proposal is noncompliant.)

8. Technical claims not substantiated with tangible data.

9. Difficult to read: straight text, no bullets, no headings, poor graphics, no white space.

10. Overuse of boilerplate. The response is not tailored to the business needs of the client or agency issuing the RFP.

## The User

The user bases his or her recommendation on criteria that are less specific and technical than those used by the gatekeeper. The user evaluates the probable impact of your solution on performance: Will this work? Will it actually make things better around here? Does it look easy? Reliable? Simple to maintain? Quick to learn? Does it meet our needs?

The user has a lot of power, sometimes much more than the gatekeeper, because the user will end up actually using the product or service. And the user knows that lots of solutions that meet the technical specs established in an RFP don't actually do the job when they're installed or implemented.

## The Ultimate Authority

The person who makes the final decision, who has veto power over the project, usually derives his or her power from direct access to or control over the money. The ultimate authority—the economic buyer—is the boss, the owner, the CEO. And the ultimate authority's criteria are usually the needs of the business. What will be the bottom-line impact of this solution? What kind of return will this investment provide?

# 9    Fluff, Guff, Geek, and Weasel:

## The Art of Saying What You Mean

As READERS, WE ALL KNOW WHAT WE LIKE: CONciseness. Clarity. Simplicity. Unfortunately, when we sit down to write, we too often fail to deliver anything like that. We produce lengthy, verbose, and complicated documents. Especially when writing proposals, many people subscribe to the "bulk" theory. Pile on the paper and the reader will give in out of sheer exhaustion. Got some documentation? Throw it in there! Got some testing plans? Throw them in, too! Put it all in. Who knows—if we put enough stuff in our proposal, something is bound to click with the evaluator and we'll get the job.

That's ridiculous, of course. When we lard our proposals will irrelevant junk, we irritate the reader and make it more difficult for him or her to find the content that actually matters. To my knowledge, nobody has ever made a buying decision based on the thud factor—which proposal makes the loudest noise when dropped on the desk. It's true, of course, that an analytical decision maker will want quite a bit of detail, but even for the analytical reader the details must be focused and relevant. Details in and of themselves have no value.

In a simple experiment we conducted, we asked people who make their living evaluating proposals to review three sample proposals. Actually, we weren't interested in their reviews at all. We just wanted to see which proposal they picked up first. One of them was 25 pages long, one was 50 pages, and one was 100 pages. Which one do you think they reached for first? That's right—the short one.

Why does that matter? Well, let's suppose that you produced the short proposal. And you organized it using the NOSE pattern, so you have focused on the client's Needs, detailed their Outcomes, recommended a Solution, and substantiated with convincing Evidence that you can do the job on time and on budget. In addition, you've developed a payback calculation that's quantified and based on the client's own data, and you've linked that payback both to your differentiators and to credible evidence suggesting that this client is likely to see the kind of return you're forecasting. If this is the proposal your client reads first, what will he or she think of the bloated, unfocused, unpersuasive proposals that come second and third? They will appear worse by the contrast and will be evaluated even more harshly.

Lots of people pay lip service to short, direct, clear writing, but the reality is you don't see much of it. Within the business, scientific, and academic communities there seems to be a cultural bias against clarity and simplicity. Some of that may stem from insecurity. Not feeling confident about his or her knowledge, experience, or company reputation, the writer tries to impress the reader with big words, long sentences, and lots of extraneous content. Sometimes bad writing stems from laziness. Sloppy, careless writing takes less time and effort, even when it produces longer documents, than carefully edited writing. And sometimes bad writing is the result of bad training. Many of us remember English classes in which "good" writing seemed to be synonymous with big words, complicated syntax, and convoluted thinking.

Overcome your anxiety and insecurity. Make the effort to write the kind of prose you want to receive—clear, compelling, and concise. And put behind you the bad training and wrong-headed advice you received from your English teachers. Your proposals are too important to your career and the success of your business. You must write them so that the decision maker understands them, feels comfortable with them, and is motivated to adopt your recommendations. That means writing as clearly and economically as possible.

## Eliminate the Fluff, Guff, Geek, and Weasel

Most lousy proposals have a few characteristics in common. By now, I'm sure you know what they are as well as I do: They're product focused rather than client focused. They're factual rather than persuasive. They're disorganized. They lack a clear value proposition. But there's one characteristic we haven't looked at yet: They use Fluff, Guff, Geek, and Weasel to impress or intimidate the reader rather than writing clearly to communicate.

***Fluff*** is the language of grandiose claims, vague assertions, and hype. We see this kind of writing too often in marketing materials, on corporate Web sites, and in proposals and sales letters. People must think this writing is persuasive, because they use it so often. But in reality it's exactly the opposite—it annoys the readers and discourages them from doing business with us. Here are some examples of words and phrases typical of Fluff. Does anything look familiar here?

- World class
- Best of breed
- State of the art
- Compelling
- Leading edge
- Quality focused
- Uniquely qualified
- Innovative
- Highly available

- High performance
- Commitment to excellence
- Synergy
- User friendly
- Integrated
- Partnership
- Seamless
- Robust
- Proven

*Guff* is the language of bureaucrats. It's needlessly complex, pompous, and dense. It depends on long, complicated sentences, lots of big words, and lots of passive-voice constructions to create an almost impenetrable barrier to understanding. Rather than clarifying or persuading, Guff is used to intimidate people. The implicit message is, "I'm much smarter than you are, so don't question me about anything." How's that for increasing cognitive dissonance?

Here is an example that came from an actual executive summary:

*The dimensionality of expected project problems coupled with the limited time available for preparation means that choices will have to be made to assure viability of the most critical analytical processes. Thus, a leveraging of problem similarities and process relationships to allow sharing of resources and solutions, will be needed to contain cost and staff expenditures and assure maximum payoff from effected solutions.*

Notice that the two sentences total 63 words, for an average sentence length of 31.5 each. That's about twice as long as educated adult readers find comfortable to decode. Also, there are 18 words with three or more syllables—about three times as many as we should be using on average. Finally, both sentences contain passive voice constructions: "choices will have to be made . . ." and "a leveraging . . . will be needed . . . ." Made by whom? Needed by whom?

*Geek* is language that's too technical or too obscure for the intended reader. People lapse into Geek when they write to themselves instead of thinking about what the reader needs. We recognize Geek when somebody from a field other than our own writes it, but we are often deaf to it in our own writing. Here's an example:

*We propose a method that gives evolved programs the incentive to strategically allocate computation time among fitness cases. Specifically, with an aggregate computation time ceiling imposed over a series of fitness cases, evolved programs dynamically choose when to stop*

*processing each fitness case with minimal damage to domain perfor-
mance.*

**Weasel** is language that sounds wishy-washy, even sneaky. It avoids
saying anything directly or definitively. Instead, every assertion is qualified to oblivion. Weasel makes heavy use of passive voice and subjunc-
tive constructions. Here's an example of Weasel:

> *We believe that we have proposed an effective solution, based on the
> information we have at this time. We look forward to exploring details
> of the project at greater depth in the future, but for now we hope that
> this initial proposal will suggest that there is a compelling case for con-
> sidering us to receive this contract.*

Unfortunately, the more you're exposed to this kind of gobbledy-
gook, the more you tend to mimic it in your own writing. Often the
RFPs you receive are written so poorly that it's hard to figure out what
they mean. You probably receive dozens of e-mails each day, many of
which are confusing and hard to understand. Internal documents, policy statements, contracts, instruction manuals, even things you'd reasonably expect to be clear, like training materials or articles in
professional journals, are so dense, so hard to read, that you wonder if
the authors themselves know what they are trying to say. When you're
swimming in a sea of Fluff, Guff, Geek, and Weasel, it's hard to keep
your head above water and communicate clearly.

Assuming that you subscribe to the linguistic version of the Golden
Rule, "Send unto others what you would like to receive yourself," the
question arises: How can you write proposals that are clear and easy to
understand? After all, anybody can say, "Write clearly." The tough part
is explaining how to do that. And what is clarity, anyway? How do you
know if something is clear or not?

Here's my definition of clear writing: the reader understands what you
wrote after reading it once. That's it. If the reader has to go back over something in your proposal and reread it to figure it out, you messed up.

Let's avoid that kind of mistake. Here are a few simple techniques
that will help you maximize your clarity:

1. Avoid writing long or overly complicated sentences.
2. Avoid using passive voice constructions too frequently.
3. Put your key points up front, which is the most prominent position for them.
4. Follow Sant's Law in each sentence you write.

Let's take a look at each technique in more detail.

## Avoid Long, Complicated Sentences

Have you ever found yourself reading something complicated, straining to understand, when your brain suddenly goes "blue screen"? You go back to the beginning of the passage and start over again. You reread the material, not because it was so enjoyable going through it the first time that you want to savor the experience once more, but rather because your brain just couldn't fuse it into anything that made sense. Usually when that happens, you have run up against a poorly constructed, overly complicated sentence, and your brain simply goes into overload. When you pick the sentence apart and look at it carefully, you realize that what it's trying to say isn't all that difficult. It was just badly expressed. The sentence was too complex to make sense.

Sentence complexity is a function of two elements: length and syntactic structure. They both play a role.

**Length** is simply a matter of how many words your sentences contain (not much more than 15 words for maximum readability). But let's look at a whopper:

> *For this program, it is proposed that the kickoff meeting be one day in length with the first half of the day consisting of the following activities: [list follows]*

*It is proposed that . . . ?* By whom? *One day in length?* As opposed to what—one day in width? This bloated sentence is bordering on silliness. Here's a rewrite that cuts it from 27 words to 12 and gets rid of several other problems, too:

> *We propose a one-day kickoff meeting. The first half will cover: [list follows]*

**Syntactic structure** is a matter of how many embedded elements the sentence contains. A simple sentence contains one idea, expressed in one subject and one verb. A compound sentence contains two [or more] related ideas, with multiple subjects and multiple verbs. A complex sentence contains one or more dependent clauses that are attached to a simple sentence, and a compound/complex sentence includes every permutation you can imagine. The more complexity in your sentences, the more difficult they are to decode. Please understand that I'm not suggesting you write in a Dick-and-Jane style. But unnecessary complexity and sloppy syntax won't help you win any deals, because they are likely to confuse, even alienate, the reader.

Often the quickest way to simplify your writing is to break a long, complicated sentence into a couple of shorter, simpler ones. Take a look at this example, drawn from a real proposal but modified to protect the author from embarrassment and me from a lawsuit. Nova is a name I made up, but the original company provides IT consulting and outsourced help desk services:

*Nova, Inc. has been an industry leader in strategic business programs related to the interaction of the needs of our customers and our philosophies towards Total Quality Management. Our goal is to be able to provide a business program that meets two specific criteria:*

*To meet the business requirements of the customer by providing complete flexibility, the highest level of customer service and responsiveness, decreased operating expense, increased profit and,*

*To provide a financial benefit to Nova which will assure Nova's ability to be a long-term business partner*

Somebody's trying to sound smart here. But they're not succeeding. By writing such a convoluted mess, they have actually implied several things I'm sure they don't mean. First, I doubt that their business is focused on the interaction of customer needs with Nova's TQM philosophies. I think they mean something like this:

*Nova, Inc. has become an industry leader by focusing on meeting our customers' needs and by implementing the most rigorous quality methodology in the Help Desk field.*

The next sentence is okay, although the phrase "business program" seems unnecessarily vague. But when you look at the two criteria, it's a bit of a mess again because the first criterion actually contains four distinct criteria and the second criterion sounds like an indirect way of saying "we want to make as much money as possible." The whole thing would be easier to understand and more convincing if it read something like this:

*We will provide you with a Help Desk program that delivers the following:*

- *Flexibility in setting up and managing the program so that it meets your needs*
- *The highest level of customer service*

> ✦ *Fast answers to your employees' questions and problems*
> ✦ *An overall decrease in your operating costs by providing you with a quality service at a lower price than you could do it yourself*
> ✦ *Increased profitability for your organization through higher employee productivity*

Notice how spreading out the bullet points gives them a little more impact. Using bullet points or enumeration is a good idea, by the way, because the brain decodes them as discrete syntactic units—as if they were separate little sentences. But they still need to be short and they should be written in parallel form.

## Avoid Passive Voice

In English, you have two options for creating declarative sentences (that is, sentences that make a statement): the active voice or the passive voice. The term *voice* is a piece of grammar jargon that refers to the relationship between the subject in a sentence and the verb. In the active voice, which we use the vast majority of the time, the subject does the action expressed in the verb. For example:

*Our sales team visited the client's site.*

"Sales team" is the subject. And they're the ones who did the visiting.

To say the same thing in the passive voice, you put the recipient of the action in the subject slot. That inverts the typical relationship between subject and verb. For example, here's our sentence above, rewritten in passive voice:

*The client's site was visited by our sales team.*

Here "site" is the subject and it received an action, namely it "was visited." There's nothing ungrammatical about that sentence. It's perfectly legal. And if your meaning dictates that you should focus on what got visited, rather than who did the visiting, it's a good choice. (Consider a sentence like this: "Interstate 75 is being repaired just south of Dayton." Do you care who is doing the repairs? No. You just want to know the location so you can avoid it.)

So what's wrong with using passive voice? The main problem is that because we don't hear it or read it very often, it's harder to decode. Our brains do a little skip step to sort things out. In passive voice, the normal relationship of cause to effect is reversed, so we have to rethink it to figure out who did what to whom.

Another problem with passive voice is that you don't actually have to say who did anything. Passive voice is the language of nonresponsibility and is frequently used as a way to communicate bad news:

*A decision has been made to terminate your employment.*

(I'll bet that if you got an e-mail or a memo with that statement in it, the first question you would have is "Who made that stupid decision?" Since the sentence is in passive voice, there's no way to know. Nobody made it, apparently. It just happened somehow.)

Combine these weaknesses of passive voice with a long sentence, throw in some big words and some jargon, and you have a recipe for incomprehensibility. In fact, you have Guff.

People normally use passive voice about 10 percent of the time. That's a good percentage for your writing, too. If you run the grammar checker in your word processor, it will identify passive voice constructions for you. Most of the time it's right, although occasionally it will confuse a present or past progressive tense for passive. If it highlights a passive voice sentence, try to switch the syntax around into active voice. Otherwise, you're forcing the reader to decode a sentence structure that's less familiar than the common active voice patterns, and you're possibly writing in a style that evades responsibility. As a result, your proposal will seem less convincing, less persuasive, than it would otherwise.

## Put the Important Stuff Up Front

It's a good idea to put the most important facts, information, opinions, or observations up front—that is, the things that are most important to the decision maker. This applies to the document as a whole, to sections within a document, to paragraphs, even to sentences. It's another example of the phenomenon we called the primacy principle in Chapter 6.

*Proposals and presentations* will be most persuasive if they are organized in terms of what matters to the decision maker. That's why the NOSE pattern works. Most of your clients are concerned first about their own problems, needs, issues, or opportunities. Next, they are concerned about using their money and time wisely, investing into activities that yield the highest rate of return. As a result, both your cover letter and your executive summary should focus on those two elements of content first. (You can see why it's deadly to start a proposal with your company's history or an overview of your products.)

*Sections of proposals* will be easier to read and understand if they start with an overview. The overview should indicate what this part of the proposal is about and how it's organized. You can summarize the key points presented in the section. But don't make the section introduction purely descriptive. Be sure to put a strong selling statement at the outset of each section, too.

*Paragraphs* make more sense when they start with a clear topic sentence. This is pretty basic stuff. You were probably introduced to the concept of topic sentences way back when, probably in the seventh or eighth grade. But since you may have been noticing the opposite sex for the first time about then, it's possible you missed it.

*Sentences* also benefit from following the primacy principle. For example, consider this:

> *Providing senior leadership during some of the recent projects presented in the table below is Mr. Ralph Brown.*

Doesn't that sound odd? (It sounds like Ralph is in the table, doesn't it?) If we put the important point, namely Ralph's leadership, up front, it will read much better:

> *Mr. Ralph Brown provided senior leadership for some of the projects listed below.*

## Apply Sant's Law to Every Sentence

What is Sant's Law? Well, in all modesty, it's the most important breakthrough in writing clear, direct prose since the invention of the simple sentence. Okay, maybe I'm not being all that modest. Or all that honest, either. But it is a technique that can help you identify whether your sentences are well constructed. And it's pretty easy to use.

Here it is in a nutshell: *To write a clear, direct sentence, make sure the key idea is embedded in the heart of the sentence.*

What's the heart of the sentence? How can you determine whether your idea is properly embedded there? If you think back to English class in about the eighth grade, you may have vague memories of being called to the front of the room to diagram sentences on the board. At the time, you probably thought it was a stupid way to ruin a perfectly good afternoon. I know I did. But it turns out that it can be useful.

Remember the first step in diagramming a sentence? You had to draw a straight, horizontal line. And what went on that line? The subject of the sentence, the verb, and the complement—usually the direct object or indirect object. So suppose you were asked to diagram this sentence:

*A bright red car hit my mother's new pickup truck broadside.*

The first thing you would do is draw that horizontal line and write down the subject, verb, and complement:

*car | hit / truck .*

That's the first step and, to apply Sant's law, the only step you have to take. You probably remember that the rest of the words in the sentence dangle down below the horizontal line, depending on which part of the sentence they modify. Who cares? All that matters is this: Does the subject/verb/complement communicate the key idea? In this case, yes. A car hit a truck. That's the main point, isn't it?

Perhaps you'll run across a sentence like this in one of your proposals:

*It would appear that enhanced access to the database on the part of our key executives is desirable.*

Can you even find the subject and verb in that thing? Well, the grammatical subject is "It" and the verb is "would appear." Not too exciting, is it? Not very clear either.

Try to rewrite the sentence so that the key ideas are in the key grammatical slots. Something like this would work:

*Our key executives need better access to the database.*

If you apply Sant's Law, what do you get? The subject is "executives," the verb is "need," and the complement is "access."

*Executives need access . . .*

Is that the key idea? I think so.

## Simple Words:
## The Traps to Avoid

The English philosopher John Locke wrote in *An Essay Concerning Human Understanding:*

*Vague and insignificant forms of speech, and abuse of language have so long passed for mysteries of science; and hard and misapplied words, with little or no meaning, have, by prescription, such a right to be mis-*

*taken for deep learning and height of speculation, that it will not be easy to persuade either those who speak or those who hear them, that they are but the covers of ignorance, and hindrance of true knowledge.*

Even though Locke was writing in 1690, it sounds like he was pretty sick of people who use pompous language to impress others instead of to communicate. I guess it's just another sign that some things never change.

In their effort to be impressive and to sound smart, writers often fall into a number of verbal traps. Sometimes they are covering their own ignorance, sometimes they are trying to pretend that they have "deep learning." Sometimes they just can't write worth a darn.

Here are some common traps to avoid:

## Trap 1:
### Using Jargon

What does using jargon accomplish for us? Well, it slows down the sales cycle, undercuts the rapport we've tried to establish, and raises doubts about our integrity and competence. Great.

The problem is that our sensitivity to in-house jargon, that sharp awareness of it that we have as new employees, quickly fades. As we attend more and more meetings and read truckloads of e-mails, as we attend training classes and participate on projects, we begin to absorb some of the meanings and connotations of the jargon we encounter. Somehow, almost imperceptibly, what was unknown and confusing becomes familiar and comfortable. *Their* jargon becomes *our* jargon. At that point, we have successfully completed one of the most important processes of socialization—acquiring the group's language. Instead of being a barrier that kept us out, jargon has become a useful tool that proves we are "in."

And that's when jargon becomes dangerous for you as a proposal writer. When you no longer recognize jargon for what it is—the specialized technical language of a particular company, department, industry, or field of experience—you are most likely to misuse it. Unfortunately, sometimes you need to use it. So how can you introduce jargon into your proposal text without confusing or alienating the reader? You must focus on the functional meaning of the jargon, not merely its lexical definition. By that I mean it's not enough to simply explain what the letters of an acronym stand for, nor is it enough to define a term's meaning by substituting other jargon in its place. Help your customer understand the term's significance at the outset of your proposal. Then you can use it throughout.

## Trap 2:
## Dangling Your Participles

When I was teaching English at UCLA, a student in one of my composition classes submitted a paper in which he asserted:

*After rotting in the cellar for weeks, my brother brought up some oranges.*

I had a hunch I knew what he really meant to say, but then I hadn't seen his brother and in Southern California one never knows. I wrote in the margin of the paper: "Please do not allow your brother to visit this campus."

In grammatical terms, that's a dangling participle; in human terms, it was an embarrassment.

## Trap 3:
## Creating Noun Clusters

I had to invent the term "noun cluster" because such a construction didn't have an official name when I first started complaining about it. Other writers have called them "jammed modifiers" or have referred to these constructions as "noun stacking" or "nominalization." What are they? A cluster of nouns all wadded together, a bolus of incomprehensibility.

To form a noun cluster, you simply string a bunch of nouns together. That's it. There's no special talent required for this activity. In fact, it probably helps to have no talent, or at least no ear, for language.

You see noun clusters frequently in technical proposals and technical documentation. Since we all like to sound smart and high-tech, they're spreading into more mundane areas as well. Now you see them in banking, finance, manufacturing, even advertising. You will see them in job titles, department designations, and those too-clever names sometimes given to in-house software applications, names specially constructed so that they form a nifty acronym that spells a word. And the place you will probably see them most frequently is in the title of proposals, especially technical proposals.

For example, here's a title that appeared on a proposal I received

*FAX TRANSMISSION NETWORK ACCESS COST*
*OPTIMIZATION PROPOSAL*

Isn't that a jewel? Or how about these beauties:

✦ *Last year, we published the earth resources satellite field station implementation, maintenance, repair manual.*

✦ *It is a direct drive remote terminal software modification package designed by our internal software applications development management group.*

Bear in mind, it's always been legal in English to use one noun to modify another noun. The first noun functions as an adjective in such a construction and is usually called an "attributive noun." Examples are *telephone company, cellular phone, bus stop, marriage certificate, book store,* and *materials laboratory.* The problem arises when many are crammed together. The reader has to go back through, figure out which nouns are functioning as nouns, which are adjectives, what goes with what, and try to make sense out of it.

If you catch yourself writing a noun cluster, what should you do? First, identify the key noun in the sequence. Then put it up front in the sequence. Look for an opportunity to use a verb and don't hesitate to link your words with a few prepositions.

Take the first example, the proposal title. As you can see, there's no verb at all in the title. What is the writer trying to say? That we can "optimize" the costs of accessing network service for transmitting faxes? Maybe. But do we want to "optimize" costs? That's ambiguous enough that it might mean costs are going up. After all, optimized costs from the vendor's perspective would be higher, right? Anyway, let's assume the writer is trying to suggest that his or her proposal will enable us to save money when we send faxes over their network. Instead of using the buzzword "optimize," let's try some ordinary English:

> *REDUCING THE COSTS OF NETWORK ACCESS*
> *FOR TRANSMITTING FAXES*

Or maybe something even simpler:

> *REDUCING THE COST OF SENDING FAXES:*
> A PROPOSAL TO ENHANCE YOUR NETWORK SERVICE

### Trap 4:
### Using Knotty Words Incorrectly

I remember reading a cover letter that stated how much the RFP had "peaked" the writers' interest. Hmmm. I don't think so. It probably didn't "peek," either. Maybe what they were trying to say was that the RFP had "piqued" their interest.

Another proposal writer slipped into the common mistake of using a currently popular buzzword in his writing without really know what it means or how it's spelled. He wrote: "This application is ideal for use in a nitch market." *Nitch?* Have you ever seen a "nitch market"? Do you think one could buy a nitch on sale there? Of course, the writer meant "niche." But the damage is done.

Okay, I admit it. There are lots of confusing words in English. Both of the previous examples come from foreign languages and are spelled in unusual ways. Sometimes words look like other words but mean something different. Or they can be correct in one context but not in another. The problem is that using these difficult or "knotty" words incorrectly can diminish your credibility and even distract the reader. (Of course, it's always possible the evaluator won't know how to use them correctly, either, and from the evidence contained in a lot of RFPs, that's probably a safe bet. However, it's not worth taking the chance.)

So what's a proposal writer to do? Use a dictionary, for one thing. Don't depend on your word processor to edit your usage. It won't. Whenever you're not sure about a word, what it means, or how you should use it, check it in a good (i.e., hardbound) dictionary. This is especially smart if you've been rummaging through the thesaurus looking for nifty new words. Check their full meaning, including their connotations, before you use them. *Stubborn, obdurate, pig-headed* and *firm-principled* are all listed as synonyms in the thesaurus, but they don't mean the same thing. (The boss is firm-principled. The jerk two cubicles over is pig-headed.)

Here are some knotty usage problems that can pop up in proposal writing—you might have run into them in your own work. Maybe a few of them bother you, too.

### Affect/Effect

This pair drives people nuts. *Affect* is usually a verb: "Your choice of a motorized log splitter will inevitably affect the logging camp's productivity." *Effect* is usually a noun. "Your choice will also have an effect on safety." One way to remember which is which: think of *"the effect."* "The" can't precede a verb, so link the "e" at the end of "the" with the "e" that begins "effect." (Sometimes people who speak in psychobabble use "affect" to refer to a person's emotional state. And sometimes lawyers like to use "effect" or "effectuate" as a verb, meaning "to bring about or execute." Ignore these people. Nobody ever learned to write clearly by imitating lawyers' or psychologists' styles.)

### Anxious/Eager

People often write that they are "anxious to work on this project." To which the reader might reasonably ask, "Why? What aren't you telling me?" *Anxious* means nervous or concerned. You will communicate more forcefully, with less ambiguity, if you say that you are *eager* to work on the project, not *anxious.*

### Assure/Ensure/Insure

All three of these words mean about the same thing: "to make certain or secure." *Assure* refers to people, though, and suggests putting someone at ease, reducing anxiety or worry. *Ensure* and *insure* both mean "to secure from harm," but *insure* has a stronger implication. If you *insure* something, the reader may take that as your guarantee of a positive outcome, whereas *ensuring* or *assuring* may imply serious effort on your part but no guarantee.

### Compliment/Complement

Have you ever seen a menu that promised an appetizer or salad that would "compliment" your meal? But when you ordered it, what happened? Nothing. It didn't say a word. No compliments. No pleasantries at all. *Compliment* means "flattery" or "praise." A *complement* is something that completes a whole: "The program modules complement each other."

### Data is/Data are

Everybody who took Latin in high school, and even a few former altar boys and girls, love to pounce on your throat if you say, "The data is in the computer," or whatever. "Data," they snootily inform you, "is the plural form of datum. Therefore, it must take a plural verb." Yeah, well . . . Maybe that's why Latin is a dead language. Those Romans were too uptight about these things. In fact, *data* as used in English is a "collective singular noun," which is grammar jargon for such words as *jury, committee, team, staff,* and *humanity.* If the data you're writing about is a homogenous whole, use a singular verb: "The billing data is backed up daily." But if the data in question is a hodgepodge, use a plural: "They discovered that their sales and customer support data were located in different parts of the system."

### Imply/Infer

Inference is a mental process. You *infer* something when you reach a conclusion on the basis of observations. Only people can infer: "The client inferred from our documentation that system training would proceed quickly." Implication is a state of being. Data of any kind, including the attributes of people, can *imply* things: "The disheveled condition of my desk implies that I am a slob. The disgusted looks on your faces imply that you are not."

### Incent

Management has been using incentives for years to motivate employees. But what genius decided to create a new verb by backing *incent* out of incentive?

This is a weird word, one that I urge you not to use. It's not accepted standard usage, although maybe it will be someday. It sounds like *incite,* as in riots. It also sounds a little like *incense,* as in infuriate. Here's some advice: Don't use incent in your proposals, or you may so incense your readers that you incite them to throw it away.

### Interface

Computer systems, hardware, mechanical parts all *interface.* That's fine. The word *interface* has become an accepted bit of IT jargon, although *connect* or *link* might sound less pompous. But people don't interface. It sounds ludicrous to say, "Our technical team will interface with your project management team." Besides, these days you can't be too careful about interfacing with strangers.

### Its/It's [also, Whose/Who's]

One of these is a contraction, one is a possessive pronoun. The contraction is the one that has an apostrophe in it. It's a shortened version of *it is* [or *who is*]. I think the confusion arises from the fact that in English we form possessives with nouns by adding *'s,* as in John's coat, the chair's padding, the company's financial reports. But we don't use the apostrophe when we form a possessive from a pronoun: *ours, yours, hers, theirs, its,* and *whose.* Why? Don't ask. It's a tale of greed, stupidity, and squalor that has been an embarrassment to grammarians for hundreds of years.

## Lay/Lie; Raise/Rise; Set/Sit

These are about as knotty as words get. People make mistakes with them all the time, and usually their readers or listeners aren't certain what's correct, either. The second of each pair, the ones with an *i*-sound, are all intransitive verbs. Big help, right? Well, what that means is that they do not take an object. Each of them is something you do to yourself: "You lie on the couch. You rise for dinner. You sit at the table." (Or somebody else does these things to himself or herself: "She lies on the beach. They rise from their pew. He sits on the board of directors.") The first of each pair are transitive verbs, meaning they are actions performed on something else: "I lay the book on the table. They raise orchids. She set the bags of fertilizer on the driveway." Good luck.

## Lead/Led/Lead

The preceding heading looks like a typographical error, but it's not. There are two different words spelled *lead*. And that's the source of the problem. The first form of *lead* is a verb, pronounced with a long *e*-sound, meaning "to show the way," "to guide," or "to direct." The past tense of the verb *lead* is *led*, which is pronounced exactly the same way as the second form of *lead*. That *lead* is a noun, is pronounced with a short *e*-sound, and refers to a soft, dense metal. The point is that thousands of proposals every year say something like, "Many of the projects listed below were lead by Dr. Stanhope." No, they weren't. They were *led* by Dr. Stanhope.

## Oral/Verbal

*Oral* means with your mouth. *Verbal* means with words. Spoken language is oral. Hence, people give "oral presentations." But both written and spoken language are verbal (unless you write in hieroglyphics or ideograms). A verbal contract could be either spoken or written. An oral contract is spoken only.

## Parameters

This word means a variable or a constant in a mathematical expression. If you have a system characterized by a number of variables and you hold them all constant except one, you will obtain parametric data for that one variable. Fine. So if you're writing about parameters in that sense, go for it. But if you're using the word because it sounds kind of smart in a high-tech sort of way, and if you're using it very loosely to mean "scope" or "limits," then shame on you. You're thinking of *perimeter,* a different word entirely.

### Principal/Principle

This pair of words is demonstrable evidence that the people who invented English had a shocking lack of imagination. Why have two words that are pronounced exactly the same and differ only minutely in spelling, and yet mean totally different things? Maybe it was laziness. Anyway, most of us recall from grade school that "the principal is my pal." (At least until you were sent to his or her office, that is.) It might be better if we also remembered "the principal is the main thing." Because that form of the word *principal* means the main or primary element. The *principal* is the chief administrator in a school. Your *principal* is the main amount of money on which you're earning or paying interest, and the *principals* in a law or accounting firm are the chief partners. *Principle* means a basic truth, an axiom, a guideline, a firm belief. In the wake of the Andersen affair, we could say, "Some principal partners had no principles."

### Serve/Service

Do you *serve* your customers or do you *service* them? I suppose it depends on what kind of business you're in, but since you're worried about creating effective written proposals, I'm going to assume that you are interested in serving your customers. I read in a proposal, "Every facet of our company is oriented to servicing you, the customer." I don't know about you, but being serviced with a facet sounds painful to me. Here's the point: *serve* is a verb; *service* is a noun. "We will serve the interests of our customers and shareholders alike by delivering the best customer service possible."

### Simple/Simplistic

Don't write in your proposal that your solution is "simplistic." Don't say, as I saw in one executive summary, that you have spent extra time developing a "simplistic project plan." Being *simplistic* in this context is not a good thing. *Simplistic* means shallow to the point of stupidity, and simplistic solutions ignore the complexities of reality. I think this mistake arises because people mistake *simplistic* for the superlative form of the word: This is *simple,* that's *simpler,* and that is *simplistic.* Wrong. *Simple,* among other things, means uncomplicated, direct, free of clutter.

Writing or speaking simply is a good idea. In fact, it's a very good idea in every proposal you prepare.

## Trap 5:
### Converting Verbs into Nouns

Here's something odd: For no apparent reason, people like to take perfectly good verbs and turn them into rather puny, ineffective nouns. For example, they convert:

*discuss* into *have a discussion*
*meet with* into *hold a meeting*
*act* into *take action*

There are many more examples of this phenomenon. Replacing strong verbs with weak nouns is not a good idea, because most business writing is woefully short of strong verbs anyway. Taking the few good ones we have and turning them into nouns drains the vitality right out of prose. Avoid this tendency.

## Trap 6:
### Riding the Cliché Pony

*Our firm is uniquely qualified for this project. We offer best-of-breed products and world-class service in a state-of-the-art package that will deliver exceptional results in enhanced airport security.*

Are you impressed? Probably not. We've heard it before. It's the same old marketing fluff. Your built-in B.S. detector is probably going off. But why? What is it about this writing that sounds so bad?

The main problem is that it's built on tired, meaningless clichés.

This is a lazy way to write. These claims lack any substantiation or proof whatsoever, so the customer is not likely to believe them. They may even get the subtle impression that you are conning them.

To avoid creating such a negative impression, prove your claims and avoid using clichés. Suppose the sentences were written as follows:

*Our firm has successfully installed more than 500 airport security systems in North America, more than any other firm. We offer the latest technology, including digital scanning and face recognition systems, and we back our products with a one-year, unconditional guarantee and a service department that is available 24 hours a day, 7 days a week. As a result, by implementing our recommendations, you will achieve three important outcomes: First, your facility will be in full compliance with new federal safety regulations. Second, the installation and training process will be handled seamlessly. And third, your total cost of owner-ship and operation will be the lowest possible.*

Now you'd be a bit more impressed, right? It's all in the details.

# 10 Weaving Your Web:

## *How to Pull It All Together Right from the Start*

OVER A QUARTER CENTURY AGO, RESEARCH INTO a particularly serious form of epilepsy revealed a startling fact. The two halves (or hemispheres) of the brain function quite differently from each other. The left hemisphere in most people controls most forms of sequential thinking, including language. The right hemisphere controls visualization and holistic or global thinking. (This hemispheric differentiation is sometimes reversed in left-handed people.) Equally interesting is the fact that people tend to be dominant to one hemisphere or the other. Just as you prefer to pick up a pen and sign your name with one hand over the other, you prefer to process information and "think" using the cognitive patterns of one hemisphere over the other.

What does this have to do with writing proposals? Just this: If you are a right-brain thinker, you may be able to conceptualize quickly and creatively but then have an excruciatingly difficult time communicating your thoughts because putting those thoughts into language requires sequential processing. You have to put one word in front of another, one sentence ahead of the next, and it all has to flow logically and make sense. For the right-brain thinker that's a two-step process, whereas for the left-brain thinker, it's an integral part of the thinking process itself.

It would be interesting to track how many hours people spend in front of their computers, watching the cursor blink, trying to come up with a good opening sentence. Here's a technique that will cut that time for even the most right-brained thinker.

## Cognitive Webbing

After witnessing people struggle to present their thoughts in clearly written form, I thought of a way to help right-brain proposal writers get their ideas onto the page quickly. I call it *cognitive webbing*. It's a nonlinear process of capturing what you know, what you believe, the key points you want to emphasize, and the examples and illustrations you want to include, with the final output being a writing plan.

It's different from another process often used to develop proposals, called *storyboarding*. Storyboarding is a technique borrowed from the film industry, in which each scene in a movie is represented by an image with the key points of action or dialogue noted below the image. Directors use storyboards to lay out a film (or TV ad or music video) so that they don't waste a lot of time and tape shooting footage they won't need or can't use. Some proposal processes have adapted the storyboarding approach to laying out a complex proposal document. Key sections or subsections of the proposal are represented by an image or two, with the critical content in bullet point format below those images. Often the pages containing these sketches and notes are taped to a long wall so that everyone can "see" the flow of the document.

Personally, I've never been a fan of storyboarding for proposals. The reason it works for a movie is that you already have a script before you start creating the storyboard. The storyboard is an integral step in moving from text to visualization, an obviously important process since movies are visual media.

But when it is used to create a proposal, the storyboarding process actually precedes the creation of the text. So the proposal team spends a lot of time putting pages up and taking them down, rearranging the sequence, adding and deleting content points, and so on. What seems even odder to me is the fact that in trying to use storyboarding processes to create the proposal outline, the team is using a technique designed for visualization to produce what is primarily textual output.

The goal of the cognitive webbing process is to create a writing plan as quickly as possible. It can jump-start the process, leaping over the writer's block that is so often characteristic of the first stages of a writing task.

A couple of other advantages of cognitive webbing: First, you can do it by yourself or you can do it as a team exercise. It's particularly effective when the entire proposal team participates in building the web, so I recommend doing it during the kickoff meeting. And it's very easy to do over the Web using a conferencing tool like Live Meeting or WebEx.

Second, you can use the process to create a writing plan for the entire proposal, or just for a section, such as the executive summary. I strongly recommend doing a cognitive web for the executive summary first. It will help everyone who is contributing to the proposal produce a road map for their own section.

This is such a powerful tool that a couple of the companies to whom I have shown it have made it a standard part of their sales or business development process. In fact, in one case the company's sales professionals actually use the technique in collaboration with their clients. Their account manager gets the client to share in the process of creating their own proposal outline. As Bill Geddy, senior director of sales at CIBER explains it, "Working through the cognitive web with a large retailer and large hospital proved to be the ultimate in consultative selling techniques in both cases. We gained insight and their own internal teams gained a unified view of why they were undertaking this complex project and what direction it needed to go. The process was so powerful, it enabled us to overcome a significant price differential because we showed them that other solutions had left out some important details."

Even if you never use this technique in conjunction with a client team, it is still one of the most powerful means I know of to pull all the loose strands of thought and insight associated with a deal together and then braid them into a unified, powerful, client-centered message.

## How to Create a Cognitive Web

You need to follow three steps. The first time you do it, the process may seem a little awkward, but after you've done it three or four times, it will seem like second nature to you. The three-step process is:

1. Write down the **end result** the customer seeks
2. **Brainstorm**, writing down every point, idea, example, and detail you think of supporting the basic notion that you will help the customer achieve that desired end result
3. **Organize** the points, using two principles:
   + The NOSE pattern
   + The customer's own priorities

We'll go through each step in detail so you can see how it works.

### Step One:
### Identify the End Result the Customer Seeks

Ask yourself, What outcome or end result does this customer want to achieve? Write that end result in the form of a phrase or brief sentence in the center of a sheet of paper, on a whiteboard, or on a flip chart. Circle it. That's your starting point: understanding what the customer wants to accomplish overall.

Avoid mistaking your products or goals for the end result the client desires. (This is the same kind of temptation that we discussed in Chap-

ter 5 in regard to confusing the client's needs with our products or services.) If you get the first step wrong, you'll find you have made a
convincing argument for something the customer doesn't want.

Starting with the end result allows the brainstorming to stay more
client centered. I also find that the end result statement can often become a call to action—a strong way to end the executive summary.

Let's pretend that you're proposing a system integration project for
Urban Bank Corporation. After careful consideration, you create the following end result statement:

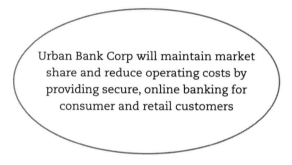

Urban Bank Corp will maintain market
share and reduce operating costs by
providing secure, online banking for
consumer and retail customers

### Step Two:
### Brainstorm

The next step is fun. You get to be creative, you get to generate ideas at
random, and at this point there are no wrong answers.

Answering the seven questions described in Chapter 6 is a good starting point. What is the client's problem or issue? Why is the problem one
that's worth solving? What does the customer seek in terms of results?
Which results matter the most? What do we have that will solve the
problem and deliver the right results? Of the various solutions we can
offer, which is the best fit? And, finally, what makes us the right choice?
Those questions will produce good information for your outline.

Another way to generate insights and content is to ask yourself the
traditional journalistic questions: Who? What? When? Where? Why?
How? Who on our staff has done this kind of work before? What exactly
will we implement? Why does the client need to find a solution? When
does the client want this work finished? Where will the work be done?
How does their desired implementation date affect our project plan? Is
that date tied to some other critical event? How will we help Urban Bank
achieve that outcome? Have we done anything like this before for another customer? Have we done other important projects with Urban
Bank? Which of their competitors have already undertaken similar initiatives?

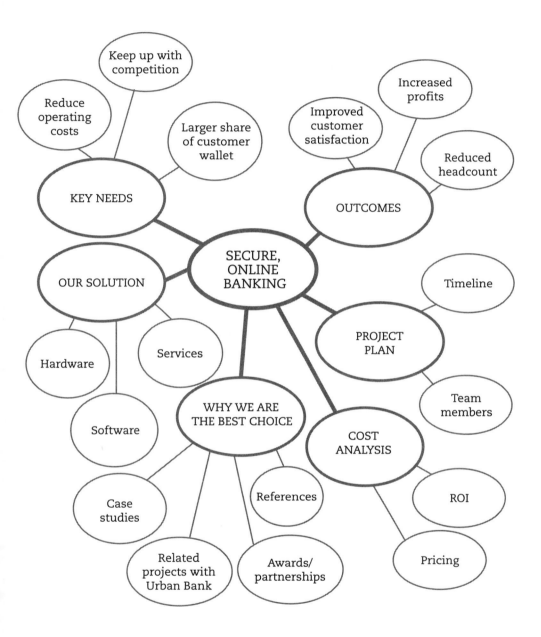

**Figure 10-1.** Sample Cognitive Web.

You can also use the Six Sigma technique of asking five Whys. If a member of the sales team tosses out that the prospect needs to implement an integrated communications platform, note it and ask, "Why?" If another member of the team says that the prospect wants to simplify communications across multiple platforms, ask "And why is that important now?" And so on.

The more you come up with during the brainstorming phase, the better. If you're facilitating this process, resist judging contributions at this point. Let each member of the team contribute ideas as they pop to mind. You're better off not excluding or rejecting any contributions now.

As you come up with all of this material, you link the ideas to the end result and to each other, grouping them into clusters of related points. Draw lines connecting related ideas or facts. Connect the key points or content groupings to the end result you wrote down first. These are the main spokes of your cognitive web. That's where the "webbing" element comes in. Your output will now look something like Figure 10-1 (although yours will have many more elements and a lot more detail).

At this point, you may want to combine some elements, discard some, redraw the connections so that what was an element of the solution becomes part of the project plan, and so on.

### Step Three:
### Prioritize

Generating all of this potential content was a nonlinear process. It didn't matter if the first thing you thought of was your change management process, the customer's "as is" situation, or a really good case study. But the order in which the customer sees the content does matter. So you need to prioritize it.

First, look for the four components of the NOSE pattern: Needs, Outcomes, Solution, and Evidence. Use those for your main groupings of content and label them in that order. Is one of them missing? Add it now. Is it hard to fit some of the points in your web into one of those four categories of content? Perhaps they really aren't relevant to your proposal.

Once you have the main categories of content identified in terms of the NOSE structure, look at the details within each category. Which detail is the most important to the customer? You've done your audience analysis work earlier, so you should be able to put yourself in the audience's place. Enumerate the points and subpoints in terms of what matters to the audience. When the task of prioritizing is complete, you will have a cognitive web that looks something like Figure 10-2.

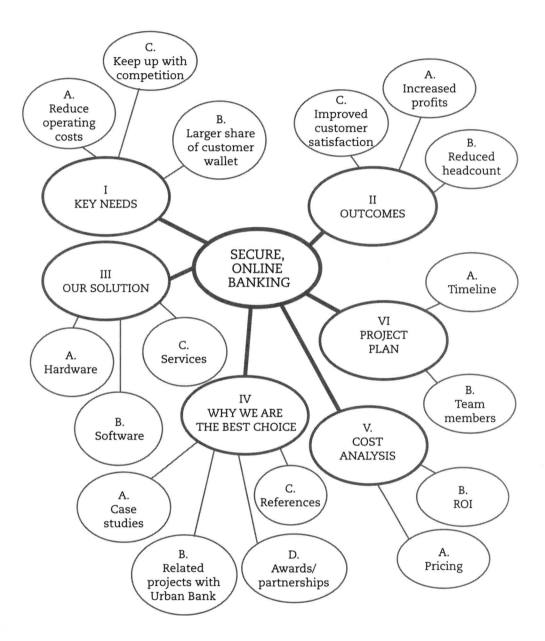

**Figure 10-2.** Sample Cognitive Web after prioritizing

If you're working on a sheet of paper or on a whiteboard, you probably have quite a mess by now. That's good. Now you can copy this mess neatly on another sheet of paper, putting point number one first, followed by its subpoints, and so on, in nice linear fashion right down the page. Presto! You have an outline for your document. And it was fairly painless, wasn't it?

Our sample cognitive web looks like this when transformed into an outline:

**I.** Urban Bank Corporation's key needs:
  **A.** Reduce operating costs
  **B.** Gain a larger share of customers' banking business
  **C.** Keep up with competitors who have Internet-based banking services

**II.** Key outcomes Urban will look for from a successful project
  **A.** Increased profits
  **B.** Decreased headcount
  **C.** Improved customer satisfaction surveys and better service

**III.** Our recommended solution
  **A.** Hardware components
     (Lots of details here)
  **B.** Software components
     (Lots of details here, too)
  **C.** Services
     Application development
     Testing
     Etc.

**IV.** Why we are the best choice to do this work
  **A.** Case studies
  **B.** Recent projects with Urban Bank
  **C.** References
  **D.** Awards and partnerships

**V.** Cost analysis
  **A.** Pricing
  **B.** ROI

**VI.** Our project plan
  **A.** Timeline
  **B.** Key personnel

Weaving Your Web: How to Pull It All Together Right from the Start    121

From this outline, we can write the executive summary for a formal proposal. (Take a look at the example in the sidebar.) We can repeat the process, as necessary, for each section of the proposal, focusing our cognitive web on the technical specifications, functional specification, project management, and other topical areas.

---

### • EXECUTIVE SUMMARY

*The following is a sample executive summary based on the outline we developed in the preceding section.*

Urban Bank has identified an opportunity to use Web-based technology to improve the bank's financial performance and deliver more value to your customers. Specifically, your research indicates that if you can provide secure, online banking services for both your retail and commercial customer base, the bank will address some important challenges:

First, you will be able to reduce operating costs. The more transactional business you can move to the Internet, the fewer clerks and ATMs you will need. If you can move 5 percent of your current routine activity to the Internet, you can save in excess of $4 million annually through reduced salaries, benefits, and rental fees associated with ATMs.

Second, you will have the opportunity to gain a larger share of your best customers' banking business. The transactional records that you can store from Internet-based banking services are more extensive and easier to consolidate and mine than other records. By tracking activity online, you will be able to identify opportunities to cross-market other services to your best customers. For example, if you have a high net worth individual with a home loan through Urban, you can market investment opportunities, checking plans, or auto loans via email.

Third, you will stay competitive with other banks in the region who have introduced Internet-based banking services. Customers do not usually switch banks because of differences in basic service delivery models, but over the next few years there is no question that Internet-based banking will become standard. Failing to develop a means of providing secure, online services could gradually erode the bank's reputation.

Addressing these challenges can have an important impact on the bank's financial performance and market share. Specifically, Urban Bank can increase profitability (since reductions in operating expense go directly to the bottom line), can reduce headcount or relocate employees into more productive work, and can actually improve customer satisfaction and account retention. In fact, for many of your customers, banking online is much more convenient than going to a local branch or finding an ATM, so their perception of the service Urban is providing will improve.

As we detail in this proposal, we recommend a combination of technology and services that will meet your need for a reliable, secure online presence. We are experienced in establishing exactly this kind of system for the financial industry. We recommend creating an online banking system built on a hardware platform of . . . The software components we recommend include . . .

Of course, choosing the right hardware and software is only part of the solution. You also need the services to execute the project on time and on budget. We are recognized as experts in the area of application development for banking systems, and have received commendation for three consecutive years from North American Bank Technology Monthly, the leading independent journal serving the banking industry. Our professional services include development and customization of the applications you need, testing of those systems, phased introductions, and back end support. In addition, we will train your own IT staff to manage and maintain the system so that you are completely self-sufficient. All of these services are detailed in Section 3 of our proposal.

Our project plan takes into account two factors. First, delays in cutting costs mean delays in generating more profit. Therefore, we have developed an aggressive timeline in order to accelerate Urban Bank's return on investment. Second, doing the job right the first time is always better than fixing the job later. Therefore, we have allowed enough room in the timeline to study your infrastructure thoroughly and to develop the right solution for Urban Bank.

The leader of our project team, David Williamson, has developed and installed online banking systems for some of the region's largest financial institutions, including . . . Williamson was a featured speaker at the recent International Conference of eCommerce Strategists, where he presented our methodology for successfully designing and implementing online banking systems. He used five different projects that he had managed as examples of the right way to handle these projects.

We have included case studies that cover several of these projects. In them we document not only the systems we implemented for our clients, but the impact those systems had on their profitability and market share.

Over the past several years, we have had the opportunity to work with Urban Bank on a number of important and exciting projects. For example, we were the lead in developing the Urban Extranet, which has enabled you to clear funds in half the time it previously took. We also were the designers and implementers of the Urban eLearning system, which has cut training costs for new employees by 70 percent. These projects have established our reputation for quality work. In addition, we have included references from other clients who have benefited from our pragmatic approach to innovative solutions.

As an award-winning technology provider, we have partnerships with and certifications from all the major technology firms, including Oracle, Microsoft, IBM, HP, Cisco, and many others. You can trust us to provide well-trained, experienced people who can complete your project in a timely and cost-effective way.

We urge you to move forward on this important opportunity. The Internet has transformed banking as we know it in this country. In the process, it has transformed the nature of competition, the way banks work, and cost structures that underlie them. As a regional bank in a highly competitive market, Urban must take advantage of competitive opportunities as quickly as possible. We are ready to help.

Does this method work? Yes! It really does. In seminars we usually create a cognitive web based on one of the attendees' real opportunities. From the initial moment of volunteering to summarizing the executive summary, we can usually complete the exercise in 20 minutes. People have told me repeatedly that it has cut their writing time on letter proposals from several hours down to thirty minutes or so. Even some left-brain writers use it, because it also helps them become more creative and do a more thorough job of analyzing the opportunity. Try it!

# Section III

## The Art of the Part:
### *Where to Put Your Effort*

# 11 Letter Proposals

ADHERE TO THE GOLDILOCKS PRINCIPLE OF PRO-
posal writing: provide only as much content as the decision maker needs and nothing more. Strive to make your proposal "just right" in terms of size. (Or, as we stated in Chapter 4, observe the maxim of quantity, to use Paul Grice's phrase.) For example, you can often meet your prospect's needs for a clear recommendation and sufficient supporting detail just by writing a letter, especially if you've simply been asked, "Why don't you put together a proposal for me so I can take a look at what you're thinking?" Such a letter proposal may be as brief as a single page or as long as three or four pages with attachments. The exact salutation you use, the particular format you choose (block, modified block, whatever), the complimentary close—none of that's really important. What is important is that your letter proposal clearly address the four essential elements of the NOSE pattern:

**The client's Need or problem.** Get right to the point. Don't waste time with cliché openings. In fact, mark it down as an infallible rule: any sentence that begins *"Per your . . . "* is a bad sentence. Even more common and just as dreadful is an opening sentence like this:

> *"We would like to take this opportunity to thank you for allowing us to submit our proposal for your consideration."*

What's wrong with that? First, it sounds like the writer is groveling. *". . . thank you for allowing us"*? The proposal is supposed to represent a business offer to solve an important problem, made between relative equals. The client may be a lot bigger than your firm, but all the same they're the one who has a problem. You're the one who has the answer. So it's more or less balanced. The other problem with that opening is that it is what is called a *conditional* sentence. If you read it carefully you realize that you're not actually thanking anybody for anything. You're saying that you would *like* to thank somebody, but . . . but what? You can't because you were up all night trying to get your proposal done and you're not feeling all that grateful?

Other bad openings start out telling the prospect about our emotional state: *"Amalgamated Chemicals is delighted to provide the following proposal in response to your RFP . . . "* Not to be harsh, but who cares if you're delighted or not?

Okay, so what's a better opening?

Well, you can still start with a "thank you" if you want to. Just focus it on something that helps you get right to the point. For example, *"Thank you for providing the information we requested so that we could complete our proposal and develop the right solution for your situation. You have indicated that there are three primary issues that are driving your decision to consolidate operations in one location: . . . "*

Or you can start by referencing previous meetings, contacts, or the client's RFP:

*"Based on the meeting held at your offices the first and third weeks of June, plus several phone interviews with other members of your team, we have developed an approach to solve the three specific challenges you identified."*

But the best opening is usually one that gets right to the point, focusing on the specific problem or need that is affecting the client's profitability or productivity:

*"Physicians and nurses working in your hospital say that the current process for recording case notes is awkward, time consuming, and inaccurate. As you explained to us, it represents a legacy system, which has long been out of date, and which contains a number of patches and additions created in-house."*

Or like this:

*"Your decision to provide an online option for your customers is very exciting. Those customers who cannot or prefer not to shop at one of your three retail outlets will have the option to order the finest in golf equipment, balls, and clothing at any time of the day or night and from any location. But it also means your Web site must be overhauled to be more user friendly, more secure, more interactive, and more compatible with your e-commerce strategy."*

Besides focusing on problems, you can also base your proposal on an opportunity. But you are more likely to get a decision maker's attention if you talk about needs and problems. Real pains focus an individual's attention much faster than potential gains.

***The Outcomes the client seeks.*** You get the client's interest by talking about their problem, but you motivate them to take action by showing that there is a significant payoff that comes from fixing the problem or meeting the need.

Don't confuse the benefits of solving the business problem with the benefits of your product or service. (Those are more accurately called *features* and should be included in the next section, in which you explain your solution.) Quantify the value of the outcomes, if you can, to make them more compelling and credible. For example, if we look at physicians and nurses who are spending too much time entering notes in their patients' files, the benefits paragraph might read something like this:

*Simplifying the process of updating case files, entering patient care notes, and documenting treatments can save Rutherford Psychiatric Hospital hundreds of hours and thousands of dollars every week. In fact, we estimate it can save your physicians a total of 120 hours weekly and your nursing staff a weekly total of 1,650 hours! Here's how we calculated the savings:*

|  | Dictation/writing time per week | Review time | Patient load | Total time |
|---|---|---|---|---|
| Physician | 10 min./patient | 5 min./patient | 20 patients | 5 hours |
| Nurse | 20 min./patient | 10 min./patient | 30 patients | 15 hours |

*The table above summarizes the average time a typical physician and nurse respectively spend recording and reviewing notes on patients each week. Multiply that by the number of physicians on staff (24) and the number of full-time equivalent nurses at Rutherford (110), and you're looking at a huge drain on productivity. Add in the staff of clerks who do nothing but type up physician notes because the existing system doesn't work well and you're looking at a massive expense that contributes nothing positive to patient care.*

If you knew what the average charge rate was for physicians and nurses at the Rutherford Hospital, you could calculate exactly what that expense is. But you can see how marshaling the numbers makes the analysis of impact more convincing, particularly compared to just offering generalities about *"dramatic improvements in productivity"* from replacing the existing system. And by the way, there is absolutely no reason not to include a graphic, table, or diagram in a letter proposal.

***The Solution.*** The presentation of your solution in a letter proposal should contain:

- ✦ A high-level description of the product or service you are recommending
  - ➤ Focus first on what you are recommending from a functional standpoint before mentioning specific products, technologies, or services
  - ➤ Do not use product or service names until you have explained what the solution will do for the client. Remember that product names are just another form of jargon.
  - ➤ Include just enough detail to show how the features of your solution address the issues the customer is concerned about
  - ➤ Differentiate your solution or your ability to deliver it to elevate it above the level of a commodity offering

- ✦ A specific, clear recommendation to act
  - ➤ Use phrases like *"I recommend . . . "* or *"We urge you to move forward . . . "* or *"Based on our experience, we recommend . . . "* so there is no doubt where you stand
  - ➤ Too many proposals merely describe a solution rather than actually recommending it; descriptions don't motivate anybody to do anything

You might also consider covering alternative solutions very briefly. Typically, you will cover them not to recommend them but to show you have considered them and concluded that they aren't as desirable as what you are recommending. This creates the appearance of thoroughness on your part, something the analytical decision maker values. More important, by briefly considering and dismissing alternative approaches you have the opportunity to anticipate your competition's approach and point out its weaknesses without engaging in disparagement. This technique is sometimes called "ghosting" the competition, perhaps because it raises issues that come back to haunt your competitors.

***The Evidence.*** The final part of your letter proposal should provide evidence of why you are qualified, proof of your value claims, and details on your project plan or implementation schedule.

Provide evidence that you can deliver the solution successfully. You can mention a couple of key customers or point the reader toward case studies that are included as attachments. If your firm has won awards or received special recognition from industry experts, you can cite that evidence, too. Or you can mention previous successful engagements you have had with this client. You don't want a lot of detailed evidence in the letter, but you do need to include enough to make the buyer feel comfortable about recommending you.

This section is also a good place to articulate the cost/benefit ratio. You can relegate line item pricing, if it's even necessary, to an attachment, but within the body of your letter itself you should use a graph or other vivid demonstration to show that the return on investment, payback period, or total cost of ownership offered by your solution are extremely compelling. You want to show the client that the benefits of moving forward far outweigh the costs. Your cost/benefit ratio will compare the price of your solution to the value of the benefits calculated in the outcomes section of your letter proposal. Don't forget the intangibles—the intangible costs, such as training, or necessary equipment upgrades, and the intangible benefits, too, such as higher employee morale, regulatory compliance, better customer service, elimination of maintenance and repair costs, and so on.

Finally, in this section you can provide basic information about the implementation schedule, project plan, and deliverables. If this information threatens to become lengthy or very detailed, include just the key dates and put the rest in an attachment. Mention any assumptions you have made that could affect the schedule, and indicate how the responsibilities will be shared between your firm and the client's.

## A Few Tips on Writing Winning Letter Proposals

Here are a few suggestions to improve the effectiveness of your letter proposals:

✦ *Don't let the tone become too stuffy.* For some reason, when people write business letters and proposals they often lapse into that pompous tone I called Guff in the previous chapter. You'll sound more sincere, maintain a higher level of rapport, and produce more readable proposals if you simplify the tone. Avoid long sentences and inflated language. Use the customer's name throughout the letter. Refer to the customer as "you," not "it" or "they."

✦ *Similarly, don't let your legal department include language that will alarm or offend your customer.* The corporate attorneys have the mission of keeping your company out of trouble. Unfortunately, that sometimes leads them to do things that violate common sense. For example, I have seen letter proposals (and cover letters for formal proposals) that included paragraphs saying, "Nothing in this proposal should be construed as a binding promise to deliver nor a commitment to any particular schedule or pricing, until such time as Customer has executed a purchase order and/or agreed in writing to contractual terms." What an exercise in dissembling! If you read that, would you want to bother reading the rest of the proposal? No, me neither. You can find a positive way to make that kind of statement or can include it as a separate attachment of terms and conditions, but putting it on the first page of your letter proposal is a bad tactical mistake.

Other attorneys and senior managers, in a misguided attempt to protect proprietary interests, have added language like this to letter proposals: "This proposal may not be reproduced and may not be shown or shared with any individual not directly authorized to review and evaluate proposals." Wow. That's warm and friendly. If I understand it correctly, it's saying we want your business but we don't trust you and we think you probably want to rip us off. But we're on to you, buddy, so watch out! Protect your proprietary interests, but don't use language that sounds adversarial to do it.

✦ *Avoid the clichés of business writing.* In particular, avoid clichéd openings such as the one I mentioned earlier in this chapter: "*I would like to take this opportunity to thank you for considering the enclosed proposal . . . blah, blah, blah.*" Other clichéd openings that need to be retired:

> "*Pursuant to your request, we are submitting our recommendation . . .*"
> "*Attached please find . . .*"

Get to the point.

✦ *Use a strong close.* Avoid the all-purpose closing that everybody uses: "*If you have any questions, please feel free to call.*" That's been done to death—so bury it. Don't ever use it again. I know it's easy, and I know everyone does it, but think about what it says: Basically, it tells the reader, "Look, I know I don't write very well. I always confuse people. So if I've confused you, don't worry about it. Give me a call and together we'll figure out what I was trying to say." Also, notice that if you use that closing, you have turned over control of the sales process to the customer. Your job is to sit by the phone and wait until the customer comes up with a question. What a lousy way to end your proposal!

The final paragraph of your letter proposal is your last chance to motivate the reader to do what you want him or her to do. Don't waste it with meaningless banalities such as, "Thanking you in advance for your cooperation" or "Let me know if I can be of any help."

To close effectively, ask for the business. Set a date when you will contact them to discuss next steps, or express eagerness to win the contract and deliver the solution. Return to your primary value proposition: financial gain, improved quality, infrastructure improvements, risk avoidance, competitive advantage, or whatever the buyer seeks. Tell the reader what he or she must do to gain this advantage. And make the action something that's easy to do—the easier the better.

Strong closings ask for the sale ("Please sign the enclosed contract and return it to us, so we can begin implementing a solution that will save your manufacturing operation more than $15,000 a month in maintenance costs"), or ask a question ("After all, if you can save more than $6,000 a month in computing costs, can you really afford to wait?"), or create time pressure ("Please remember that the special pricing we have offered in this proposal will be available to you only through the end of the quarter, so please don't hesitate"), or suggest specific action ("Just return the enclosed authorization statement, signed at the bottom, and we will schedule a free analysis of your energy consumption and potential for savings").

Finally, close with confidence. Avoid expressions like "I hope that" and "If it would be all right" and "We believe that." When you have said what you wanted to say and have asked the customer for appropriate action—stop.

Figure 11-1. Sample Letter Proposal.

<<Date>>


Ms. Jane Woods
Sr. Vice President
Information Systems
Diston Drugs Corporation
8333 Dairy Creek Road
San Francisco, CA 94133


Dear Ms. Woods,


Thank you for meeting with us and helping us understand the Diston Corporation security infrastructure in greater depth. Based on our meetings with you and your staff, we propose to conduct a security review of your environment, develop security checklists, and develop an overall information security plan. Our approach is based on our understanding of your needs and on Waugh Security's experience with similar clients in the retail industry. As you requested, we have made the project scope and pricing scalable.

**Understanding Your Security Needs**

Because of numerous mergers and consolidations during the past three years, Diston's environment has become complex to manage. Although this has affected every aspect of the firm's operations, from corporate headquarters down to the store level, one of the most challenging areas has been information security:

- Because you have inherited a variety of legacy systems, Diston is currently utilizing several different computing platforms, including DEC, HP, IBM and Tandem, and a variety of operating systems including Windows, UNIX, and VM.
- In addition, the corporation communicates through an extensive network that includes external connections to wide area networks, virtual private networks, and the Internet.
- Departments throughout the corporation, regional offices, and retail outlets in widely dispersed locations currently all have different security policies, different procedures for managing

each system, and different understandings of security requirements across the business units.

## Achieving Bottom-Line Results

Your goal is to standardize security within the corporation and to develop a program that will give you more proactive control of your systems and operating environments. In addition, you want to establish a blueprint for a security organization that will keep the corporation's systems as secure as possible while remaining flexible enough to adapt to future security requirements. You also want to keep your security environment current as requirements evolve.

Based on the figure you provided us and on information obtained from previous security assessments we have conducted, we estimate that Diston will see cost savings from increased efficiency of more than $500,000 a year. More significantly, through threat reduction and enhanced security procedures, the company will avoid information losses valued at more than $2 million annually and will reduce fraud by an expected 35%. These figures are based on estimates derived from experience with other firms in the retail space. We will calculate actual risk avoidance values for Diston as part of our deliverables.

## Project Scope and Deliverables

Diston relies on the availability and integrity of your business systems and network to operate more than 500 retail outlets throughout North America. You recognize the need to take proper measures to protect the sensitive information—including financial transaction data and customer information—that moves through your network. Waugh Security will help you identify risks in the environment and will recommend controls to mitigate any security exposures.

From an execution standpoint, the key objectives of this project are to:

- Conduct a comprehensive security review of your environment
- Develop checklists to ensure consistent application of security procedures
- Develop a plan for implementing recommendations resulting from the review

The project will include the following activities:

*I: Conduct a Security Review.* This review will include an assessment of:

- Security processes (e.g. auditing, event escalation, user administration, etc.)
- Windows, UNIX, and Novell server operating systems
- Windows and NT workstations
- Network security provisions
- dial-up security
- routers, intelligent hubs
- security of network management and network monitoring systems
- external connection security

To complete this review, we will use our automated security assessment tools including special tools for NT and UNIX. Due to the short project time frame, we will look at a representative sample of high-priority systems. This will include all five UNIX systems at headquarters and five Novell file servers. We will also assess points of entry into the network, including dial-up and external connections. These entry points exist at headquarters, stores, and the data center. Interviews, documentation reviews, and on-site tours will be critical to the security review.

Areas that are out-of-scope of this review include the Lexington mainframe operating system, the Internet connection via QwikLink, application security controls, and the operating system of the in-store processor systems.

At the conclusion of this review, Waugh Security will provide Diston with a report detailing your security strengths and weaknesses. This report will also prioritize recommendations for improving security, and will quantify to the extent possible the risks associated with not implementing the recommendations.

*II: Create a Data Inventory.* We will conduct a high-level inventory of the types of data in the Diston network and will document the current controls and risks for each data type. This inventory will help spot areas of weakness, where additional controls are necessary to protect sensitive data or to assure regulatory compliance.

*III: Analyze Roles and Responsibilities within the Security Organization.* As Diston begins to formalize a security organization, the entire corporation needs to understand the roles and responsibilities. This analysis will serve as a blueprint for building the security organization and assuring its effective integration into the corporate culture as a whole. We will also create a job description for a Diston Information Security Officer, which will help ensure that you hire an individual with the correct skills.

IV: *Develop Checklists of Best Practice in Security Procedures.* Waugh Security will develop security checklists for Diston covering the following areas:

- Novell Netware
- UNIX
- External access (firewalls, gateways, dial-up, etc.)
- Network (routers, network administration, encryption, etc.)
- PCs (Windows 7 and NT)
- System audits
- Virus control
- Security provisions appropriate for generic applications

The Diston Information Technology team can then tailor these checklists further to bring common controls to the entire Diston environment.

**Deliverables** for this project will include:

- High-level data inventory detailing controls and risks
- A report itemizing current security strengths and weaknesses
- Quantification of current risks and recommendations for mitigating weaknesses
- A cost/benefit matrix for implementing the security recommendations, identifying key tasks, benefits, and representative implementation costs
- Recommendations for setting up the Security Organization, including roles and responsibilities
- Security checklists for your major systems, including Novell Netware, UNIX, Windows, VMware, external access, network, PCs, system audit, virus control, application security
- A presentation to Diston management of our findings and recommendations
- Project working papers

### Project Methodology, Staffing, and Schedule

**Methodology.** Waugh Security has developed a unique methodology for managing security reviews. This methodology, which we call Comprehensive Assessment of Security Matters (CASM) has been recognized by independent, third-party evaluators as the most effective process of its kind in the industry. For Diston the CASM methodology will save time and money while assuring you of a thorough review and complete set of actionable recommendations.

Our process will begin with an assessment of Diston's current procedures and security gaps. During this phase we will interview key personnel, review current security documentation, conduct on-site assessments at headquarters and key retail stores, and use automated security assessment tools to probe the Diston environment. From this assessment, Waugh Security will document the strengths and weaknesses in each area we assess. We will then develop recommendations to improve security controls and will quantify the risks associated with not acting on the recommendations.

**Staffing.** To complete this project in the timeframe you indicated was necessary (i.e., before June 1), we will assign a three-person core project team:

Dr. Richard Hsiung will lead our team, participating on a part-time basis and providing technology oversight. Dr. Hsiung is the senior manager of Waugh Security's Infrastructure Assessment Group. He has more than 20 years' experience in developing systems solutions to real-world problems. In particular, he is recognized as an expert on information security and authentication issues and was a senior member of the U.S. government's task force on Public Key Infrastructure issues for corporate security.

H. William Jones will serve as project manager. He will provide the day-to-day project supervision. Mr. Jones has extensive experience in strategic planning of information management systems for retail and manufacturing environments. He most recently had the lead role in developing e-commerce strategies for one of Waugh Security's largest retail clients, Heartland Clothing Inc. We have attached a case study reviewing this project.

Clark Johnson will complete the Waugh Security team. Mr. Johnson will oversee assessment activities, will gather data from our automated tools, and will conduct interviews with Diston managers and employees. Mr. Johnson is a technology specialist with more than five years' experience in using security assessment tools and conducting assessment activities.

From Diston, we will need the full-time participation of Charles Vincent, senior quality assurance manager. Besides Mr. Vincent, other Diston personnel will participate in this project as described in the attached description of project assumptions. Given the short timeframe of this project, timely participation of your personnel will be critical to its success.

*Schedule.* Based on the scope, approach and staffing described above, as well as the attached Project Assumptions document, we estimate this project will require five weeks to complete. We are prepared to begin on April 13 and to complete the work no later than May 23. The chart below outlines the project phases and work. We have attached a project plan that describes the phases, tasks, and resources for this project in more detail.

We propose the following project timeline:

| Project Phase | Week 1 | Week 2 | Week 3 | Week 4 | Week 5 |
|---|---|---|---|---|---|
| Project Organization | █ | █ | █ | █ | █ |
| Security Review | █ | █ | █ | █ | |
| • *Review Background Material* | █ | | | | |
| • *Document Assets* | | █ | | | |
| • *Identify Threats* | | █ | | | |
| • *Calculate Potential Loss* | | █ | █ | | |
| • *Document Environment* | | | █ | █ | |
| • *Document Controls* | | | █ | █ | |
| • *Develop Recommendations* | | | | █ | |
| Prepare Data Inventory | | █ | █ | | |
| Analyze Roles and Responsibilities | | █ | | | |
| Create Checklists of Best Practices | | █ | █ | | |
| Present Project Results | | | | | █ |

**Estimated Project Fees and Expenses**

We estimate our professional fees will be $182,000. Travel and living expenses and appropriate out-of-pocket expenses will be additional. Based on our preliminary estimate of cost savings from enhanced efficiency, this project will pay for itself within the first six months. If you factor in risk minimization and avoidance of loss, the payback is even faster.

We will submit an invoice to you at the end of each month for fees and expenses incurred during that month. If circumstances suggest that the scope of our work will change from what we have described in this letter, we will obtain your written approval prior to incurring fees in excess of those noted above.

I will call you on Wednesday, March 28, to discuss the next steps. We look forward to working with you to create a more secure environment at Diston Drugs and to preserve the information assets that are such a vital part of the corporation's capital.

Very truly yours,


Jeffrey Christiansen
Vice President
Waugh Security

*Attachments:*
1. Project assumptions
2. Project plan and Gantt chart
3. Case study: Assessment of Information Security Vulnerabilities for Heartland Clothing
4. Waugh Security standard business terms

# 12 The Structure and Key Elements of Formal Proposals

SOMETIMES YOU NEED TO WRITE A FORMAL PRO-posal rather than submit a letter proposal. You may decide to do so, for example, if the document is too long to fit comfortably in the letter format (that is, more than four or five pages), if it's proposing a costly or complicated solution, or if a formal, sectioned response has been mandated by the RFP to which you are responding.

Formal proposals will vary, depending on what's appropriate for the given audience and what the customer has specified in the request for proposal or invitation to tender. But, as a general rule, all formal proposals will contain three broad categories of content: the business case; the detailed solution and substantiation; and the supplementary attachments and appendices. Figure 12-1 explains what each of these categories typically contains.

The reason you want to structure your formal proposal this way is to provide the right kind of content, written at the right level of expertise, for all of the various evaluators who will look at it:

**Senior executives** will want the basics. They want to know: Are we getting what we need? Do these recommendations make sense? Is there a compelling reason for us to do this? What do we gain from choosing these people? What differentiates them? How much will it cost? What kind of ROI can we expect? Often the senior executive is looking for strategic impact that transcends the specific solution. The RFP may be asking for a plan to coordinate digital marketing campaigns in both Europe and North America, but what the senior executive may want to see is evidence that your approach to providing that coordination will increase market share or bump revenues upward.

| | | |
|---|---|---|
| *The Business Case* | Cover letter<br>Title page<br>Table of contents<br>Executive Summary<br>• Customer needs<br>• Customer desired outcomes<br>• High-level presentation of solution<br>• Key value-added components or uniqueness factors<br>Pricing and payback analysis | **Accessible:** by all audiences, but focused on the top-level executives and financial buyers<br><br>**Content:** Overview, high-level content focusing mainly on business issues, bottom-line factors.<br><br>**Graphics:** ROI charts, payback analysis, focus boxes to highlight key text |
| *Solution and Substantiation* | Solution in significant detail, including:<br>• Deliverables<br>• Operational description of the equipment or system proposed<br>• Training<br>• Documentation<br>• Implementation<br><br>Scope of work<br>Project plan/master schedule<br>Timeline<br>Project team, resumes, organization chart<br>Subcontractors<br>Pricing/cost analysis<br>ROI or payback calculation<br>Value-added components<br><br>Detailed evidence, including:<br>• References<br>• Case studies<br>• Testimonials<br>• Uniqueness factors<br>• Accolades and awards<br>• Warranties, service-level agreements<br><br>RFP response<br>Compliance matrix<br>Question and Answer section | **Accessible:** primarily by technical reviewers<br><br>**Content:** Details addressing how the system works, establishing value, differentiating your offering from competitors'<br><br>**Graphics:**<br>• product illustrations<br>• flow charts<br>• process diagrams<br>• schematics<br>• CAD drawings<br>• Gantt chart<br>• cost comparison table<br>• photos of team members<br>• brief resumes of key team members<br>• copies of testimonial letters<br>• copies of certifications |
| *Attachments and Appendices* | Terms and conditions<br>Sample contract<br><br>Glossary/nomenclature<br>Relevant marketing materials<br><br>Other attachments (digital media with sample code, video, photo tour of prospective facility, etc.) | **Accessible:** varies; usually a highly specialized reviewer<br><br>**Content:** Specialized information to facilitate the decision process |

**Figure 12-1.** Content Categories of Formal Proposals.

**Gatekeepers** and **technical evaluators** have more specialized interests. They want specific, detailed content that addresses their areas of responsibility and concerns.

> A gatekeeper, who often performs the initial screen of all proposals to eliminate as many as possible, is looking for issues of compliance. Are we getting what we asked for? Has this vendor answered all of the questions? Did they follow our instructions? Is their pricing realistic? Often a gatekeeper is more interested in finding reasons to dismiss a submission than to recommend one. If they have received 20 or 50 or even 100 submissions, they need to whittle that stack down to something manageable quickly.

> A technical evaluator is looking at the proposed solution and all the factors surrounding it, including issues of installation, implementation, training, support, and so forth. This evaluator wants to know: What are they proposing? How does it work? What are the risk factors? Do they have sufficient experience? How will it fit into our operation? The technical evaluator is attempting to determine if the solution you are recommending will work in their environment. They want to know if it will make life inside their cubicle easier or harder. Rather than strategic issues, the technical evaluator is more likely to be looking for more tactical impact—increased operational efficiency, the automation of something that is labor intensive, or reduced risk of noncompliance with regulatory standards, for example.

By writing your proposal with three distinct components in mind, you can satisfy the information requirements of these different audiences. The Business Case, particularly the cover letter and executive summary, is your primary channel for addressing the senior executive. The Solution and Substantiation section is more likely to speak to the technical evaluator's concerns. Your proposal's compliance matrix and pricing and your accuracy in following instructions will be important to the gatekeepers. The Attachments and Appendices are also more likely to appeal to technical evaluators or to other specialized roles, such as legal or procurement.

## Protecting Your Proprietary Interests

Before we look at the parts of a formal proposal, let's take a minute to consider an issue that worries a lot of people. How do you write a proposal that presents a creative solution and that may contain information that is confidential or proprietary to your business without having your solution and your proprietary content taken by an unethical client, shared with a competitor, or otherwise misused?

The first and most obvious answer is to know your client. If you have concerns about their ethics, you should conduct a careful bid/no bid analysis. (Bid/no bid processes are discussed in Chapter 18.) If you still want to go after the business but you're worried they might steal your ideas, you have a few options:

✦ Limit the amount of specific technical detail you provide. If you can describe your solution in general terms without revealing exactly how you will execute it, you may prevent someone from deciding they can do it themselves. Similarly, if you provide aggregated pricing instead of line item, detailed pricing, you make it a little more difficult for somebody to use your proposal as a shopping list. The downside to this approach, of course, is that you also lose a little credibility because of the vagueness and you may lose an opportunity to differentiate your approach.

✦ Seek a nondisclosure agreement and/or a letter of understanding before you submit. Ask the client to sign a nondisclosure agreement in which they acknowledge your ownership of the content in your proposal and agree not to share it with anyone outside the evaluation team without your written consent. Some firms ask the customer to sign a letter of understanding, especially those that must invest heavily in information gathering or research and development activities as part of their proposal process. This letter states that the customer intends to buy the products or services being proposed and will make a preliminary commitment to you for purchasing them, subject to a careful review of the proposal and pricing. These letters usually aren't binding, but they do require the customer to make a statement of serious intent.

✦ Mark your proposal "Proprietary" or "Business Confidential." Put these warnings on the pages of your proposal that actually contain proprietary content. Don't put them on every page, because if you mark content proprietary that is actually in the public domain or that belongs to the client, you invalidate your proprietary claim in general. You can also put a separate statement of proprietary rights in your proposal. I recommend putting it on a separate page, preferably at the back, and not trying to fold it into your cover letter, title page, or executive summary.

✦ Copyright your proposal. To do that, simply put "Copyright <<year>> <<Your Company Name>> on the title page or in the footer. You don't have to file any paperwork to establish a copyright. Legally you don't even need to put the notice on the page. The second you write it, it's copyrighted. But by putting the notice on the document, you alert people that you are asserting proprietary rights. If somebody uses your material without your permission, it's then up to you to tell them that they have violated your copyright and demand that they stop doing it or that they compensate you appropriately. The main purpose of copyrighting your proposal is to make a clear claim of ownership to the intellectual property it contains.

✦ Submit at deadline. If you submit early, who knows what will happen to your proposal while the client waits for others to arrive. Those pesky documents have been known to sprout legs, walk themselves down to the copy center, and reproduce like fruit flies. Of course, submitting early is usually not your worry; getting the thing done on time is the big concern. But I've seen situations in which a team worked hard to meet a deadline, only to learn that another vendor had requested and been granted a delay. Since the new deadline applies to everyone, and since your proposal is done, the temptation would be to go ahead and submit it anyway. Don't do it.

✦ Build your proposal on your differentiators, so that there's no way a customer can do it themselves or give it to a competitor to do it. That can be difficult if you don't have strong differentiators, but it's ultimately the best way. If you possess true uniqueness factors, and those are intimately connected with a compelling value proposition, stealing your stuff essentially becomes impossible.

# 13 Writing the Business Case

Writing a formal proposal can be a daunting task. Some of them may be hundreds, even thousands of pages long, but even if they are much shorter, they are still complex documents. As the old proverb about eating an elephant says, you can only get the job done one bite at a time.

The most important bites are the ones that appear up front—your cover letter, title page, and executive summary. Allow yourself enough time to do a good job with those parts and you'll at least create a positive first impression.

## The Cover Letter

The cover letter is your firm's official transmittal message. Serving as a formal introduction and statement of commitment, it presents your company's offer to your client. Because it speaks on behalf of the company, it should be signed by an executive of sufficient rank to bind the company to a contract. Ideally, it should be signed by someone in your organization who is the peer of the person who will make the buying decision in the client's organization. (That may not be the same as the person to whom the cover letter and proposal are addressed, obviously.) What about having the salesperson or account manager sign the cover letter? You can do it that way, but it will not have the same impact as having the president or a senior vice president sign. If you wish, you could have both the senior executive and the salesperson sign the cover letter.

The cover letter is part of the total proposal package and should help sell your solution. Think of the cover letter as a mini executive summary. Include the customer's key need or needs, one or two important outcomes from meeting those needs, your basic approach or solution in a sentence or two, and your two most important differentiators. If your proposal was written in response to an RFP, reference the RFP by name or number. Indicate in the cover letter the effective period for the pricing, staffing, and implementation schedules offered in the proposal.

End with a specific call to action and, if possible, a statement of what you will do next: "I will call you on Thursday to schedule an appointment to present this proposal in person and discuss the implementation steps necessary to meet your deadline." Avoid clichés such as, "Please feel free to call if you have any questions."

The cover letter is also a place where you can thank individuals in the client's organization who have been helpful to you.

If your proposal is a revision, indicate that in the cover letter. You may want to point out specific sections where you have made changes.

Avoid making statements that undercut rapport and trust, such as this one that appeared in the cover letter of an actual proposal:

*All assumptions are considered preliminary until the final proposal, SOW and vendor management responsibilities for each study is approved.*

Would that sentence make you feel confident that the vendor will stand by what they are proposing? Or do they already seem to be looking for wiggle room?

Figure 13-1 offers an example of an effective cover letter.

**Figure 13-1.** Sample Cover Letter.

[date]

Mr. Samuel Taylor, CPA
Chief Financial Officer
Kallaher Financial Group
123 E. Fourth Street, 5th Floor
Los Angeles, California 90094

Dear Mr. Taylor:

The enclosed proposal responds to your request for audits of the following facilities:

- the Patriot Center for Rehabilitative Medicine in San Luis Obispo, California
- the Phoenix City Hospital in Phoenix, Arizona

- the Moreno Valley Wellness Center in Sunnymead, California
- the Playa Vista Health Care Center in Los Angeles, California

Our proposal addresses your need for thorough audits of all four operations, but we have also gone a step further, taking into account your broader objectives. We have developed an overall plan to help you gather the necessary data to turn the properties around financially and protect the value of your investment. We have also outlined our services in the event that one or more of these properties cannot be made profitable and must be sold or liquidated.

We recommend handling the audits by means of a partnership between ourselves, through our headquarters in Los Angeles, California, where we have extensive experience in real estate audits, and James J. Harrison, CPA, & Company, a firm with offices in Phoenix, Arizona, with recognized expertise in supporting the health care industry. This partnership is uniquely qualified to handle the audit and provide additional services as may be required.

We bring some distinct advantages to the process of handling your audit:

1. As medium-size firms, we have the flexibility and responsiveness to meet all deadlines, especially those imposed by third parties and regulators. We offer you the level of service and commitment that the national firms save for their largest clients.

2. At the same time, we have the resources, specialized knowledge, and experience to handle complex audits of long-term care facilities quickly.

3. Senior partners of both firms will be personally involved in conducting your audits.

4. We provide the highest-quality services at a cost-effective price.

We seek to handle all four audits because it is important to develop a total picture of the financial situation for all four facilities. In addition, by handling all four audits, we can save you money. For these reasons, our firms would decline to participate in a split or partial award.

We are eager to work with you on this project. May we schedule a time to present our proposal to the entire management team?

Sincerely,
Donald Miller, CPA    Nancy Jamison
Partner    Business Development Manager

# Title Page

The title page should include a title for the proposal, the name of the recipient, the name of the preparer(s), and the date of submission. You can also put the client's logo and your company's logo on the title page. It's a nice way to personalize the title page, but don't do it if the client is touchy about anyone reproducing their logo. Ask permission first.

Never title your proposal "Proposal." That doesn't say anything your clients can't figure out themselves. (It's a little like writing a book and titling it "Book," isn't it?) Oddly enough, "Proposal" is the most commonly used title for proposals in the English-speaking world. Also, avoid using generic titles such as "A Proposal for New American Corporation." Finally, avoid any proposal title that is basically nothing more than the name of your product or service: "Proposal to Analyze Internet Security Requirements." "Proposal for the TurboEncabulator Model 5000." All of those are losers.

You'll get better results if you create a substantive title that states a benefit to the client or focuses on the primary outcome the client desires. Try to construct a title that does the following:

+ Describes your recommendation in terms of its outcome or impact on the client organization
+ Contains a verb that expresses a beneficial state of change for the client
+ Focuses on results, not product names
+ Avoids any use of your own in-house jargon

Here are some examples of effective titles:

REDUCING DATA TRANSMISSION COSTS
A UNION TECHNOLOGY SOLUTION FOR AMERIBANK CORPORATION

IMPROVING PRODUCTIVITY THROUGH ONLINE INVENTORY ACCESS

INCREASING CUSTOMER LOYALTY THROUGH ENHANCED SERVICE OPTIONS

CUTTING COSTS IN THE ACCOUNTS PAYABLE AREA
WITH AUTOMATED WORKFLOW PROCESSES

Some federal, state, and local government programs and some RFPs prepared by consultants specify a format for the title page or even provide a form for you to complete. In that case, do what they ask.

Figures 13-2 exemplifies a complete title page.

**Figure 13-2.** Sample Title Page.

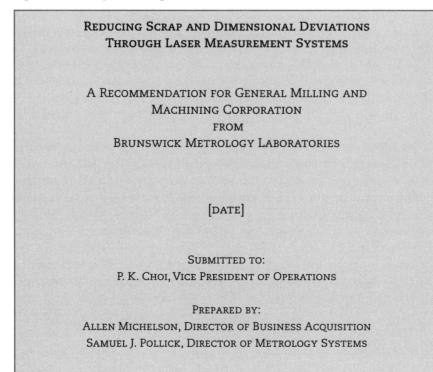

REDUCING SCRAP AND DIMENSIONAL DEVIATIONS
THROUGH LASER MEASUREMENT SYSTEMS


A RECOMMENDATION FOR GENERAL MILLING AND
MACHINING CORPORATION
FROM
BRUNSWICK METROLOGY LABORATORIES



[DATE]



SUBMITTED TO:
P. K. CHOI, VICE PRESIDENT OF OPERATIONS


PREPARED BY:
ALLEN MICHELSON, DIRECTOR OF BUSINESS ACQUISITION
SAMUEL J. POLLICK, DIRECTOR OF METROLOGY SYSTEMS

## Table of Contents

One of the key principles of successful proposal writing is to make your proposal easy to use. People are more likely to view your submission positively if it seems easy to understand. The table of contents is a helpful tool for achieving that goal.

Does your proposal need a table of contents? It probably does if it contains more than four or five pages of content or if it is divided into two or more sections.

List the title of each section and the headings of each major subsection in your table of contents. That will help the reader see the logical structure of your proposal at a glance. Numbering the sections and subsections in your proposal can help show that structure, too. If the RFP uses a numbering scheme or a particular nomenclature for sections or division of content, mirror it in your table of contents.

Make sure the table of contents includes page numbers. Surprisingly, a lot of them don't. Number the pages consecutively through the entire proposal. Don't start renumbering the pages with each section.

Figure 13-3 shows the structural clarity a table of contents can add to your proposal.

**Figure 13-3.** Sample Table of Contents.

# Executive Summary

The executive summary is the single most important part of your proposal. It's the only part that's likely to be read by everybody involved in making a decision. In fact, it's the *only* part of your proposal that some decision makers may read. And it's the part they look at first, which means it creates the first impression for your proposal.

Calling it an "executive summary" is a bit of a misnomer, but we're stuck with it now. The name is misleading because this part of your proposal doesn't really summarize the rest of the document. Think of it as a business overview or a management case. That will help you include only the content that matters.

Here are some additional guidelines:

✦ Use the NOSE structure, explained in Chapter 5, to organize the content of your executive summary. Do not focus on your company, your products, or your feelings ("We are delighted to have the opportunity to respond . . ."). Instead, start by addressing the customer's needs and what they stand to gain. Recommend a solution and provide brief evidence indicating why your firm is the right choice to solve the problems, deliver the value, and successfully implement the solution.

✦ Write the executive summary so that it is accessible to anyone from the janitor to the chairman of the board. Focus on organizational issues and outcomes, and keep technical content to the essential minimum. Challenge the use of acronyms and jargon.

✦ Present your value proposition and your top three or four differentiators in the executive summary. You will develop and substantiate them elsewhere in the proposal, but make sure they are clear and prominent parts of the executive summary.

✦ The executive summary should be about the customer, not you. Count how many times the customer's name appears and compare that to the number of times your firm's name appears. The ratio ought to be 3:1 in favor of the customer.

✦ Keep your executive summary short—approximately one to two pages for the first twenty-five pages of proposal text and an additional page for each fifty pages thereafter.

Remember that the last comment regarding length is just a guideline, not an absolute rule. Write an executive summary that tells your story clearly and persuasively, even if that takes an extra page or two.

The structure of the executive summary is almost identical to the structure of the letter proposal. Both are based on the persuasive pattern, both use a minimal amount of detailed substantiation, and both are primarily concerned with defining the customer's problem or need correctly, articulating the positive outcomes that will come from solving that problem, and recommending a solution. Keep your executive summary focused on the bottom-line issues the customer cares about the most. Write it as though it were titled, "Why My Company Is the Right Choice to Solve Your Business Problem [with Whatever]." A sample executive summary is presented in Figure 13-4.

**Figure 13-4.** Sample Executive Summary.

---

### • EXECUTIVE SUMMARY

General Hospital is coping with a daunting combination of opportunities and challenges: comprehensive health care reform, a lackluster economy, the rising cost of medical care, and an aging population. In response you have introduced sweeping change throughout the organization. These changes are designed to help you improve the quality and quantity of health care you deliver and to increase the shareholder value created by every employee. Your goal is to improve innovation, affordability, accessibility, and simplicity in the delivery of health care to your market.

Technology is a key element in your plans to deliver these improvements. However, your existing content management and collaboration solutions, built on older platforms, have not kept pace with evolving business requirements. As a result, you have launched a program of significant technology transformation.

*Addressing Your Key Challenges*

The primary challenge for any CIO or IT manager is to meet the organization's diverse business needs while minimizing system complexity and cost. In updating General Hospital's technology platform, your goals are ultimately to increase employee efficiency, reduce manual processes, and enhance organizational agility. For example, you recognize the need for a cost-effective solution to make your authorization and claims processes faster and more responsive. You also need a system that is more flexible so it can keep pace with the changing demands of your users.

During our discussions, you indicated that the most pressing challenges you face include the following:

- *Eliminating manual authorization processes.* Your current process for managing authorizations is almost 100% manual, is costly, does not scale, and is frustrating for referral specialists to complete.
- *Simplifying claims administration.* Today you handle approximately 40% of your claims volume via fax, which is very labor intensive. You need a streamlined, automated process that is workflow driven.
- *Overcoming the lack of integration.* Your current process does not effectively handle the volume of faxes and does not integrate them into an automated workflow. You need to overcome that

lack of integration so that no patient or provider waits for an answer.

### Achieving Bottom-Line Impact

In this economy, General Hospital's investment in technology transformation absolutely must produce bottom-line value. As a result, we have developed a solution that will help you achieve the following goals:

- *Automated reporting and reduced costs.* We are recommending a single authorizations and claims processing platform to eliminate manually generated reports. Based on the data you provided and on our experience with other hospitals of similar size, we project that General Hospital can reduce the time spent on manually completing reports by 1,500 hours a month. Assuming an overhead charge rate of $20 an hour for administrative support, the system we are recommending can save General Hospital approximately $360,000 a year.
- *Integrate your critical business systems.* Our solution will give every functional area of the hospital a unified view of patient/provider/eligibility data. This will eliminate interdepartmental barriers so that your entire team can focus on delivering the best quality care in the most cost-effective manner. An integrated view will improve overall performance, including clinical outcomes.
- *Increased productivity and organizational responsiveness:* Through smart automation of key processes, you will enable your referral and claims associates to manage authorizations and claims more easily and provide better service to your clients. Your employees will no longer need to be experts in multiple systems because they will all use a single solution that allows them to view all the data they need in one place. As a result, you will increase employee efficiency and maximize the usability and convenience of your investment in tools and technology.

### Our Recommendation

Continental Claims Systems recommends that General Hospital simplify and automate information processing throughout the hospital. We recommend moving General Hospital from your current manual environment to an integrated, fully automated platform, a solution that will have a dramatic impact on business performance and employee productivity. In addition, Continental Claims Systems is an experienced deployment partner. We have conducted hundreds of similar projects, so you know the job will be done right and will meet your unique needs.

The heart of our proposal is the implementation of the Continental Millennium II system, a product that will give you the capabilities you need to manage the entire life cycle of unstructured authorization and claims content from creation to expiration on a single unified platform. These capabilities include document management, records management, Web content management, and forms solutions.

To get the full value from your use of Millennium II, we also recommend a deployment plan to transition you from your current manual environment into a fully integrated environment. The first phase of that plan is an engagement for discovery and planning. Based on our experience with hundreds of clients similar to General Hospital, we have found this is the most effective way to assure quick and accurate delivery of the system you need. Specifically, our solution involves the following scope of work:

1. **Discovery Phase:** Continental consultants will perform a discovery workshop to review General Hospital's enterprise architecture and network environment. In addition, the consultants will work closely with your team to determine an optimal production environment for Millennium II. Upon completion of the Discovery phase, General Hospital will have an understanding of the network, hardware, and software configuration you need to maximize your results.

2. **Execution Phase:** Continental consultants will work with General Hospital's subject matter experts to understand your current processes, and then define and develop future processes using Millennium II. This phase will continue until we have created:

   - Detailed functional requirements for authorization and claims automation
   - System and application architectures
   - A user interface prototype
   - A detailed project plan for the remainder of the project

   Upon completion of the Execution phase, General Hospital will have an installed Millennium II environment, and a detailed design for automated authorization and claims processes.

At the end of this initial engagement, Continental Claims Systems will provide an estimate for remaining work and a project plan outlining the remaining activities, resources, and timeframes necessary for successful completion.

*Why Continental Claims Systems is the Right Choice for General Hospital*
There are four reasons that Continental Claims Systems is the best partner for you on this project. These reasons are core strengths of the Microsoft team, strengths that differentiate us from the competition and enable us to deliver the most value for General Hospital:

1. **Ranked #1:** We manufacture the #1 authorization and claims system in the industry *(source: Health Technology Reports, February 2011)*, Millennium II, a product that you already own. Industry analysts have stated that Millennium II is an enterprise-class platform that easily integrates with a variety of back-end systems.

   > *"We decided to work with Continental Claims Systems' consultants because we thought, 'Who would know how to use this technology and integrate it with others better than the people who created it?'"*—WAYNE LOPEZ, SENIOR MANAGER OF BUSINESS APPLICATIONS, ROGERS HOSPITAL

2. **Unique tools and project accelerators:** We have developed specific tools and project accelerators to get the job done faster at the highest quality. Checklists, configuration project templates, supportability reviews, and sustainability are all built into our delivery methodology. In addition, lessons learned become "inputs" for all new projects so that we avoid or mitigate risks and issues early.

3. **A record of successful past performance with General Hospital.** You chose us to implement a pilot system for claims authorizations at your Meadowton facility, stipulating that the system had to be in production within five months to meet your internal requirements. We successfully met that aggressive timeline, achieving what Meadowton CIO Sally Robertson called "the cleanest launch in hospital history."

4. **We have an unmatched record of delivery successes.** With over 500 customers implemented, we have more experience in han-

dling large-scale deployments and migrations for customers than any other firm in the world.

*Summary*

We appreciate your choice of Continental technology products to help you run the business side of your hospital. We take pride in our technology, and we are equally proud of the professional services we offer to help customers get the greatest return on their IT investment. We are eager to work with the General Hospital team to simplify workflow, automate labor-intensive processes, improve the delivery of care, and reduce the cost of operations. We are confident we have the right solution for you in the combination of our award-winning platform and our delivery expertise.

# 14 Recommending and Substantiating Your Solution

ALTHOUGH THE EXECUTIVE SUMMARY IS THE single most important part of your formal proposal, the body contains the details of your solution and the evidence to substantiate your ability to deliver it. What should you cover in this section? How should you organize it? Following are some suggestions, but remember that the overriding rule should be that you provide exactly what your client wants to see in the order in which he or she wants to see it. Avoid the temptation to "bulk up" your proposal by including lots of extraneous detail.

In most cases, the body of your proposal should include:

+ The technical section, which may include the technical details, functional analysis, operational description, design specifications, and implementation programs associated with your recommendation
+ The pricing section, which will include detailed costs and an analysis of return on investment or another form of cost justification
+ Detailed response to the questions and requirements of the RFP
+ Case studies, success stories, and past performance summaries
+ Related applications that have been successful
+ References to satisfied clients
+ Testimonials
+ The management plan, including project schedules, critical milestones, and the allocation of responsibilities among your firm, the customer's organization, and other vendors, if any
+ Brief resumes of key personnel who will oversee or work on the project
+ Logistical and support issues
+ Warranties, service-level agreements, and risk-sharing options, if any
+ Documentation
+ Training plans

Not every proposal needs to contain all of this content. In fact, most of them won't. Include the elements that are of most interest to your customer and deal with them in their order of importance as the customer sees it. If technical competence is not much of an issue, put it later in the proposal and address something that's more important up front. If you are responding to an RFP, use it as your guide. It may specify an order for the content in your proposal. Even if it doesn't, look at the sequencing of issues in the RFP and mirror that in your proposal.

# Section Introductions

One of the most important areas of your proposal is the introduction you write to each major section. A short introductory paragraph, particularly if you highlight it with a box or shading, focuses the reader's attention, provides the reader with a transition from one major idea to the next, and gives you an opportunity to state your key themes.

Why are they so important?

+ They make your proposal easier to read and understand. That's always a good thing.
+ They allow you to state the benefits of your recommendation up front.
+ They are a perfect place to present your win theme(s).
+ They help readers figure out quickly whether a particular section is relevant to them.

Here's an example:

> The following section addresses the specific features of our software and how users can customize the interface to meet their own requirements or preferences. Specifically, this section discusses the tools included in the standard package that make it easy for a user to modify the view of data. These tools reduce the time it takes to locate and process data, thereby increasing productivity.
>
> This section also discusses how a system administrator can enable users to make modifications at the desktop level or can make modifications that affect the entire enterprise. This capability allows you to match the software to your specific work environment and requirements, eliminating the need for customization and reducing the amount of time the administrator spends configuring the product for individual users.

# Recommending Your Solution

Of the thousands of proposals I read each year, the majority do not recommend anything. Most of them lapse into informative writing and simply describe a product or service. Descriptions have their place, but they can come across as evasive in a proposal. In addition, descriptions typically consist of standard verbiage that provides a general understanding of the product or service, but nothing specifically relevant to the customer. An effective solution links specific features of the product or service back to the customer's needs and outcomes, constantly answering the question, "So what?" In a solution, each feature has relevance. It either solves part of the customer's problem, or it delivers value, or both.

Here are some guidelines to help you write an effective solution recommendation:

✦ Stay focused on the controlling strategy you established in the executive summary. Even though you stated your value proposition there, you need to repeat it and build on it in the body of your proposal. Repetition is the key to making certain the client sees it, understands it, and remembers it.

✦ Be objective. Don't allow your enthusiasm to carry you away into using wild superlatives or making unsupported claims. Be careful about using language that implicitly guarantees results (unless you really are guaranteeing them contractually), or that predicts outcomes you're not sure you can deliver. (Note: This is important. There are legal implications to anything you write in a proposal. If you win the contract, your proposal becomes a legally binding document and you could be held to the promises or claims you have made in it.)

✦ Use specific, concrete language. Use details. Simply saying that a system is "efficient" or "ideal for these purposes" is not enough. Go into detail: "This system achieves 99.96% up time, the best in the industry, as documented by the independent journal *Manufacturing Monthly*."

✦ Support your claims with substantive evidence. Statistics, third-party validation, test results, awards, and other forms of evidence are more convincing than generic claims. Case studies that showcase successful applications of your products or services are very effective. References to satisfied customers also help, particularly if they come from well-known firms in the same industry as your prospective client.

## Explaining How Your Solution Works

In the solution section of your proposal, you may need to explain how the equipment or mechanisms you are recommending work. Here's a simple outline that will keep your discussion organized and make it easy for your reader to understand:

**I.** Introduction: Start by focusing on what the equipment will do for the client—the problem it will solve or the benefit it will deliver.
  **A.** Define/identify the mechanism or equipment:
  **1.** Indicate its function or purpose, linking it to customer needs or issues.
  **2.** Describe its general physical characteristics (including a comparison or analogy to a more familiar object).
  **3.** Divide it into its principal parts.
  **B.** Indicate why the mechanism is important to the reader: this is another good spot to introduce or reinforce your value proposition.

**II.** Provide a part-by-part description.
  **A.** Part number one:
  **1.** What the part is (definition)
  **2.** Function or purpose of the part
  **3.** Physical characteristics (including comparison)
  **4.** Division into subparts
    **a.** Subpart number one
      **(1)** What the subpart is
      **(2)** Its function or purpose
      **(3)** Appearance
      **(4)** Detailed description
        **(a)** Relationship to other parts
        **(b)** Size
        **(c)** Shape
        **(d)** Methods of attachment
        **(e)** Material
        **(f)** Finish
    **b.** Same as "a" above for subpart number two
  **B.** Same as "A" above for part number two.

**III.** Closing*:* Link the product or mechanism to your value proposition.
  **A.** To bring the description to a close with an emphasis on function:
    **1.** Briefly describe the mechanism in a complete cycle of operation.
    **2.** Mention variations and options of the mechanism.
    **3.** Indicate the importance of the mechanism to the customer's operating environment.
  **B.** To bring the description to a close with an even more persuasive slant:
    **1.** Compare the mechanism to other makes and models, in terms of features and advantages—this is a chance to "ghost" the competition by pointing out important differentiators or design features without disparaging your competitor.
    **2.** Calculate the probable gain the customer will see from implementing the product or mechanism—quantify the increase in productivity, the reduction in maintenance costs, or whatever measure is most compelling.

## Describing Processes

Your proposals may also need to recommend processes and operations, particularly when the solution is primarily a service. The pattern follows the same kind of logic that is effective in presenting products and mechanisms:

**I.** Introduction: Link the process to your customer's general concerns—the problems they want to solve or the needs they want to address—and introduce your value proposition or a supporting win theme here. Answer the question: why is this process important?
  **A.** Define or identify the process:
    **1.** Formal definition: what is the process?
    **2.** Statement of significance: Why is it done? Why does it happen? (This is an excellent place to remind the client of your value proposition or key differentiators, such as cost savings, superior reliability, and so on, by indicating how this process is an improvement over what the customer is currently doing or what the competition is offering.)
    **3.** Underlying principle that governs this process. (For a natural process, such as a chemical reaction, we want to indicate that the process is essentially inevitable. For a human process, such as a training method, we want to indicate that the process is

based on research into best practices or based on other forms of empirical evidence.)

**B.** Indicate the time, setting, operators, equipment, and preparations necessary.

1. Time and setting: when and where it is done or how it happens in a natural setting
2. Personnel: who (or *what* for automated processes) performs it
3. Equipment: what is needed
4. Necessary conditions: the requisite circumstances

**C.** Indicate the point of view from which the process will be considered.

**D.** List the main steps.

**II.** Present the steps in detail.

**A.** Step number one

*Note: Each step is itself a process. Organize it by following the format outlined in the Introduction above.*

**B.** Key step number two, etc.

*Note: The simplest and most logical way to organize a process description is chronologically. For a cyclical process, simply choose a reasonable starting point and follow the complete cycle.*

**III.** Closing: Return here to your value proposition and emphasize any differentiators your process may have.

**A.** Techniques for closing the description:

1. Simply stop after the final step—this is effective for a short description.
2. Summarize the key steps again—this is effective for a lengthy, multipage description. *However, if you use this approach, emphasize the value of following these steps or the importance of expert knowledge in executing the steps correctly.*
3. Comment on the process's significance, particularly in the context of achieving the customer's objectives.
4. Indicate the process's place in a larger scheme of operation.
5. Mention other methods by which the process can be performed and why you are recommending this method. (This is an opportunity to ghost the competition.)
6. Discuss the consequences of modifying time, setting, operators, equipment, or other conditions (another ghosting opportunity).
7. Predict or forecast improvements in productivity, cost efficiency, etc.
8. Recommend implementing or using the process.

## Linking the Customer's Needs and Goals to Your Solution

Customers do not automatically recognize that the solution you are proposing will give them the results they want. You must clearly, explicitly link the elements of your solution to their needs and to the outcomes the client seeks. This is particularly important for a highly complex or technical recommendation. Imagine the client asking after each mention of a feature, "So what? Why should I care?" If your proposal answers those questions, it's on the right path.

To create solution presentations that are more persuasive and client focused, use the structure presented in Figure 14-1 as a basic guideline in organizing descriptions of products and services. Figure 14-2 provides an example of a solution description that follows this structure.

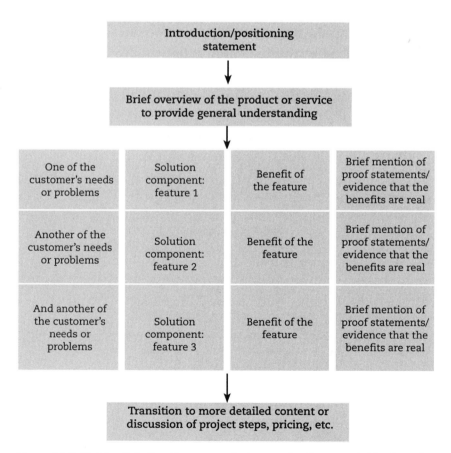

**Figure 14-1.** Linking Solution Recommendations to the Customer's Needs and Outcomes.

### The DataMaster System from ComStar

We at ComStar recommend using the DataMaster system as a platform for developing American Cellular's EtherSwitch system. The DataMaster system is a new generation of data management tools, designed specifically for the cellular marketplace. Its design incorporates all of the elements of traditional call management and billing systems, but is based on a new, modular platform that allows for easy customization to meet unique needs.

You indicated to us that you are looking for a vendor who can address four specific needs in your business:

- Capacity to handle current and projected volume of transactions without requiring system add-ons or expansion
- Enhanced customer support and service
- A customizable solution
- A complete solution, including service bureau options

The DataMaster system, in conjunction with our services, provides you with exactly what you want.

| | |
|---|---|
| *Capacity to handle the volume of billing transactions your business needs* | ComStar is the only provider of cellular billing systems with existing capacity to handle the volume you specify in your RFP. With our combination of software designed specifically for the cellular market and our extensive service bureau capabilities, we can provide American Cellular with the right mix of products and services regardless of the volume your business demands today or in the future. |
| *Enhanced customer support and service* | Your billing systems are a fundamental part of your total customer support and service system. By outsourcing the management of billing to a third party, you must feel confident that your customers will receive the highest-quality service and that the relationship will be transparent. ComStar has received awards from industry groups for the quality of our customer support. In addition, because the DataMaster system is customizable, it can provide your customers with exactly the kind of billing information they want. Finally, as your first line of customer support, we handle all customer inquiries in a timely fashion with a documented 97.9% closure rate on the first call. |
| *Customizable solution* | Everyone wants choices. Unless your business partner can offer you a wide range of options, you may feel that you are forced to take less than or something other than what you really need. ComStar offers a broader range of product and service offerings than any other provider in the wireless market. The DataMaster system was specifically designed as a modular, N-tiered application with a mathematically infinite number of potential configurations. |

| A complete solution | ComStar is a pioneer in creating and providing cellular billing systems and we continue to be the industry leader. But we are also the largest provider of service bureau operations with the ability to handle the complete range of customer billing, service and support functions, including problem resolution, collections, marketing, and more. As a result, we can tailor a solution specifically to your needs. |
| --- | --- |

As you can see, the use of the DataMaster platform addresses your four primary objectives. In addition, it delivers all of the technical functionality you have specified in your RFP. In some cases, we provide the functionality that you specify, but because that functionality will be delivered from an innovative platform, the system architecture may not conform exactly to the design specifications you have included in the proposal. These differences will be invisible to the user. However, we do want to be clear that in some instances we deliver the functional requirement but do it in a different part of the system or with a different logical flow of processing steps.

We believe it makes good business and technical sense for American Cellular to use DataMaster as the platform for your EtherSwitch. It will provide you with a comprehensive, flexible, high-quality product at a much lower cost than would be possible if the entire system were created as a custom product.

Figure 14-2. Sample Solution Description.

# 15 Persuasive Answers to RFP Questions

Remember that RFPs almost never identify the business issues that underlie the proposal as a whole, nor do they indicate why a particular question is being asked. But those factors matter. You'll improve your chances if you address both the business issues that underlie the RFP and the critical questions in particular. Simply "answering the mail" and providing factual statements is usually not enough.

Evaluate the questions being asked and divide them into three categories:

**1. *Pro forma questions***: This is stuff they have to ask, but won't make much of a difference to winning.

**2. *Tactical or narrowly focused questions***: These questions often address infrastructure, technical, or contractual requirements, but the client is often willing to overlook noncompliance on these matters as long as they are getting what they need otherwise.

**3. *Strategic questions***: These are the ones that really matter, the ones that get at the heart of the solution the customer seeks.

Spend most of your time on the strategic questions.

RFP answers can require all kinds of writing—simple statements of fact (for example, answering the question "When was your company founded?"), process and product descriptions (for example, responding to "Explain your disaster recovery protocol"), team resumes, brief case studies, references, and even opinions ("What do you consider the most important trends in the industry and how will you help us address them?"). Regardless of the kind of writing required by a given question, however, and no matter whether the question is pro forma, tactical, or strategic in nature, your focus should always be on clarity and persuasiveness.

## A Dozen Recommendations

Here are twelve quick tips to help you get maximum points from evaluators when they read your answers to the questions in their RFP:

**1. *Do not change the order of the questions and do not rewrite them.*** Respond to them exactly as they were written. Changing the order makes the evaluator's job harder, and rewriting them is a pretty clear indication you think they're incompetent.

In a survey of proposal evaluators, we asked what really irritates them in the responses they get. The number one answer? The vendor did not follow the instructions in the RFP. Now, these are people who are not above specifying what font your proposal should be in and how wide your margins should be. Clearly, rewriting the RFP and rearranging the order of the questions isn't going to go over well.

**2. *Repeat the question as written in your response, then answer it in a different format.*** Change the font, use bold for their question and regular type for your answer, or change the color. Just make it obvious which is theirs and which is yours. I've seen proposals in which the authors decided to write a complete narrative, weaving in the answers to RFP questions along the way. What a disaster.

**3. *Include a compliance matrix*** at the start of your response or at the start of each major section within the response. A compliance matrix is a table that lists the requirement or question, your level of compliance ("Exceeds," "Fully complies," "Partially complies," "Takes exception," "Not available" are typical options), and perhaps includes the page number where the detailed answer can be found. Evaluators love compliance matrices.

**4. *Do not send your reader off to another part of your proposal to find the answer.*** For example, never write, "Answered above." Or, "See section 3 for this answer." In the first place, you come across as lazy and inconsiderate. In the second place, they might not have the rest of the proposal, since it's pretty common for reviewers to divide up the document and score only their part.

**5. *Answer the question. And answer it each time they ask it.*** It's amazing how often proposals contain so-called answers that have almost nothing to do with the question they are supposedly answering. Here's an example of an answer that doesn't really answer anything:

*What is the underlying database architecture and version of your cash management system?*

> *Since GlobalBankNet has been developed internally by GlobalBank, there is no relevant version number for the service. As changes and upgrades are made to the service, all users automatically use the latest release when they next log on.*

Okay, that sort of covers the version number issue, but it seems like the important part of the question had to do with database architecture. The writer has ignored that part.

**6. *Focus on what the client cares about first, not on your product or service details.*** Most buyers are interested in what our product or service will do for them, not its inner workings. Unfortunately, when answers are written by subject matter experts, the text is often too technical and too product focused. Reviewers tend to skim proposals and as they glance at our answers, they will sweep their eyes from the top down. If the opening paragraph doesn't immediately engage them, we may have lost the opportunity to get maximum points.

**7. *Use the A / P / S format for important answers.*** When we look at a question in an RFP, the logical impulse is to plunge in and start regurgitating facts that sort of answer it. But if it's an important question—one that addresses a fundamental issue, that gets at a key evaluation criterion, or that probes for your differentiators, for example—don't do that. Instead, write your answer using A / P / S: Acknowledge that the question is significant, make a Persuasive statement about what you have done in this area, and then Substantiate with details.

Here are two answers, one written as a factual response and one written in the A / P / S format. Which one do you think is more persuasive?

*Question: What information appears on the Explanation of Benefits form? Can EoB information be customized? Please provide a sample of an EoB form.*

Answer 1:

> *See enclosed. Generally all EoB messages are pre-defined for all clients to meet readability, accuracy, and legal requirements. Limited customization is available, including the addition of logos and personalized remarks in the remarks area.*

Answer 2:

> *Plan members need to understand how their benefits were determined. The Explanation of Benefits (EoB) form is an important tool in our overall effort to provide good communications and to avoid confusion when plan members file a claim.*

> *United Health has designed our EoB forms for maximum readability and accuracy. In addition, we have created layouts and content in our forms to address certain legal requirements. However, within that framework we can also provide customization. For example, we can add your logo to the form, or we can provide personalized information in the remarks area.*

> *The enclosed EoB is a sample of what we will provide to your members.*

I think you'll agree that the two answers say essentially the same thing. But the first answer sounds perfunctory, doesn't it? And do you detect a tone of negativity? They don't seem interested in customizing the EoB if they don't have to. The second answer says the same thing exactly, yet it manages to sound positive and cooperative. It's basically a matter of the structure of the answer. By following the A / P / S format, answer number two says it much more effectively.

**8. *Weave your value proposition into your answers and include key differentiators.*** Tie their business or technical need to the value or outcome you are delivering in explicit language:

> *You indicated that one of your most important needs is to reduce operating costs. As a result, we have included as a component of our solution a strategy for reducing your energy consumption by 15% to 18%.*

Then link that promise of value to a differentiator so that your competitors can't say, "Me, too."

> *That decrease in energy consumption will come as a direct result of implementing our gas and electric rationalization software. This software*

*automatically manages your energy costs to assure that you pay the lowest possible price 24 hours a day. The only system of its kind, our software has been proven in controlled studies to reduce energy bills dramatically.*

Finally, offer some proof so they feel confident in believing your value proposition:

*For example, when Leeds Smelting implemented the software, they saw an immediate reduction in energy costs of more than 20%. Similarly, Birmingham Hospital reduced energy costs by 17% during the first year of using our system.*

**9. *Keep the writing simple and clear.*** Keep your average sentence length around 15 to 18 words, minimize the use of passive voice constructions, and challenge jargon and acronyms. In Chapter 20, on editing, I will show you how to use the readability calculation tool that is built into Microsoft Word. This will instantly tell you whether your answers are clear and easy to understand.

**10. *Provide time to edit answers written by subject matter experts.*** People who seldom interact directly with customers have no way to know if their explanations make sense to outsiders. As a result, they may produce language that is too dense, too technical, or that makes too many assumptions.

A key problem for subject matter experts is the tendency to overuse product names and in-house jargon. Because they don't present to customers very often, they don't realize that the language that works so well within the organization is totally confusing to outsiders.

**11. *Watch your tone. Keep it friendly.*** Avoid sounding curt or peremptory, especially when the answer is just "Yes" or "No."
*Do you currently provide cellular service for Amalgamated Chemical?*

Yes.

*Are bank charges reports available online in English and are charges reported in AFP format?*

No.

A little more information, please!

**12. Simplify.** Challenge the Geek and Guff, as explained in Chapter 9. Ask yourself, "Would someone outside the business understand this answer?" If not, simplify it.

## Typical Writing Problems with RFP Answers and How to Fix Them

The first problem that plagues many RFP answers is lack of clarity. On the left in the following text is an answer that appeared in an RFP response. On the right is a revision that is clearer.

| | |
|---|---|
| AllCall Telecommunications is committed to managing fraud risks by proactively identifying potential exposures, facilitating and participating in the resolution of exposures and increasing the awareness of fraud-related issues across not only the AllCall Telecommunications Network, but the wireless communications industry as a whole. | Fraud associated with the misuse of telecommunications and Internet systems is a serious, potentially costly, problem. Your risk of fraud will be reduced dramatically if you select AllCall Telecommunications, according to research firm Sylver and Brown. Why? Because we manage fraud aggressively by testing our networks, identifying potential weaknesses, and proactively resolving them. |

The version on the left is not clear because it is one, long, convoluted sentence; because it is focused entirely on the vendor, not the client; and because it contains no evidence. The version on the right consists of four sentences, including one that is a single word. It addresses what the customer cares about first and it includes a bit of evidence to support the claim that they do a better job in preventing fraud.

The next problem is the tendency to write **self-centered content**. Instead, try to keep the answers client centered. Again, the bad one is on the left and the better one is on the right:

| | |
|---|---|
| *AllCall Telecommunications Premium Corporate Care<sup>SM</sup>* The Premium Corporate Care (PCC) program has been developed to provide a unique level of customer service to large corporate-sponsored accounts who manage their AllCall Telecommunications Service through centralized telecom management.<br><br>    This program is intended to reduce involvement in customer service issues so you can focus on your primary mission. To this end, it is critical that the Advocate and the customer establish a one-on-one relationship. | *Getting the Industry's Best Service: Premium Corporate Care<sup>SM</sup>* Your company relies on effective communications, but that isn't your core business. As a result, you need excellent service that responds immediately any time you have a problem.<br><br>    The answer is AllCall Telecommunications' Premium Corporate Care plan. If you have centralized telecom management in place, we can assign a dedicated resource to your account who will be your single point of contact for all service issues. The result is speedy resolution of problems and greater peace of mind. |

The version on the left starts out by naming the service plan (and including an acronym that is never mentioned again), then describing it in very generic terms. In the third sentence, the answer mentions an "Advocate" but never defines who or what that is. We can guess, but guessing creates uncertainty and doubt. The version on the right starts by addressing what customers are more likely to care about—being able to focus on their business without being distracted by telecommunications issues. The service plan is then presented as an answer to that problem. We left out the acronym and the jargon term "Advocate" because they don't seem to add anything.

## The Compliance Matrix: Simplifying the Evaluator's Job

Tip number 3 in the preceding list mentioned the importance of including a compliance matrix in your response to an RFP. So what's a compliance matrix? It's a chart that makes it easy for the evaluator to determine which proposals are worth looking at and which can be discarded. Remember that the evaluator's first job is to reduce the number of proposals to a manageable few. An easy way for a gatekeeper to do that is to glance through your proposal to see if it complies with the basic requirements. The presence of a compliance matrix shows the evaluator that your response is worth keeping and looking at in detail. The absence of one may suggest that it's not.

In addition to showing the evaluator how well you meet the requirements of the RFP, your compliance matrix should make it easy to locate more detailed information. In the following sample (Figure 15-1), the page numbers are hot links that jump directly to the relevant answers.

---

*Our Proposal Is Fully Compliant with Your Requirements*

The compliance matrix below illustrates graphically the extent to which our solutions match up with Urban Bank's key requirements. Detailed answers and explanations for each question or requirement can be found in the following pages, as indicated by the page numbers.

COMPLIANCE KEY:
EX = Exceeds the requirement
F = Fully complies
P = Partially complies
N = Non-compliant

| Question | Extent of Compliance | | | | Page | Comments |
|---|---|---|---|---|---|---|
| | EX | F | P | N | | |
| Urban Bank Corporation needs to streamline the proposal generation process. | | ✓ | | | 21 | Our recommendations will eliminate 11 steps from the current proposal process at Urban Bank. |
| Internet accessible and mobile proposal and presentation generation capability integrated with a product and price configuration system. | | ✓ | | | 22 | We offer a Web-based (not merely Web-enabled) system that includes presentation capabilities. We provide built-in integration with the pricing tools Urban is considering. |
| Produce consistently high-quality customized proposals, request for proposal responses, and customer presentations. | | ✓ | | | 24 | Our system produces the full range of documents in an easy-to-use format. |
| Automated interface to configuration systems. | | ✓ | | | 25 | Our system accepts output from configuration systems if formatted as an Excel or Word file. |
| Knowledge transfer. | | ✓ | | | 26 | |
| Guidance leading to a prospect/customer needs analysis and solution. | | ✓ | | | 27 | Our system coaches the user to define the opportunity, including needs and solution. |
| Supplemental product support. | | ✓ | | | 29 | We provide exceptional technical and customer support. |
| Catalog product and service proposal language, promotional text, graphics, and promote the Urban Bank brand ID. | | · ✓ | | | *31* | Our system serves as a library for all types of content and automatically formats documents to match Urban identity requirements. |

**Figure 15-1.** Compliance Matrix.

# 16 Presenting Evidence and Proving Your Points

W HEN WE WRITE PROPOSALS OR CREATE SALES presentations, we typically try to establish the superiority of our recommendations by offering some kind of proof. In the world we work in, there are four kinds of proof we can offer to a prospect: the things we say about ourselves; the things our clients say about us; the things third-party, outside experts say; and the documented experience we can point to. Let's consider each type of proof.

***Things we say about ourselves.*** Every proposal contains some of these statements. "Our software is designed to be user friendly." "We are passionate about customer satisfaction." "We are a leader in developing effective treatment regimens." And so on.

Do they work? No, not very well. Customers and prospects are likely to be skeptical of claims we make—after all, why wouldn't we say positive things about ourselves? The other problem is we often lapse into clichés to communicate these claims—"best-of-breed products" combined with "state-of-the-art implementation" and "world-class support" producing "synergy and partnership" that results in "bottom-line impact."

The best way to put some teeth into these claims is to ditch the clichés and back up each assertion with a bit of proof. For example, instead of saying we offer "best-of-breed products," why not say "we offer products from the seven largest manufacturers of molding equipment, including three products that received the coveted 'injection molding machine of the year' award"?

Other things we say about ourselves—the number of ATM outlets in our network, the number of employees who work for the company, the number of clients we have in the higher education sector, or the fact that we were named one of the best places to work in South Dakota—are effective only if those statements are relevant to our prospective customer.

***Things our clients say about us.*** These claims, which typically take the form of quotes, references, and testimonials, are more compelling. After all, your clients don't have to say anything at all. The fact that they're willing to do it is somewhat impressive.

On the other hand, there's the psychological phenomenon known as "hindsight bias." We're all aware of it, even though we may not know the technical name for it. When people make a choice, they then become much more convinced it was the right thing to do and will start recommending it to others, even though they originally weren't that sure about it and even though the actual results may not justify that level of commitment.

As a result, our clients and prospects are likely to be a little bit skeptical about the things our clients say about us. Their skepticism is balanced to some extent by the fact that people think a decision is more sensible when they see others are also making it. Based on experience, we know that we make fewer mistakes when we do what others are also doing. The strongest way to buttress the value of quotes, references, and testimonials is to leverage another psychological principle: the concept of social proof. People are more comfortable listening to and believing what they hear from people who are similar to themselves. As a result, the best proof statements will come from clients who are in the same industry, who have the same job title, and who had similar challenges and got them resolved by working with you.

***Third-party proof.*** One of the ways to gain influence over others, as explained in Robert Cialdini's book *Influence,* is to leverage the phenomenon of "submission to authority." Perceived authority carries tremendous inherent persuasive power. As a result, if you can cite an outside source—a governing body, a recognized expert, or some other authority—it can have a strong impact on prospective customers. Similarly, if you've won awards, achieved a difficult status in your field, or had your excellence certified by a third-party agency, it's very much to your advantage to cite that proof.

The problem, of course, is that every industry has its "experts for hire," who will evaluate your product and rate it, partly based on how many of their publications you subscribe to at outrageous fees. This whole field is about as open and honest as figure-skating competitions used to be. So, once again, a shiny endorsement from a group of quasi-experts may provoke yet another bout of skepticism in the prospect. But not always. And when it does, the skepticism is likely to be much lighter.

***Documented experience.*** One of the best kinds of proof is the case study or past performance write-up. These work well because they often combine all three of the previous forms of proof statement into one concise package. You describe work you successfully accomplished for another client, quoting that client if possible, and citing figures showing the positive impact your work had on the client's organization. You also mention any awards or recognition you received as a result of this work. In my opinion, well-written case studies are the single most effective form of proof you can include in a proposal or sales pitch.

## Writing Effective Case Studies

Case studies (which are often called "past performance qualifications" or "Quals" in government bidding circles) give you the opportunity to build your credibility and demonstrate relevant experience, while also helping the decision maker develop a "vision" of the results you can produce.

Keep your case studies short. Usually one or two pages is plenty. A common mistake in writing case studies is to lapse into informative writing and provide a detailed project summary. That usually doesn't work. Instead, a good case study will highlight the productivity gains a customer achieved, not the products you installed. Focus on the success your previous client achieved, not on the details of the project you managed or the product you delivered.

Choose case studies that feature customers who are similar to the company or agency to which you are proposing. Match a municipality with a municipal or county government client, for example, or use a bank with another bank or financial institution, and so on. It is also helpful to at least use a client that is similar in size and that had a problem similar to the one your prospect has. That way the prospect can more easily see themselves in the case study.

In recent years, complex contract vehicles issued by the U.S. federal government have asked for little more than an executive summary and a handful of Quals. This often happens when the government agency or department is issuing what is called an IDIQ—an acronym that stands for "Indefinite Duration, Indefinite Quantity." In other words, the people issuing the RFP don't know exactly what they need, how much of it they need, or how long they will need it, but they would like you to bid on it anyway. That's an oversimplification, of course, but essentially an IDIQ is a means of identifying a few vendors who have the broad qualifications and experience to handle whatever the government agency may need in a particular area of support—information technology, for example. The RFP will typically list a lot of task areas on which approved vendors will be asked to bid. The Quals you provide will need to show that you can do most of those tasks.

Regardless of whether you are writing case studies to win a hundred-million-dollar IDIQ or a simple case study to win a contract to paint the church down on the corner, you will get the right results if you organize them effectively. Structure your case studies using the P / A / R format: Problem / Action / Results. Figure 16-1 provides an example of a case study that follows the P / A / R structure.

**Problem:** Briefly describe the previous customer's situation, the problems they were facing, and/or the objectives they had in mind. The first part of the case study should provide your prospective customers with enough information that they can identify with the one being described.

It's most effective to name the previous customer, but you don't have to. You can use a general description: "A large, international biotechnology firm with complex requirements for warehousing and transporting volatile compounds and controlled substances."

**Action taken:** What did you do to help them solve their problem or meet their objective? Be as specific as possible about the solution you provided, particularly highlighting steps or processes that are among your differentiators.

Obviously, the actions you took should be the same as or very similar to the actions you are recommending in this proposal. Otherwise, your case study will demonstrate that you are competent in ways that aren't particularly relevant to the current opportunity.

**Results obtained:** Specify the results the customer obtained. Whenever possible, quantify the impact: 15 percent reduction in total project length, 20 percent lower operating costs in the outbound telemarketing function, 17 percent higher productivity among hourly employees.

If quantifiable results are not available, or if the existing customer won't let you share them with others, the next most convincing kind of evidence is a quote from a key executive within the customer organization.

---

**What our client needed:** In the highly competitive executive recruiting business, success is based on who you know and what you know about them. REX Recruiting found that they were not able to keep track of their contacts and leads in a systematic way. As a result, opportunities to place executives were sometimes lost.

**What we created:** After investigating costly, high-end products designed for sales forces or customer service organizations, REX Recruiting contracted with Mustang Software to create a data storage and tracking tool that was right for them. REX Recruiting defined exactly what kind of information they wanted to store, how they wanted to use it, and how they needed to access it.

Mustang took it from there. Creating simple data screens that required no knowledge of databases, we created a user-friendly system that was compatible with REX Recruiting's Microsoft-centric environment. Each executive, each job opening, and each company for which REX has previously provided an executive is available in the system. For each of these categories the company defined significant attributes and details that needed to be tracked. The user can search on any of those categories or attributes or can combine any number of them to create a custom report format simply by clicking on the screen. When one of REX's recruiters receives an inquiry from a client, he or she can generate a report that lists all available candidates with the right qualifications. Recruiters can also generate candidate profiles and status reports to keep clients informed about the status of the search and document effort.

**How it worked**: REX Recruiting has seen 17% growth since the system was implemented, which is all the more remarkable since it coincided with a general downturn in the economy. With seven new offices on the West Coast, REX has grown to be the largest firm specializing exclusively in executive placements.

**Figure 16-1.** Sample Case Study.

## Creating Persuasive Resumes

Research conducted among evaluators for the U.S. Department of Defense and the National Aeronautics and Space Agency found that they have certain distinct preferences regarding the resumes or profiles of proposed project team members. (Evaluators in the commercial sector have a similar set of priorities.) These evaluators thought the following content was most important (listed in order of priority):

+ Recent, relevant experience
+ Education, particularly in specific skills or technologies applicable to this project
+ Professional licensing or accreditations
+ Professional affiliations
+ Publications, presentations, or patents

Obviously, providing specific examples of relevant experience is more important than any other factor. As a result, when you write a resume for use in a proposal, it should not look like the kind of resume you use when you're seeking a job. Don't organize it chronologically, listing every job the person has held back to the days when he or she was junior barista at Starbucks. Instead, focus on assignments that are specifically relevant to the project being bid.

Keep the resumes short. Two or three paragraphs will usually be enough. But edit them or rewrite them so that they really match up to the opportunity being proposed. Using the same resume every time you include someone in a project is a bad idea. Each resume needs to be modified to suit the particular opportunity.

Some companies resist putting any resumes in their proposals at all. They worry that the people they are quoting may not be available when the project actually starts, causing difficulties with the client. The concern is understandable, but it's a mistake to leave resumes out. The people who are part of your team are among your absolute differentiators. If they're well qualified, they should be highlighted. Include language in your proposal indicating that this is the team you are proposing, assuming a prompt contract award and timely start. If there are delays in getting the project started, some team members may not be available. Your clients are commercial people. They understand that you cannot keep your best contributors on the bench, not generating any revenue, in the hope that their project will get started someday.

# 17 Gathering and Tailoring Reusable Content

Sometimes we have to depend on other people and it's frustrating. As proposal writers, for example, we often have to turn to subject matter experts or salespeople for the content we need. As sales professionals, we often need colleagues in marketing or the proposal operation to find specific content that we can use in making our case to a prospect.

The first problem with this situation is that people often don't write very well. If you are asking them to create something from scratch, what you get may not be usable. A subject matter expert may answer a technical question in an RFP with a torrent of Geek. When subject matter experts write, they often don't have much sense of how to communicate to non-experts. They don't have any real experience in developing customer-oriented content.

What to do? Give them a form to fill out. That will simplify the process for both of you and will reduce the amount of rework you end up doing. If you need a subject matter expert to describe the features of a new product, for example, and you want to make sure he or she doesn't just describe the technical aspects of those features, consider using a page like the following:

| Feature:<br><br>Name:<br><br><br>Description:<br><br><br>Function in the system: | **Why it matters to a customer:**<br>*(Greater reliability? Increased through-put? Reduced maintenance costs? Etc.)* |
|---|---|

If you need a sales rep to write up a case study, give him or her a form that focuses on the key bits of data you need:

| Customer's problem: |
| --- |
| *What was the situation the customer was dealing with? Why was it a problem? Why did they need to fix it?* |

| What we did: |
| --- |
| *In 3 or 4 bullet points, identify key actions we took, services we provided, products we installed, etc, that solved the problem:* |

| Results: |
| --- |
| What happened after we provided our solution? Can we quantify the impact? (For example, 15% increase in customer retention; 22% increase in new enrollments; etc.) Can we get a quote from a key executive? |

By making the job a little easier, and by guiding their thinking to include the kinds of information we need to write persuasive proposal content, we're likely to get better results.

But there's still a second problem. The subject matter experts don't want to be bothered answering your question about migrating the application from SQL to Oracle. Effusive flattery may help, aided by a promise, backed up by action, that if they answer the question once, you'll never bother them again. That's one advantage of having a well-managed proposal automation system in place. You can store their input in a library from which you can retrieve it in the future, not bothering them again. (Of course, you may need them to check it for technical accuracy every six or twelve months, but that's more acceptable to them than asking them to re-create the whole thing because you lost it.)

# Section IV

## How to Manage the Process Without Losing Your Sanity

# 18 Deal or No Deal?

## Qualifying the Opportunity

PROPOSALS ARE EXPENSIVE. THEY CAN SUCK UP huge amounts of resources and time. And the most expensive ones never seem to win. In fact, in some ways the worst thing that can happen to you is that you finish second. Your investment is probably equal to that made by the winner, but your return on it is zero. As my friend Tom Amrhein used to say, "The best way to improve your win ratio is to stop bidding for work you have no chance of winning." That's great advice, but often surprisingly hard for people to take.

## Deal or No Deal?

Qualifying an opportunity at the outset helps you determine whether it's worth pursuing at all, and, if it is, with how much effort. At a minimum, you need the answers to five questions:

1. Do we know enough to figure out whether this is a good opportunity or not?
2. Is the client serious?
3. Is it worth winning?
4. Do we have a competitive solution?
5. Can we win?

It's worth noting that you can change the answers to each of these questions except the second one. You can request a meeting, do some research, develop a coach so that you acquire enough insight to assess the opportunity. Theoretically you can modify your solution, team up with another vendor to fill in your gaps, or even help the buyers redefine their understanding of what they need so that your solution is competitive. And there are any number of ways you can increase your chances of winning—you might develop a compelling value proposition, offer compelling payment terms, or identify differentiators that set your offer apart. But if the client isn't serious about conducting a fair and open competition in the first place, there is nothing you can do.

I've heard the protests myself: *They must be serious! Why else would they have sent us the RFP?* One way to test whether what you've received is real is to call the prospective client and ask for a meeting. Tell them that you're excited to receive the RFP and you would like to schedule an hour with the right people so that you can develop an appropriate solution. If they are serious about considering your submission, they will probably say yes. On the other hand, if they tell you just to answer the questions and they will see about scheduling a meeting after you have submitted, you probably should pass on the opportunity. They're not serious. (This approach is impossible for government bids, of course, because they typically shut down all contact with the contracting officer and other personnel once the RFP has been issued. Trying to meet with them during the mandatory silent period will disqualify you from consideration.)

Some companies have created scoring rubrics by which they qualify their opportunities. If the deal scores more than a minimum number of points, it's considered a strong candidate and you should write the proposal. If it's below that minimum number, it's probably not worth pursuing. Sometimes there's a middle range where the final Go/No Go decision can be turned over to an executive committee. Creating a score sheet is a good idea, because it forces you to think through the deal characteristics most often associated with good opportunities and because it makes the decision process more objective. Of course, if you don't enforce the method, if there are no teeth behind using it, it won't accomplish much.

The generic scoring sheet shown in Figure 18-1 addresses the remaining four key questions from the preceding list. Adapt it to suit your own business.

## Do we know enough?

+ What do we know about this customer and their concerns?
+ Can we provide an accurate and detailed customer overview, including size of deal, potential revenue generation, market trends, probable scope of solution?
+ Have we met with the key decision makers?
+ Do we know what the customer is trying to achieve?

+ Who is the incumbent provider? What kind of relationship do they have?
+ Do we have other clients in this industry sector?
+ Is the company on our target account list?

If you are confident you have enough information, answer the questions in Figure 18-1.

| | Yes | No |
|---|---|---|
| **Is this a real opportunity?** | | |
| 1. Does the prospect have a compelling need to move forward? | | |
| 2. Has the client established a budget for addressing this need? | | |
| 3. Is the budget realistic and sufficient to fund the project or purchase? | | |
| 4. Has the prospect assigned people to work on the process of choosing an appropriate vendor? | | |
| 5. Will the prospect engage in pre-proposal discussions with us? | | |
| **Is it worth winning?** | | |
| 6. Can we generate a good margin on the work? | | |
| 7. Is there a prospect of substantial follow-up business? | | |
| 8. Does this client tend to continue relationships with vendors rather than automatically putting work out to bid? | | |
| 9. Is this work in line with our strategic plans? | | |
| 10. Can we deliver this work without straining our resources or incurring unacceptable risks? | | |

| Can we compete? | | |
|---|---|---|
| 11. Are we talking to the key decision maker or decision influencers? | | |
| 12. Do they understand our capabilities and expertise? | | |
| 13. Can we provide a solid solution that works in their environment? | | |
| 14. Can we differentiate ourselves from the competition in ways that matter to this customer? | | |
| 15. Do we have good personal contacts within the prospect organization and will they coach us? | | |
| Can we win? | | |
| 16. Is the client driven by decision criteria other than price? | | |
| 17. Is there a strong bias in favor of a competitor? | | |
| 18. Can we steer and control the steps to close? | | |
| 19. Can we affect the decision criteria? | | |
| 20. Can we offer substantial business value? | | |

**Figure 18-1.** Sample Scoring Sheet.

How many *Yes* boxes have you checked? You might rate the results of your scorecard like this:

| | |
|---|---|
| **1–5** | Keep looking |
| **6–10** | Marginal pursuit |
| **11–15** | Potentially qualified |
| **15–20** | Solid opportunity |

This kind of score sheet may not work for you, but you should implement some form of structured, flexible bid/no bid analysis. Some of the issues you may want to take into account in developing that process include the following:

✦ *Are we the incumbent provider of the product or service being requested in this RFP?*

Statistically, in government contracting, incumbents win about 90 percent of all rebids. The percentage is lower in the commercial sector, but regardless, if you're the incumbent vendor, you should have a pretty good shot at winning the competition. If somebody else is the incumbent, your chances are very low. Can you overcome those odds? I'm not saying you can't, but it will require a proposal that demonstrates extraordinary value to turn a decision maker away from a proven incumbent vendor.

✦ *Is the customer happy with the incumbent's performance?*

Even when the incumbent has done a poor job and the decision maker is unhappy, the incumbent still wins almost half the time. But common sense tells you that you have a much better chance to win if the current provider has messed up.

✦ *If the customer is unhappy with the current vendor's performance, was the RFP issued to deal with those problems?*

If the RFP was issued to solve problems inherent in the current vendor's performance, this is a good sign. You've got a chance. The client is telling you that they're really fed up. Of course, it's still possible they're just using the RFP as a stick to beat the incumbent with and aren't really committed to making a change. But it's definitely worth giving it a shot.

✦ *Do we have a strong relationship with the customer?*

One global consulting firm found that the single factor most predictive of a successful proposal was the existence of a strong relationship with the customer. If they had a relationship, their win ratio was over 40 percent. If there was none, the win ratio was below 10 percent.

✦ *Does this RFP play into one of our strengths?*

Do you have provable differentiators? Can you cite compelling evidence of successful prior experience?

✦ *Does the RFP appear to be slanted toward a competitor?*

Do the requirements strongly favor a competitor? Is there language in the RFP that comes from your competitor? It's possible your competition gave the prospective client a sample RFP, parts of which ended up in the one that was issued, but the presence of content that favors one provider should be a caution signal.

✦ *Is this project or acquisition already funded?*
Make sure there's money behind the opportunity. There are people who see nothing wrong with having you create a proposal even though they know the project isn't funded. Maybe they think if your proposal is good enough, it will help them get the money. Maybe they just think it'd be nice to receive a bunch of proposals to "see what's out there." Don't waste your time.

✦ *If not, are funds available within the client's budget?*
Maybe the money has been allocated for the next fiscal year's budget. This will be a judgment call, but if you can get confirmation from two or more executives in the client organization, particularly if they have financial responsibility, then you have to assume the funds probably will be there.

✦ *Will completing this project or deliverable require heavy investments of time and money on our part?*
This doesn't mean you shouldn't bid. But it could affect the potential profitability of the deal. And if you are a small company or an individual, winning the proposal could preclude you from pursuing other opportunities for a while.

✦ *Would winning this contract further our own goals?*
Where do you want to move your company? What markets do you want to be in?

✦ *Is this client likely to be a strong partner or reference account in the future?*
Landing a trophy account who is willing to be a reference or a case study may be invaluable to you downstream.

✦ *Would winning this opportunity be particularly damaging to our competitors?*
Do you have the chance to steal away one of your competitor's most important accounts? Can you shut them out of a region or a market?

✦ *Are there strong political considerations affecting our decision to bid?*

If you "no bid" an opportunity, will you be removed from the approved bidders list? Is the key executive at the client organization a close friend of your firm's CEO?

## Determine the Appropriate Level of Effort

The second important decision you have to make, after you decide whether or not to bid in the first place, is how hard to work on the opportunity. Traditional bid/no bid processes usually produce simplistic output—*Yes or No? Go or No Go?* Rather than settling for a binary answer, you might try to develop something more nuanced that helps you determine how hard you should work. Some deals are worth pursuing, perhaps, but not worth making your maximum effort. Other deals are so valuable or so likely to produce a win, you should hold nothing back.

This is also an important exercise if you are running a proposal operation and have more requests for support than you can realistically meet. You need to know which deals should receive full effort and which ones can safely be relegated to a more perfunctory response.

A decision tree, perhaps based on some of the questions in the preceding list or others that you would normally use in a bid/no bid analysis, can help you determine how much effort to put into responding. For example, the decision tree in Figure 18-2 answers the first question in the list: "Are we the incumbent provider (vendor)?" If the answer is Yes, that leads to a second question, which might be, "Is the customer satisfied with us?" If that answer is Yes, we're moving into a realm where our probability of winning is high. However, if the answer to the first question is No, we are not the incumbent vendor, our chances are somewhat lower. The follow-on question in that case might be, "Is the customer satisfied with the current vendor?" As you can see, a "yes" or "no" answer to that question will make a big difference in our chances of winning. In Figure 18-2, opportunities in the upper right quadrant (labeled A) have a high probability of being successful. Opportunities in quadrant D (lower left) are almost guaranteed losers. The other two quadrants have probabilities somewhere in between, with a slightly stronger likelihood going to those opportunities in which you are the incumbent (quadrant C).

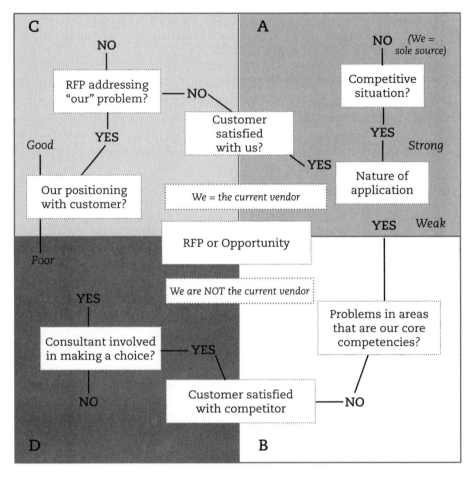

**Figure 18-2.** Determining the Level of Effort.

By developing this kind of decision tree, you will be able to determine how much effort to put into an opportunity. At the top level (quadrant A), your very best opportunities call for dedicated commitment and focused effort. You will create a formal proposal that is highly customized to the client and the opportunity. The time you spend on this proposal may range from several days to several months, but your calculations should indicate that the investment you make in producing a quality proposal is very likely to be rewarded with a profitable contract.

The next notch down (quadrant B) is an opportunity for which you believe the competitive playing field is open and fair, but your likelihood of winning is substantially lower. Perhaps you are up against an unusually strong competitor; perhaps this represents a new market for you; or perhaps it's a perfect fit that has suddenly appeared out of no-where and you have no relationship with the decision makers. For such an opportunity, you would be wise to spend a little less time and effort, but still try to deliver a customized proposal. The difference is that you will rely heavily on boilerplate and spend less time during the editing process on customizing the content. The time you spend on such a pro-posal may range from a few hours to a few days, but it will be substan-tially less than the effort you put into your best opportunities.

At the next level (quadrant C), you may be in a zone where there are lots of caution signs. You have the contract but the client is very un-happy with your performance. Or you suspect that the RFP has been is-sued to check pricing and apply pressure to the favored vendor. You are unable to get answers to basic questions or are not allowed to meet with senior managers who are important members of the decision team. The client's infrastructure does not match your solution's requirements. There may be any number of warning signs, and when you come across them, you need to be realistic and respond accordingly. In this situation, you are perilously close to a "no bid," but if you decide to respond or if you are ordered by senior managers to respond anyway, you should con-sider submitting a generic proposal or one that you have generated from a proposal-automation system but have not spent much time revising. Your focus should be on turning the proposal around extremely quickly, in no more than a few hours, and the effort should involve the absolute minimum number of contributors.

At the lowest level, of course, you have the option of not bidding at all. In that case, you simply prepare a tactful letter explaining that this opportunity does not seem right for you.

## How to Say No Nicely

When you consider whether or not to "no bid" an RFP, you must ask yourself what consequences that action may have downstream. Will a "no bid" decision limit future opportunities to bid on this customer's business? If a consultant is involved, will a "no bid" decision taint your company's relationship with that consultant? In the real world where we have to do business, political considerations may be as important as any business factors.

If you decide not to go forward with an opportunity, particularly one in which you have already moved several steps down the sales cycle, you obviously need to tell the prospect. Simply cutting off contact or not submitting a proposal will create confusion and destroy the customer's trust. So what should you do?

The short answer is that you need to tactfully walk the line between telling them you don't want their business because of something that's wrong with them (they have lousy credit, you think their management team is nuts, and so on) and telling them that you can't do the job because there is something wrong with you (you don't have the expertise, your own management team is nuts, and so on). So the best way to position a "no" is to suggest that the details don't provide a good business fit. If they press for further explanation, I'd focus first on their infrastructure requirements (you want Oracle; we only do Sybase; you want brick exteriors; we only do vinyl siding); on the timing issues (given the project plan you outlined and due to other commitments, we will not have our in-house experts available to support your project when you need them); and last on the business focus (this is an exciting opportunity, but it is not part of our core focus at this time). Those are somewhat neutral-sounding reasons. If you can deliver the message deftly enough, you can avoid long-term commitment but still remain friends.

Remember, too, that not all business is good business. If there's no profit to be made, if the customer has unrealistic expectations, if the requirements in the RFP don't make sense or don't match your competencies, or if your resources are stretched too thin, you should definitely bow out.

# 19 An Overview of the Proposal Development Process

ONE OF MY CLIENTS SHARED AN EMBARRASSING story during a workshop. It seems that after laboring on a proposal for several weeks she found herself, accompanied by a colleague, shuffling papers in the backseat of a cab as it raced across town, desperately trying to assemble three copies of a proposal in hopes of beating a 3 p.m. deadline. Along the way, their frantic efforts so distracted the cab driver that he hit another car. At that point, my client grabbed her papers and began running, in high heels, toward the client's headquarters. Snapping one of the heels off, she hobbled the last couple of blocks. She got there too late and her proposal was not accepted.

Sadly, most people who have done a few proposals have their own horror stories. These are the folks who know the location of every overnight delivery service, which ones have late pickups, which copy centers are open all night, how to save time by printing on multiple printers simultaneously, and other last-minute, time-saving tricks. Clearly, something has gone dreadfully wrong if this is the way proposal projects are managed.

Managing a complex proposal can become a real nightmare. It can threaten your sanity. At the end you may feel you've gained new insight into the concept of a Pyrrhic victory—your victory has cost you far more than you'll ever gain. But it doesn't have to be that way. This chapter addresses some of the key issues involved in managing a proposal project and in assembling a successful, cohesive team to put that proposal together.

If you're self-employed, if you're a one-person sales support operation or marketing department, or if you're a field salesperson who has to handle writing proposals and responding to RFPs by yourself, you may look at the notion of a proposal team with wistful longing. However, even when you're working alone, an understanding of the steps in the proposal development process can help you work more efficiently and effectively.

Basically, the flow of activities involved in developing your proposal should look something like Figure 19-1.

**Figure 19-1.** The Sequence of Activities in Managing a Proposal Project.

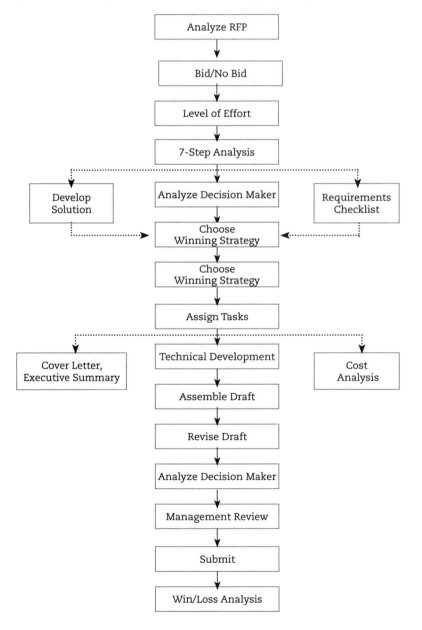

# Lay a Solid Foundation

Winning proposals have their roots in good sales and marketing. I have never believed that a proposal by itself was likely to win business if there was no prior relationship, no effective positioning or branding, no information gathering to provide insight into the opportunity. As a result, there are numerous pre-proposal activities that must be carried out long before you begin to work on the proposal. These include sales and marketing efforts to generate leads and qualify opportunities, branding and promotional activities to position your firm properly, and information gathering so that you understand the customer and their issues, your probable competitors, and the solution that is most likely to be successful.

If there is no prior relationship, if the buyer doesn't recognize you, if your sales team has no knowledge or insight about the opportunity, your chances of writing a winning proposal are roughly the same as winning the Super Lotto. It happens. It just isn't going to happen to you.

Suppose you have to write the proposal anyway. In that case, you need to scramble as quickly as you can to acquire any information and insight you can grab. We discussed methods for uncovering information and insight from a prospect's Web site and from analyzing comparable clients in Chapter 6. What are you looking for? Insight into the issues facing the firm or agency, their financial status, their objectives, the primary customer base they serve, who their chief competitors are, what kinds of values they revere in their corporate culture, the major initiatives they have launched during the past year or so, their basic organizational structure, and recent events or developments among their competitors. That will do for a start.

# Review the RFP Document or Opportunity

If you are responding to a formal RFP, you should immediately analyze what the RFP says and what you are being asked to do. (If there is no formal RFP document, as in the case of a proactive opportunity, it's still a very good idea to figure out what the client expects you to deliver.) As soon as you receive the RFP—or even a draft copy of the RFP—begin the analysis by reading carefully, separating out its requirements, and asking the seven questions to keep you client focused that we covered in Chapter 6. It will be helpful to you if you break the process of analyzing the RFP into several steps:

**1. *Read*** the complete RFP quickly to gain an overall sense of its scope and requirements.          .

**2. *Note*** any obvious conflicts or discrepancies in the RFP, either in the margins or on a separate sheet.

**3. *Burst*** (separate) the RFP contents into the following categories:

A. *Administrative information*: information regarding logistics, the time and location of the bidders' conference, if any, your points of contact, how many copies to prepare, due dates, schedules, address to which your proposal must be sent, etc.

> *This information will be vital in developing your timeline for getting the proposal completed.*

B. *Legal requirements:* clauses or specifications that govern contracts, including terms and conditions, subcontracting requirements, payment schedules, ownership of the work product, certifications and representations, etc.

> *This information is obviously important in terms of determining whether or not you can comply with the terms and conditions or other governing clauses.*

C. *Format guidelines:* information regarding the required or recommended format, including page limits, font sizes, margins, restrictions on the use of color, guidelines regarding graphics, etc.

> *This information will be important in designing and publishing your proposal and in establishing appropriate visuals, determining the length of key sections, and in managing the writing.*

D. *Content requirements:* Further specifications that will guide your development of a solution, including the scope of work, technical requirements, required sections, evaluation criteria, evidence required, management plan, and so on

> *This information is vital because it shapes your actual content. Use it to develop the compliance matrix, to determine your key strategy or win theme, and to develop your cognitive web and requirements checklist.*

**4. *Reorganize*** the RFP if it is not clearly laid out, placing the various types of information into the categories you identified in the previous step.

> ***NOTE:*** *In reorganizing the RFP, you are simply making a document that flows more logically for your own purposes. When you respond, you should **respond to the RFP as it was written**.*

**5. Develop** a requirements checklist containing each of the requirements within the categories of information you identified.

> *How do you know whether something is a requirement? Well-written RFPs will tell you what's required or mandatory and what's simply desirable. In addition, if the language states that you "shall" or "must" do something, it's a requirement. Finally, assume that issues that come up repeatedly within an RFP are so significant they constitute de facto requirements.*

**6. Define** the terminology used in the RFP
   A. Jargon
   B. Organizational names or relationships
   C. Technical terms that seem to be used in an unusual way

**7. Highlight** any requirements or instructions in the RFP that you cannot meet, including legal requirements to include proprietary or confidential information.

> *You do not have to be 100 percent compliant to win a contract. However, you must be aware of the expectations and requirements stated in the RFP and take exception to any that you can't or won't be meeting.*

**8. List** any areas of ambiguity in the RFP, any requirements that seem contradictory or incomplete, and any that seem to deviate from the functional purpose of the RFP. Some of these items may be the basis of questions you raise at the bidders' conference, if there is one. Or they might be the subject of e-mails you send back to the account team or the prospect, seeking clarification.

**9. Compile** all of the ambiguities, contradictions, inexplicable jargon, questions, and clarifications you need into a list that you can send to the client or raise at the bidders' conference.

## Create a Proposal Schedule

A proposal is like any other complex project. To ensure an on-time completion, you need to establish a schedule right away and then regularly check progress against it.

To create the proposal schedule:

✦ **Identify the "drop dead" date**—the absolutely last date by which the final draft must be completed and ready to go to production.

✦ **Schedule printing** to be completed with plenty of time for shipping or delivery of the final document. Include at least one to two extra days for production to allow for emergencies and problems.

✦ **Create a Gantt chart** for a large-scale project, using a tool like Microsoft Project. Identify the critical events or deliverables in your project.

✦ Look for opportunities to **complete tasks in parallel, not sequentially**.

✦ Don't forget to **build in time for a technical review** of the first draft **and a mock evaluation** of the final draft. The mock evaluation, or Red Team review as it's often called, should occur approximately two-thirds of the way into the schedule. (We'll discuss this process in more detail later, in Chapter 20.)

✦ **Use labor-saving tools** whenever possible, including automation software, design templates, compliance checklists, and so forth.

✦ **Empower your contributors to do a good job the first time** by providing them with all the information they need, including insights into the client, competitors, key issues, strategy and win theme, etc. A kickoff meeting is an ideal place to provide this information, but you should also build in incremental reviews to reinforce the right approach and to make sure they are heading in the right direction.

## Assemble the Team

In Chapter 24, where we discuss what's involved in setting up a dedicated proposal operation, I review the types of contributors you will want on a basic proposal team—a proposal manager, one or more writers, a graphics specialist, and one or more subject matter experts (if this is an option). It also makes sense to include the account manager, salesperson, or business development personnel who have uncovered the opportunity and who know the client best. Other participants, at least at the initial stage of a proposal project, might include senior management, financial analysts who can work on pricing issues, a contracts expert if there are unusual terms and conditions in the RFP, and perhaps a representative from marketing. If your solution will involve combining efforts from a number of departments, such as software development and customization, customer training, and customer support, those departments should be represented at the outset so that they at least have this opportunity on their radar screens.

## Hold an Effective Kickoff Meeting

Like any complex project, writing a major proposal can be intimidating at first. You can get off to a good start if you hold an effective kickoff meeting. Your meeting process should include developing an agenda, creating checklists of key requirements, gathering insight into the client, making key decisions, and generating a basic outline for the proposal quickly.

One tool that you should develop immediately, if you regularly work with a team of contributors, is an opportunity analysis worksheet. All you need is a simple template of questions and blank fields that you can print out in advance of the kickoff meeting. (See the sample questions in Figure 19-2.) Leave it blank before the meeting. Then work as a team to fill it in. The template will provide a structured process to gather all the information and insight your firm possesses. The template should include information about who the customer is, who the decision makers are, what previous business relationship exists between your company and the prospective customer, and the size and focus of the opportunity. It should also cover those seven critical questions that we discussed in Chapter 6. You also want insight into the customer's business, technical, political, economic, and social concerns; the values that will drive the selection process; the competitive landscape; the most effective strategy for positioning your firm (your best value proposition and win theme); and your firm's readiness to bid. Having said all that, let me add a word of warning: don't make it too complicated. A one-page opportunity analysis will get used. Three or four pages will be ignored.

**Figure 19-2.** Questions for a Sample Worksheet.

---

### OPPORTUNITY ANALYSIS WORKSHEET
### FOR TRUST ADMINISTRATION

*Customer's business profile*

1. Who is responsible for decisions affecting the trusts? How do they make decisions?

2. What would they change about the way the trusts are set up or administered if they could?

3. What is the main benefit they want to gain from improving the way trusts are managed?

4. What elements of the customer's business situation are driving this opportunity?

5. Is there a compelling reason why they need to move quickly in changing the administration of the trust?

6. Are we positioned with the key decision maker? Do we have access to the authorities who can make this decision? Do we have strong champions within the customer organization?

*The financial issues:*

1. How many trusts does the customer have? How large are the trusts?

2. Is the customer completely satisfied with the performance of his or her trusts?

3. Is the customer satisfied with the yield?

4. What gross return did the customer earn on the trusts last year?

5. Who is currently handling the trusts?

6. How are the funds invested? Certificates of deposit? Stocks? Bonds?

7. What is the customer's investment strategy?

8. How many different fund managers does the customer have? Who are they?

9. What trustee fee does their current trust administrator charge?

10. What investment management fee do they charge?

11. Does the current trust administrator offer profit sharing?

So it's time for your kickoff meeting. Here are some tips for making it go smoothly:

✦ **_Invite the right people,_** as outlined earlier. Don't neglect people you may need to work with later on the project. They're less likely to feel put upon if they're included at the outset, even if they choose to skip the meeting.

✦ **_E-mail everyone the relevant background information_** before the meeting, including a copy of the RFP and other useful data. This information might include:

  ✦ Nature and scope of the RFP
  ✦ Why this has been determined to be a "bid" project
  ✦ Why it's important from a strategic perspective to win
  ✦ Background information on the customer and their current situation
  ✦ Historical data on previous relationships, if any, with this customer

✦ **_Assume that no one will have looked at any of this_** information when they arrive. Hey, we're all busy, you know?

✦ **_Create an agenda_** for the meeting. However, once you provide them with the agenda, empower the attendees to modify it. That will give them some ownership into the success of the meeting.

✦ **_Briefly review the material you sent them in advance and then complete the opportunity analysis form._** This is also a good time to review the initial technical approach/solution that has been developed for this project, if there is one.

✦ **_Discuss and reach agreement as a team on the primary value proposition_** and any secondary strategies that you will use in writing the proposal. This primary value proposition should be linked to your firm's differentiators and should deliver a provable, measurable return to the customer.

✦ **_Brainstorm as a team for evidence_** to support the value proposition.

✦ **_Conduct the cognitive webbing process with the team,_** if possible, so that everyone shares a deep understanding of the business issues that underlie this opportunity or that remain unexpressed in the RFP. As I explained in Chapter 10, cognitive webbing is a technique that quickly organizes your proposal outline.

✦ *Assign team members their responsibilities,* along with milestones, due dates, accountability, and deliverables. Emphasize the importance of early reviews and sticking with the plan as developed in the kickoff meeting.

✦ *Create a requirements checklist,* either during the kickoff meeting or very soon after, in which you list every requirement from the RFP, is there is one, or everything the customer has asked you to provide. You probably have the bones of your requirements checklist from the careful reading of the RFP you did when it first arrived. Now it has to be fleshed out, because when your proposal is done, you will use the requirements checklist to make sure nothing has been missed. Remember that the easiest way to get yourself thrown out of a bid is to miss one of the key requirements.

## Create the Draft Proposal

Now that the assignments are made, contributions will start trickling in. You will need a way to keep track of them and integrate them into one master document.

If you do a lot of proposals or if your proposals are quite complex and involve a lot of contributors, invest in a proposal automation or document control system. This will enable members of your team to work simultaneously and submit their work when it is ready without any fear of overwriting somebody else's contributions.

As Figure 19-3 illustrates, the best way is to start a proposal project is by writing the executive summary. Sometimes people think they should write the executive summary last, thinking that it is supposed to serve as an abstract or précis of the entire proposal. However, that isn't the function of an executive summary. Rather, it is intended to provide an overview of the business case for the top executives. It summarizes the client's key needs and desired outcomes, offers a high-level presentation of your solution, presents a couple of key differentiators, and outlines your basic value proposition. You should be able to write this content as soon as you've done the cognitive web during your kickoff meeting.

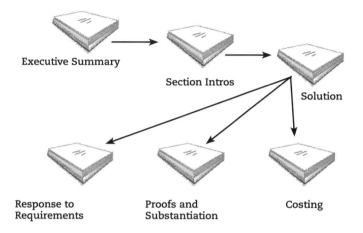

**Figure 19-3.** The Order in Which to Write.

Next, write the introductory paragraphs to each major section of your proposal or have your contributors write them. These paragraphs contain the most general information about the section and can be written even if the details of the technical solution have not been finalized.

Now write the basic description of your solution. You may need to fill in gaps later, but get as much of it done now as you can. Once you have completed this, with all of the features and benefits identified, you can move on to develop the highly detailed content—the actual response to the RFP questions or requirements, the substantiation sections, and the cost section.

Here are some additional tips on getting the first draft done quickly and efficiently:

✦ Assemble all your materials, including any research you did on the client, notes from sales calls, your requirements checklist, any reusable text that might be appropriate for the proposal, your cognitive web, and so on.

✦ Review the research you did into the decision maker and evaluators, and then try to write as though you were speaking to those individuals. Vary your style to match their preferences to the extent you know them. If you can, try to picture the customer sitting across the desk from you. How would you say this if the two of you were in a conversation? That's pretty much how you ought to write it.

✦ Write quickly. Don't stop to edit while you are writing. This is one of the biggest mistakes people make. It's so easy to "fix" things on a word processor that people start fiddling with their text before they're more than a few lines into it. Soon they've lost their train of thought, perhaps even got themselves blocked. Ignore awkwardness, grammar mistakes, mixed-up formatting. You can work on those problems later. Your goal for now is to get a complete draft done as quickly as possible.

✦ Get the basic content down. You can start writing on the part you find easiest or most interesting. You do not have to write the document in the same order the reader will see it.

✦ For each section or major part of your proposal, try to move from general to specific, from introductory paragraphs and main ideas to supporting details.

✦ If you cut and paste boilerplate or reusable text, revise it to match the win themes you are using in this proposal. Above all make sure it doesn't contain the wrong client's name!

✦ Use personal pronouns—"we," "you"—not third-person or oblique references. Call the customer by name—that is, use the company's name throughout the proposal. Never refer to the customer as "they."

✦ Challenge the acronyms and jargon. If in doubt, leave it out and use something simpler. (Using the customer's jargon and acronyms is permissible.)

## Edit Your Draft

Editing is a vital part of creating a winning proposal. All good writers edit heavily, so please make sure you allow enough time in your project plan to do some serious editing. In fact, editing is so important, I've devoted Chapter 20 to it, so we won't go into a lot of detail here.

## Print and Publish Your Proposal

The final steps in your proposal project are to print the document, bind it, and either ship or deliver it to the client. After all the work you've done to produce a great proposal, you don't want to put something out that looks amateurish or shoddy. You don't have to spend big money on printing or binders, but you do want the deliverable to look professional and competent. In my experience, using a coil binding and a heavy-weight card stock for the cover, perhaps embossed with your corporate logo, is adequate for proposals under 100 pages. Longer proposals usually need a sturdier binding.

Once the proposal is gone, take a deep breath, catch up on some sleep, and get ready for the next one. There are some postsubmission activities you should complete, too, but you're probably exhausted at this point, so we'll talk about those tasks in Chapter 23.

# 20 The Pursuit of Perfection:

## *Editing Your Proposal*

So YOU WANT TO BE A GOOD WRITER? THEN force yourself to be a rewriter. That's where good writing happens.

A lot of people apparently believe that good writers don't need to revise, that excellent proposals simply pour out of them in their complete and final forms. Trust me—that's a delusion. If you currently cling to it, you'll have to give it up. Otherwise, you'll have little chance of improving your work.

## How Much Should You Edit?

How much editing should you do? As much as you can. I know that's a bit vague, but I'm sorry to tell you that there's no magic formula, such as "five minutes per page" or "15 percent of the total time allocated to document development." If it's of any interest to you, in my own company we typically allocate about as much time for editing as we do for creating the initial draft. We think a one-to-one correlation is about right. Keep in mind, though, that we have years of experience in writing proposal text. For someone who has never written a proposal, the editing time might easily exceed the writing time.

The important point is that you must plan editing into your overall proposal project. Designate a specific amount of time for it, and resist any attempts to poach on editing time for other activities. To calculate how much editing time your proposal will need, take into account the constraints imposed by your deadlines, the availability of team members to contribute to the editing process, and your own experience and that of your colleagues in editing complex documents.

Another way of asking "how much" is to ask yourself: "How good is good enough?" When is your proposal good enough to go to the client?

First, you need to recognize that perfection is not a realistic goal. I've had writers and editors working for me whose only standard was "perfect." It took a while for them to understand that even the most stringent quality-control processes don't set perfection as their goal. Instead, the goal should be *excellence*. We want to deliver a proposal to our client that is truly excellent, that is in the top 1 or 2 percent of all the proposals he or she receives.

To define excellence, we can consider six levels of "correctness," listing them in order of increasing difficulty of achievement:

1.  There are no mechanical, spelling, or punctuation errors and no typos.
2.  There are no obvious errors of facts, content, or logic that the reader will notice immediately.
3.  The proposal follows an effective and appropriate structural pattern and has been adequately divided into functional units so that the reader can understand and use the proposal easily.
4.  The proposal writing is clear and concise, free of needless jargon, ambiguities, or possible misinterpretations.
5.  The proposal has been slanted correctly in terms of the primary audience's level of expertise, personality, and values, and fully meets that audience's needs.
6.  The proposal is complete, informed, and intelligent, written in a crisp and interesting style, and delivered in a format that makes it easy to use for multiple evaluators.

So—how good is good enough? Lots of technical or business professionals are satisfied if their documents reach level 2. If it gets by on the first reading, it's good enough for them.

From a reader's point of view, however, nothing less than level 4 will do. And for a proposal, where the reader is making a buying decision, you shouldn't tolerate anything less than level 5.

## Editing: A Five-Step Process

Perhaps an even more important issue than how much editing you should do is how you should do it. Most people were never taught true editing skills. Instead, they were threatened with F's if their papers contained more than three misspelled words, so what they learned to do was proofread.

Proofreading is part of editing, the final step before you print and deliver the proposal, but it's not the whole job. It's also not likely to improve the overall quality of your proposal nor is it likely to help you improve your writing skill. In fact, there are four other steps that must precede proofreading.

**Warning: Don't Edit Immediately After Writing.** You must let your writing "cool" before you edit it. If you look at it immediately after finishing the first draft, you'll miss a lot of errors and problems. Because you know what you *meant* to say, you are unable to see what you *did* say. You read what you think should be there, rather than what is actually on the page. In fact, it's so difficult to gain enough detachment from your own writing that you might consider having someone else edit your work while you edit theirs.

When you have gained sufficient detachment (or found somebody to do the editing for you), cover all five steps of the process, even if you do some of them simultaneously.

**Step One:** Go through the first draft quickly and ask three questions:

1. *Have I said anything obviously dumb?*
   + Misplaced modifiers, incomplete thoughts, errors in logic, the wrong client's name—all of these qualify. So do inaccurate facts, unsubstantiated claims, and wildly optimistic calculations of ROI.
2. *Have I written with a consistently client-centered focus?*
   + Challenge yourself: Is this information necessary? Does it address the client's needs, problems, interests, values? Is it appropriate for the audience's level of expertise, personality type, and role in the decision-making process?
3. *Can I cut any of this material without interfering with the reader's understanding or my ability to persuade?*
   + Be ruthless. If it's not contributing to one of the four essentials of a persuasive proposal—evidence you understand the client's problem, a compelling reason to choose your recommendation over any other, a specific recommendation, evidence of your competence to deliver the solution and to manage the project—cut it! Many proposals are bogged down with a clutter of details.

You will probably find it helpful to read through the draft out loud. When you have to say the words, you hear them more accurately and the rough spots become more obvious. Read quickly. Don't stop at this point to fix things. If you see or hear something that seems awkward, underline it or put a mark in the margin next to it. If there are words or phrases that sound odd or that seem to call attention to themselves, circle them. Again, don't stop to rewrite at this point. Just mark whatever you notice.

**Step Two:** Read through the proposal more slowly now and focus on structure and organization. You're still not rewriting. You're trying to figure out if the content flows in the clearest and most persuasive way.

1. *Structure:*
   - Have I used the NOSE pattern to structure the proposal as a whole?
   - Have I used it to structure major sections of the proposal?
   - Is the overall proposal unified? Is there one central value proposition, idea, or focus to which everything is related?
2. *Organization:*
   - Have I used the P / A / R format to organize my case studies?
   - Did I use the A / P / S pattern for my important RFP answers?
   - Does the sequence of content in my resumes put the most important facts up front?
   - Are the various parts of the proposal arranged in a coherent, logical order? Do they match the order specified by the client, if any?
3. *Is the information easy to find?*
   - Did I create logically sequenced sentences, paragraphs, and sections?
   - Are the key ideas up front whenever possible?
   - Do the major sections start with an introduction?
   - Have I used plenty of highlighting?

**Step Three:** During the third revision, work on clarity, conciseness, precision, directness, and emphasis. In particular, make sure you have adjusted your proposal to suit the audience, then take a close look at your word choice, sentence structure, and overall readability. The goal is to communicate the information so clearly that your customer can read it once and understand it.

1. *Audience:*
   - Did I slant the material toward the audience's
     - Level of expertise?
     - Personality type?
     - Role in the decision-making process?

+ Did I prioritize content so that what the audience thinks is most important appears first?

2. *Word choice:*
   + Work on the words or phrases you marked during your initial review of the proposal.
   + Challenge jargon and acronyms. Are they necessary? Are they defined clearly?
   + Review the chapter on word traps in this book. Correct any of these mistakes.

3. *Sentence lengths and patterns:*
   + Check for passive voice. Revise passive constructions into active voice.
   + Check the verbs. For sentences where the main verb is a form of "to be," rewrite the sentence so that it contains a strong verb.
   + Use the grammar checker in your word processor to determine your proposal's average sentence length. Is it near the 15–17 word range that's most accessible for adult readers?
   + Have you minimized compound/complex constructions?
   + Have you avoided long dependent clauses, particularly at the beginning of the sentence?

4. *Readability:*
   + If your word processor contains a readability tool, use it. (This is explained in the next section.) Is the readability of your proposal appropriate?
   + Spot-check the most important parts of your proposal—the cover letter, the executive summary, the section intros.

5. *Make the information easy to understand.*
   + Focus on simplicity: in vocabulary, sentence structure, and organization.
   + Keep the proposal as brief as possible.
   + Be specific: use details, not clichés, to make your points; use graphics to illustrate concepts; include examples, comparisons, and analogies to make your ideas clear.
   + Keep the proposal relevant—no tangents, nothing extraneous or unnecessary.

**Step Four:** During the fourth phase of editing, work on *style*. In particular, look for generic, bland descriptions of your products or services that you can make more vivid by linking them to the customer's business, specific needs, or desired outcomes. Also, watch for the typical business clichés. Is there a way to make your point more emphatically by using specific details? What about a metaphor or analogy, particularly for a level one reader? You might even look for an opportunity to use humor or a bit of drama.

Create a strong, compelling beginning for the cover letter and executive summary. Provide a clear call to action at the end of the cover letter and executive summary. Include concrete examples, comparisons, or analogies to clarify your ideas. Focus on business outcomes and the function of what you describe, not just the technical or operational aspects.

**Step Five:** At the fifth level of revision a writer inspects the final copy for *mechanical or typographical errors*, the mistakes of carelessness or neglect. Errors in spelling, punctuation, grammar, and other small mistakes can communicate to a reader that you are careless, hasty, ignorant, or disrespectful. Besides—such mechanical and grammatical mistakes are nothing but background noise, which can interfere with your message getting through.

1. *Proofread carefully.*
   + Is the proposal free from mistakes in grammar, spelling, punctuation?
   + Is it legible?
   + Is the format consistent throughout?
2. *Does the total package do the job it's meant to do?*
   + Is the proposal complete and thorough?
   + At the same time, is it focused and concise?
   + Are the contents accurate and well supported?
   + Will it arrive on time?

## Measuring Readability

Your car may be capable of going 150 miles an hour, but that doesn't mean it will benefit from continuous operation at that speed. Likewise, you may be capable of reading at the level of a college graduate, but that doesn't mean you'll want to all the time. Most people find it easier to read text that is a couple of grade levels below the level of reading mastery they have achieved. In a proposal, you want to focus your reader's energy on understanding your ideas, not on decoding the language. Write at a comfortable, easy level.

Readability formulas measure how difficult or easy a given piece of writing is likely to be. Most of them measure sentence length, on the assumption that longer sentences are harder to decode, and vocabulary complexity, usually as indicated by the average number of syllables in each word. The assumption is that multisyllabic words will be harder to decode.

Whatever else it may be, readability is a fairly complex phenomenon. These formulas will give you a rough numerical value, which may or may not be an accurate indicator of a passage's real level of readability. Obviously, long words aren't *always* hard to understand. And long sentences aren't *always* difficult to read. There are exceptions. Also, a passage with an otherwise excellent readability score might be full of noun clusters, faulty parallel structure, dangling modifiers, vague words, and so on.

However, as a rough guideline, readability formulas can be useful, since they measure the two fundamental components of the reading process: syntactical difficulty and language familiarity.

### Determine Readability with Your Word Processor

You can measure readability very easily by using tools built into your word processor. For example, if you use Microsoft Word, click on the Office button and then go to Word Options. In the Word Options window, click on the Proofing tab. In that section, check the option that says "Show readability statistics" and then click on "OK." The next time you run a spell check, you will get a summary chart at the end of the process that tells you more than you probably ever wanted to know about your writing. This chart, titled "Readability Statistics," tells you the percentage of passive sentences your writing contains. It also gives you the Flesch Reading Ease index and the Flesch-Kincaid Grade Level index. These numbers measure how easy or hard the writing is to decode.

When I run a spelling and grammar check on the previous paragraph, I get this summary:

| Readability Statistics | |
|---|---|
| **Counts** | |
| Words | 141 |
| Characters | 675 |
| Paragraphs | 1 |
| Sentences | 8 |
| **Averages** | |
| Sentences per Paragraph | 8.0 |
| Words per Sentence | 17.6 |
| Characters per Word | 4.6 |
| **Readability** | |
| Passive Sentences | 0% |
| Flesch Reading Ease | 64.1 |
| Flesch-Kincaid Grade Level | 8.6 |

There's a lot of useful information here. I can see that my average sentence length is about right, and that I've completely avoided passive voice constructions. But what about the Flesch Reading Ease and Flesch-Kincaid Grade Level numbers? Are they good or bad?

The Reading Ease score is based on a standard of 100. The higher the number, the easier the writing is to understand. In business writing, which includes proposals, of course, a good score would be somewhere between 50 and 70. Based on that score, my paragraph is all right.

The Flesch-Kincaid Grade Level measurement indicates the equivalent U.S. grade level of education that someone would need to read a particular passage easily. The assumption is that a person has achieved reading mastery at that level. Note that this is strictly a measurement of the complexity of the writing. It does *not* mean the content is appropriate for someone at that level. When an article or white paper or executive summary has a readability grade level of 10, that only means that the language complexity is such that someone with a 10th-grade reading ability could decode it comfortably. Whether that person understands it or not is a completely different issue.

The following chart shows you how various grade levels correlate to mass market publications. Note that grade level 12 is the danger line. Above that line, reading becomes uncomfortable for the majority of readers. Above 15, almost nobody can read easily. Just because your reader has a Ph.D. doesn't mean you should write at a grade level of 20. In fact, almost nobody enjoys reading for extended periods above an index of 10. And don't worry that your audience will feel that your writing is condescending in tone or style. They don't feel that way about the *Wall Street Journal*, do they?

| Index | Reading level by grade | Reading level by magazine |
|-------|------------------------|---------------------------|
| 17 | College post-graduate | |
| 16 | College senior | |
| 15 | College junior | |
| 14 | College sophomore | (No mass market publication |
| 13 | College freshman | is this difficult.) |
| 12 | High school senior | *Scientific American* |
| 11 | High school junior | *New Yorker, Atlantic Monthly* |
| 10 | High school sophomore | *Newsweek, Wall Street Journal* |
| 9 | High school freshman | *Sports Illustrated* |
| 8 | Eighth grade | daily newspapers |
| 7 | Seventh grade | *People* |

*Other Ways to Improve Your Readability*

Other factors besides sentence length and word choice will affect the ease with which your readers understand what you have written. Here are some you can control:

**Legibility.** Is your type easy to read? Don't use a font that's too small, because reading will become a strain. Don't print type on a colored background that doesn't offer sufficient contrast. Don't give your reader faint or spotty reproductions of your document. If your type isn't legible, you have made the job of reading more difficult.

**Interest.** If your reader is interested in what you're writing about, he or she will read comfortably at a slightly higher level than they normally would. That's another reason to lead with the strongest content, rather than starting with your company history or an overview of your technology.

**Format.** Incorporating plenty of white space into your page design can make your text seem more readable. Headings, subheadings, the use of color, the use of sidebars, and including illustrations can also help.

**Simplicity.** Presenting too many new ideas, new concepts, or new acronyms in a short space can discourage the reader. Most people have trouble, for example, keeping track of more than three or four new acronyms in a page of text before their mind goes blank and they lose the thread of your message.

# Color Your Proposal World

If you have been part of a large proposal project, particularly in the government contracting arena, you may have participated in a color team review. Color teams are established at specific stages of the proposal process to review the work completed and to provide guidance in areas where the project may have gone astray.

Different organizations have set up different procedures, but in general the commonly used color teams are Blue, Pink, Red, and Gold. Each occurs at a specific stage of the proposal development process and each has a specific focus:

The **_Blue Team_** occurs early in the business capture cycle, usually well before you start writing the proposal. It's an opportunity to analyze the sales strategy and gain insight into the potential customer, the account team's capture plan, and the likely strength of your solution. In a commercial setting, this kind of examination is typically handled by a sales manager during his or her regular pipeline review and account planning sessions with members of the sales team. In a government setting, the process is more formal and drawn out, because the agencies and departments to which you are selling usually have multiyear budget cycles and detailed program requirements that generate opportunities.

The **Pink Team** is set up after the customer publishes the RFP. The purpose of the Pink Team is to discuss the basic solution approach, the value proposition or win themes, and the storyboards, if any. This is the opportunity to make sure the general effort is pointed in the right direction. It's also an opportunity to get senior management's input, helping to reduce the temptation for somebody from the corporate suite to swoop in at the last minute and demand wholesale changes to a proposal just hours before it needs to be locked down.

A **Red Team** review is an exercise that involves reading and scoring the final draft of the proposal as if the customer were looking at it. It's a dry run that gives you the chance to improve your proposal before you send it into the fray. You assemble a team who play the role of customers, evaluating the complete draft against the evaluation criteria and the client's requirements. This is not the time to tweak sentences or niggle with wording, although the Red Team members should point out major problems, such as missing content or incorrect information. Your Red Team should consist of people who did not write the proposal, so they will look at it without any preconceived notions. Ideally, they should be individuals who can play the role of customer in terms of expertise, personality type, and priorities. That means you need to select reviewers who can simulate such a point of view. One person who is almost never included in the review process—but who could offer some extremely helpful insights—is a purchasing or procurement professional from within your own organization. Ask that person to evaluate your proposal as if he or she were buying from it and you're likely to get some practical and useful insights.

Finally, the **Gold Team** looks at the proposal after it has been completed and all revisions have been made. This is a task for senior management, a final check before submission. The focus is on contractual terms, pricing, and scheduling.

Dana Spears, a veteran of numerous color teams during his 24-year career as an officer in the U.S. Air Force and as a proposal manager for Northrop Grumman and other firms, has stated that the keys to success in using the color team approach include:

+ Limiting the purpose of each review to just two or three critical objectives
+ Putting the right people on the teams
+ Arming them with checklists asking specific Yes/No questions rather than soliciting open-ended feedback

Prepare your reviewers so they understand their role. Make it clear that they are not expected to edit, rewrite, or proofread. Their job is to score the proposal as though they were members of the customer's evaluation team. Provide them with a copy of the RFP and with the scoring system the customer will use in evaluation. Make sure that the Red Team reviewers have no contact with the proposal team while they review it.

Spears's recommendation for using a checklist—either on paper or online—is excellent for minimizing the temptation people have to rewrite the proposal so that it sounds the way they think it should. Too often that means adding Fluff, Guff, Geek, and Weasel, which you'll just have to remove again. Using checklists also prevents you from getting caught in the nightmare of having half a dozen reviewers who have each used the Track Changes option in Microsoft Word and inserted comments in their own version of the document. Trying to compare and collate all of those different versions is a sure recipe for a major migraine.

The job of the Red Team reviewers is to be as objective, factual, fair, and specific as possible. The responsibilities of Red Team reviewers, in order of priority, should include:

+ *Checking for compliance with the RFP requirements*
    ➤ Repeating the language of the RFP is usually not enough. Your proposal must offer intelligent ideas, evidence of relevant experience with similar situations, and knowledge of the client's business or agency.
    ➤ In demonstrating that you understand the requirements, show how you have helped other clients with similar problems.
+ *Checking for clear, compelling win themes and value propositions*
    ➤ Show that your proposal will produce a measurable, positive outcome.
    ➤ Describe what you will do, who will do it, what you will deliver, and how the client will benefit.
+ *Reviewing the proof statements and evidence: are they relevant and convincing?*
    ➤ Avoid vague generalities. Provide specific details to convince evaluators you can deliver quality results on time and within budget.

➤ Cite relevant prior experience. If you don't have similar projects, explain why the projects you do cite are relevant.

As they evaluate the overall proposal they might examine other issues, too:

+ Is the proposal client focused? Does it show that your company understands the customer's problems, goals, and values?
+ Are there any words or phrases that catch your attention or stand out in any way, either good or bad?
+ Are the themes consistent throughout the proposal and well integrated into the total proposal?
+ Does the executive summary use the NOSE pattern effectively? Does it make a convincing business case?
+ On the basis of the opening, what impression does the proposal create? Are you more "with" or "against" the writer?
+ Does the proposal persuade throughout or are parts of it merely informative?
+ Are there parts of this proposal that are dull or confusing?
+ Does the proposal present clear differentiators and tie them to value statements that will appeal to this customer?
+ Does the proposal convincingly show that your company offers the best solution and highest value?
+ What else do you wish you knew or had available that's not in the proposal you just read?

Next to the Yes and No boxes in your checklist, you might provide some space where the reviewers can offer constructive, specific feedback. What you want are statements such as the following:

*"Transportation planning experience is not highlighted enough in the resumes. Add a separate heading just for that category."*

*"So what? You mention these features, but how will they help? Why should a customer care? Am I paying extra for them?"*

Simply saying that a section is "weak" or "vague" doesn't help anybody.

### How Your Customer Reads and Evaluates Your Proposal

The basic process for evaluating solicited proposals (that is, proposals submitted in response to a Request for Proposal, Request for Information, Invitation to Tender, or other formal solicitation) follows a series of steps:

**1.** A responsible person—for example, the project manager, contracting officer, RFP manager, or an outside consultant—does an initial read-through of each submission. His or her job during this step is to identify any submissions that fail to comply with the mandatory terms and conditions of the bid. Proposals that fail to comply may be eliminated at this point. Evaluators are not required to read or score the entire proposal if they have identified a major weakness.

**2.** If price is handled as a separate issue, the cost volume will be separated from the rest of the proposal and delivered to the individual or team responsible for financial analysis.

**3.** Once those proposals that are clearly noncompliant have been eliminated, the survivors are often evaluated against a set of criteria. Even when these criteria are very specific, with numeric values or weights, the process rapidly becomes subjective. Evaluating proposals can be exhausting work and after the first few documents, evaluators get tired. When they are fatigued, they're more likely to be critical and to make snap judgments.

Given the nature of this process, here are some tips for getting a better score:

✦ Submit the briefest proposal possible. Because short proposals are read first, evaluators may unconsciously consider them the standard by which all subsequent proposals are judged.

✦ Make sure your proposal is easy to read and formatted so that your key points jump off the page. Your recommendations will seem to make more sense.

✦ Link your deliverables to the benefits your customer seeks and then to your differentiators. This will help separate you from competitors and will make your recommendations read more like a solution, one that the customer can get only from you.

✦ Avoid promising benefits without substantiating how you will deliver on those promises. Provide proof statements for each material feature, function, or requirement, and provide relevant references, testimonials, case studies, and statistics.

## What Evaluators Like and What They Hate

A few years ago, we conducted a survey of people who make their living evaluating proposals for the federal government. We wanted to know the things they like to see in proposals and the things that they hate. Here are some findings from that survey:

*What They Like:*

1. They like proposals that follow the directions in the RFP.
2. They like compliance matrices. A compliance matrix saves them time and indicates you've been thorough.
3. They like proposals that clearly identify the vendor's differentiators and indicate why those differentiators matter.
4. They like section summaries.
5. They like well-organized and consistent proposals. They believe a professional-looking document shows good project management and thoroughness.
6. They like to have the contract deliverables clearly labeled. That shows you understand what you must deliver and are committed in writing to doing it.
7. They like resumes that are clearly tailored to the specific project being quoted.
8. They like supplementary technical data that was not called for in the proposal, as long as it is relevant.

*What They Hate:*

1. They hate proposals that are wordy.
2. They hate poor-quality proposals—unreadable graphics, spelling mistakes, typos, poor photocopying, and so forth.
3. They hate proposals that are weak or vague in responding to the RFP requirements.
4. They hate proposals that take a poor or unproven approach to solving the problem.
5. They hate proposals that have inherent deficiencies—missed requirements, inaccurate data.
6. They hate proposals that offer alternate or optional solutions that were never requested.

# A Proposal Writer's Checklist

Here's a checklist you can use to determine if your proposal is "good enough." It covers the major points we've talked about in this book. If you can say "yes" to each of the questions in this checklist, you probably have a very good proposal. Print it and send it! And good luck!

## I. The Development Phase

  **A.** Have I analyzed the client's needs and desired end result thoroughly and creatively?

  **B.** Have I turned the statement of need into an overall strategy?

  **C.** Do I know what the customer's decision criteria are?

  **D.** Have I assembled all the necessary information?

  **E.** Have I accurately identified my audience?

    **1.** Personality style

    **2.** Level of expertise and familiarity

    **3.** Role in the decision process

  **F.** Have I developed a cognitive web for the executive summary and for the overall proposal?

## II. Style

  **A.** Have I used a natural, friendly tone?

    **1.** Have I avoided clichés and eliminated Fluff, Guff, Geek, and Weasel?

    **2.** Have I used active voice?

  **B.** Have I expressed myself clearly?

    **1.** Do I understand my subject thoroughly?

    **2.** Are my sentences reasonably short and simple?

    **3.** Have I used specific words?

    **4.** Have I adapted my vocabulary to suit the reader?

    **5.** Have I eliminated jargon?

  **C.** Have I written concisely?

    **1.** Have I eliminated unnecessary detail?

    **2.** Have I cut unnecessary technical details?

  **D.** Have I expressed myself with precision?

    **1.** Are my ideas in logical and effective order?

    **2.** Have I provided the necessary definitions, details, and examples?

  **E.** Have I written with proper emphasis?

    **1.** Did I reinforce the value proposition throughout the proposal?

    **2.** Does my executive summary make a strong, concise case?

## III. Structure

  **A.** Have I used the NOSE pattern to structure this proposal?

    **1.** Did I restate the customer's needs clearly and accurately?

    **2.** Does the proposal state the customer's desired outcomes?

**3.** Is the solution linked back to the client's needs and to the outcomes they will get from meeting those needs?

**4.** Have I offered relevant evidence to show that we can deliver the solution on time, on budget, and in a professional manner?

**B.** Have I prioritized the content from the reader's point of view, putting the content they think is most important first?

**C.** Have I highlighted my key points and made it easy for the reader to skim the proposal?

## IV. Mechanics

**A.** Have I included all the necessary mechanical and prose elements?

**B.** Are my headings and titles clear, properly worded, and parallel?

**C.** Have I keyed any tables or figures into the text and discussed them adequately?

**D.** Have I proofread the manuscript completely?

# 21 The Packaging Is Part of the Product

W E'RE AT A FLEX POINT IN PROPOSAL WRITING, I think. Traditional methods have involved writing a document, printing it out, binding it and putting it between nice-looking covers, and then physically delivering it—usually multiple copies—to the prospect. Many RFPs still specify that you must submit hard copies. State and local government agencies often require a paper submission. But increasingly RFPs call for digital submissions. Each of these modes of delivery has advantages and weaknesses.

***Traditional paper-based proposals*** have the familiar form factor that all paper-based documents have. They're easy to skim, easy to flip back and forth in, and easy to score. You can write notes in the margins, you can fold down the corner when you see something interesting, and you can underline or highlight stuff that you want to remember.

On the other hand, with paper-based proposals, given that some may number well over a thousand pages, a lot of trees have to die.

***Digital proposals*** save paper, save transportation costs, and can be delivered to the prospect almost instantaneously. There's no need to make multiple copies, because the prospect can simply forward your digital version to whomever needs to see it.

But digital documents can be difficult to work with. If the proposal has been saved as a .PDF file in Adobe Acrobat, which it probably should be, the reader will have a lot of difficulty annotating it. Skimming digital documents can be hard, too. And when you deliver a document in native Microsoft Word format, its appearance can change (and never for the better) if the recipient has the Normal template set to something unusual or is using an older version of the program.

The next generation of digital delivery sounds pretty exciting. The ability to embed video, to create hot links to Web sites outside the proposal, and the opportunity to use advanced search technology, hyperlinks, and a more creative interface all sound very cool. But there are a whole host of issues associated with the use of technology that will have to be addressed first. In the public sector, it's unlikely that submissions with embedded video, hot links to Web sites, advanced search technology, hyperlinks, and more creative interfaces will gain immediate acceptance until most organizations make use of them. Even when dealing with a technically sophisticated clientele, we've all had problems from time to time getting a video to open, a photograph to display, or a page to load properly. What happens if your evaluator has similar problems? Does he or she simply mark your submission noncompliant and move on to the next one?

## Body Language in Print

We all know that body language is a critical component of making a positive first impression. Research published by the American Management Association states that people size each other up face-to-face in about seven seconds. We can absorb the body language and other nonverbal cues the other person is sending and then decide whether to approach them or run the other way. But don't we do the same thing with documents?

What kind of first impression is our document making? As our customers first glance at it, do they want to read it or reject it? Interestingly, they probably make that decision a lot faster about a document than they do about a person. Researchers at Carleton University in Ontario, Canada, found that users form an initial positive or negative impression of a Web page in as little as 1/20th of a second—which is about how long it takes to read a single word. The researchers tested users by flashing Web pages on a screen for half a second and for 1/20th of a second, and found that the results were consistent—even at the shorter interval, observers came to similar conclusions about the Web pages based on a quick sense of the pages' visual appeal. Interestingly, the research also found that such categorization then carries over to influence how users judge the trustworthiness and quality of the Web site itself.

This supports research I did years ago, which found that customers make an initial "keep" or "discard" decision regarding proposals in about seven minutes. That means they have taken the time to register the document's initial visual appeal and have also skimmed it for bits of key content. The Canadian research adds that the initial sizing-up of the content is heavily influenced by a beginning aesthetic impression.

Nancy Webb is an expert on page architecture and design—how to make a proposal or other sales document look good in print and on the computer screen. In other words, she is an expert in the art of managing the body language of our documents. She says the first thing to choose is the font—the type family you will use for your body copy and your headings. Webb recommends using a serif font, like Times Roman or Garamond, for the body copy because it is easier to read. The serifs (the small chisel marks at the edges of individual letters) help knit those letters into word shapes, which is what the eye and brain actually read—the shapes of words, not the individual letters. By contrast, reading lengths of sans serif text quickly becomes fatiguing.

Sans serif fonts do work in headings and subheadings, however. Generally, headings have more impact if you use a sans serif font, like Arial, Avant Garde, or Helvetica. Webb recommends limiting your document to two type families. She also says to avoid Courier as well as decorative or ornamental fonts, such as scripts, gothics, and other unusual designs, which may be distracting and are often hard to read.

Next, pay some attention to your page architecture. Nobody wants to read a page that is crammed wall-to-wall with small type. That kind of layout has about as much eye appeal as the phone book. Webb stresses the importance of using white space to increase the appeal of the page and of using call-outs and simple design elements to make the page interesting.

Avoid printing your document with a justified right margin because that kind of margin makes it harder to read. She also does not recommend using the underline function, again because it makes the text much harder to read. Same thing with using ALL CAPS.

In fact, if there is a consistent theme to the tips Webb offers her clients, it is the importance of designing for readability. Whatever choices you make, remember that in the reader's mind easy readability translates into a subconscious sense that what you are telling them makes sense. If your document is poorly designed and not easy to read, the decision maker will assume your recommendations are also poorly designed and difficult to work with. The first rule of persuasion is to be clear. Focusing on document readability can make that impression.

## Creating Graphics that Suit Your Purpose

In the 1920s, Fred Barnard, an advertising executive, tried to convince his clients that adding pictures to the placards in streetcars would make their ads more effective. As evidence, he cited a Chinese proverb: "A picture is worth ten thousand words." Thus a cliché entered the English language—although the ratio of words to picture was mysteriously reduced by a factor of ten along the way.

Actually Barnard made the whole thing up and what the Chinese characters he used literally say is, "A picture's meaning can express ten thousand words." That's a different claim, one that emphasizes the in-terdependence of words and graphics. Properly chosen, words and graphics can combine to create a powerful message that transcends ei-ther medium alone.

For years I've been citing a study done at the University of Minnesota that showed the impact of graphics. Researchers gave a piece of text to a sample group and asked them to rate how persuasive they thought the text was. The researchers then took the exact same text, added a graphic, and gave it to a new sample group. The perceived persuasiveness went up 47 percent when the graphic was added! That's why I continually urge people to include graphics in their proposals, particularly in the presentation of their value propositions. There's nothing you want to be more persuasive than your value proposition, so that's the place to use a bar chart, a trend curve, or a pie chart to illustrate the positive impact your solutions will have.

Edward Tufte, author of *Visual Explanations: Images and Quantities, Evidence and Narrative* and three other books on the art and power of ef-fective visual display, has become almost a cult figure for his insightful and provocative opinions about the potential for strong graphics—charts, illustrations, and so on—to convey content quickly, persuasively, and powerfully. Proposal writers can use four of Tufte's principles to their benefit:

1. Graphics should be interesting in their own right.
2. Graphics should be content rich, dense with information, and should include multiple dimensions and variables.
3. Graphics should force us to make "wise visual comparisons" and should show causality.
4. Words, numbers, and images should be integrated on the page, never broken up by lodging all the graphics at the end of the document or on a different page from where they are discussed.

Another important point that Tufte reiterates is that your presentation—both the words and the graphics—succeeds or fails based on the accu-racy, quality, and relevance of your content. This fundamental truth takes us back to the wisdom of Barnard's phony Chinese proverb: it's the harmony of word and image that creates the most powerful impression. Here are some ideas for using color and graphics to enhance your docu-ment:

✦ *Use your customer's logo* on the title page and in the header of your proposal. Balance it in terms of size and impact with your own logo. Too many proposals go out with a cover and title page dominated solely by a vendor's logo, which comes across as self-centered and obnoxious. (However, make sure the customer is okay with your using their logo. Some companies are very touchy about it.)

✦ *If the customer has a "company color," incorporate it into your design.*

✦ *Avoid highly technical graphics,* complex diagrams, and complicated charts. Simple graphics will attract more attention and they will be easier to understand.

✦ *Orient the graphics so they read on the page just like the text.* The reader should never need to turn your document sideways to look at your graphic.

✦ *Write an active caption* that not only explains what the graphic is showing but also emphasizes a customer benefit. In long documents, it's a good idea to number the graphics, too.

✦ *Use the kinds of graphics that are appropriate to the role of the audience.* For example:

> *Senior executives* are likely to look at payback calculations, ROI charts, or gap analyses.

> *Technical evaluators* will appreciate a compliance matrix more than any other kind of graphic. (As I explained in Chapter 15, a compliance matrix lists each requirement, shows your level of compliance with it, and references where in the document the evaluator can find detailed information.)

> *The "business beneficiaries"* of your solution—that is, the people who will use it or maintain it—will be most interested in visuals showing the cycle of operation, workflow, escalation policies for handling problems, and so forth.

To gain maximum benefit, use the kind of graphic that best suits your message. Here are some ideas:

| The Point You Are Making | A Type of Graphic You Could Use |
|---|---|
| We fully comply with all of your requirements | Compliance matrix |
| Our system or approach offers better performance | Comparison table<br>Bar chart<br>Stacked bar chart<br>Pie chart<br>Trend curve |
| Our system will meet your performance expectations | Schematics<br>Flow chart<br>Table<br>Matrix |
| We will assign the right people to this project | Table of tasks with associated personnel assigned to the tasks<br>Table of personnel with associated experience, past projects, publications, etc. |
| We can meet the deadline | Critical path chart<br>Gantt chart<br>Schedule |
| We have the right experience to do this job | Tables of past projects, objectives, outcomes, dates, clients<br>Maps showing locations of similar projects |
| We have a history of successful projects | Testimonial letters scanned into the text (make sure they stay readable!) |
| We are committed to quality | Diagram of project activities, showing regular reviews and QC |
| We offer unique features, strengths, and/or benefits | Bullet points<br>Sidebars (boxed text, possibly with shading) |

Think about graphics while you're outlining or organizing your document, before you have written any text. Graphics that are thrown in as an afterthought typically look like afterthoughts.

# 22 Presenting Your Proposal

$P$EOPLE OFTEN ASK ME, "WHAT'S THE BEST WAY to deliver my proposal?"

The answer I always give: "In person."

I know what they're really looking for are tips on bindings and covers, stuff like that, but those factors are much less important than getting in front of the decision maker to present your recommendations in person. Nothing replaces human contact for maintaining rapport, enhancing credibility, and handling questions and objections.

## The Rise of Oral Proposals

On any given day, according to my unscientific estimate, about three and a half billion people on earth are giving PowerPoint presentations to the other three and a half billion. Or at least it sometimes feels that way. And most of them aren't very good.

Salespeople in the private sector have always been taught to present their recommendations, but traditionally that wasn't part of the acquisition process as you were selling to government agencies. Now it is. The Office of Federal Procurement Policy endorsed the use of oral proposals, a move that coincided with a government-wide program initiated by the General Services Administration to promote open communications between the government and industry. As a result, many federal agencies began to require oral proposals. Specifically, Federal Acquisition Regulation (FAR) 15.210 now states that such oral proposals may substitute for or augment written proposals, that they may occur at any time in the acquisition process, that they are subject to the same restrictions as written information, and that the oral presentation may appropriately focus on the vendor's capability, past performance, management plan, resources and personnel, and technical solution. Certifications, representations, pricing, and the signed offer sheet need to be in writing. As a result, the Department of Defense, Department of Energy, Federal Aviation Administration, Bureau of Engraving and Printing, and Internal Revenue Service all began to use oral proposals aggressively.

No wonder it feels like half the world is presenting to the other half!

## How to Deliver a Winning Presentation

Preparing an effective oral proposal is as complex and time consuming as preparing a written version of the same proposal. And it creates a whole new set of worries related to delivery skills.

People who feel reasonably confident expressing themselves in writing are sometimes terrified at the idea of presenting the same content in person. As a senior scientist at a highly technical firm groused during a proposal presentation class I was leading, "Apparently it doesn't matter which company is best, what matters now is who can send in the best actor to deliver the message."

Of course, it would make just as much sense to complain that it doesn't matter which company is best, all that matters is who can write the most persuasively. Or who had the best sales force. Or who had the smartest scientists. The fact is that delivering the message has always been part of winning business. But if you are a competent professional, if you understand your client and your solution, you already have the most important components. You *can* develop your presentation skills.

Here's some more good news: almost all of the skills and techniques you have already learned in this book for preparing persuasive written proposals also apply to oral proposals. For example, you still need to ask the key questions—what is the customer's problem? Why is it a problem? What positive outcomes does the customer seek? Which outcomes are most important? You need to carefully analyze the audience and you need to organize your presentation using the NOSE pattern. You will save time and produce a client-centered message if you use the cognitive webbing technique to develop your presentation outline. Editing still matters, and the Red Team process as explained in Chapter 20 can be an ideal way to rehearse so you can sharpen your presentation before it really counts.

But there are also some important differences between written proposals and orals. You cannot deliver information at the same pace or the same level of density in an oral presentation that you can in a written document. Also, you must have a clearly structured introduction and conclusion, and the entire presentation must flow together, ideally unified around a single theme or message, whereas a written proposal can present information in discrete units. And, most obviously, you must be prepared to interact with your audience, handling questions, objections, and interruptions in real time.

Never read your proposal or your slides to the audience. There's nothing more deadly than watching someone read a document to you or read the text off a screen word for word. Always present your points.

Also, never hand out copies of your written proposal until the end of the presentation. Otherwise your audience will start flipping through it, looking for pricing or studying the graphics, only half listening to you. You can provide handouts based on your presentation slides so the audience can take notes, but never give them the whole proposal. (In government settings, you may be required to provide a hard copy of your slides in advance and you will almost always be precluded from providing anything related to your pricing.)

## Oral Proposals from Start to Finish

The process of developing and delivering an oral proposal is a matter of applying common sense and the techniques of persuasion we've already discussed, plus a few unique steps necessitated by the medium of delivery.

To create an outline for your presentation, follow these steps:

**1.** Write down your key point. What exactly is your message?

**2.** List the people who will be attending and perform an audience analysis. What do you know about them? How can you find out more?

**3.** Find out from the client how much time you have for the total presentation. Then divide your time as follows:

+ *Introduction:* up to 10 percent
+ *Body:* 70 percent
+ *Conclusion:* up to 10 percent

[Reserve the remaining 10 percent or so of your total time for questions, interruptions, and digressions.]

**4.** Now, write each of the key points you will make in the body of your presentation on a sheet of paper. A key point might be one of the customer's most important needs, one of the components of your solution, a summary of three important case studies, and so forth. Usually, you can cover approximately five to ten key points in a one-hour presentation, but this will depend on the complexity of your presentation.

Next to each point indicate how much time you will spend on it. Also, if you will have more than one person deliver the presentation, indicate next to the point who will be presenting it.

Then break the points down into the subpoints or supporting evidence you will present to fill out this topic. Don't use complete sentences. Just use bullet points or phrases.

Next to each key point, note a visual aid or graphic concept that will help you communicate.

**5.** Develop an attention-grabbing opening. This is absolutely vital. Go ahead and write it out in full sentences. This is one part of your presentation that you want to get right. (We'll discuss techniques for starting your presentation later in this chapter.)

**6.** Write a strong conclusion that asks for the business and moves the presentation toward definite closure. (We'll also discuss closings later.)

You now have a basic outline for your presentation!

## Develop Visual Aids that Support Your Presentation

According to Nick Oulton, an expert in designing effective PowerPoint presentations and the author of *Killer Presentations,* the typical presentation is developed backwards. Instead of being designed as an aid for the members of the audience, to hold their attention, to help them understand, and maybe to motivate them, the slides are set up primarily as a crutch for the presenter. They are created as glorified cue cards. The typical slide consists of a big topic heading followed by five to ten bullet points. There might be some little piece of clip art stuck in the corner, but usually the slide is nothing but words. And the presenter stares at the slide and proceeds to read each bullet point. Word for word.

Talk about mind numbing!

Oulton urges his clients to use a lot fewer words and a lot more pictures for the vast majority of presentations. The goal is to create a slide that looks interesting but that isn't automatically comprehensible at a glance. There should be just a bit of mystery about it. The audience member should wonder, "What does this mean? What's the point here?" The presenter's job is to explain the point or clarify the meaning, so that when the audience looks again at the slide, it makes sense and has an impact. The problem, of course, is that using fewer words and a more visual approach puts added pressure on us when we're presenting. We won't be able to use the screen as a teleprompter any more. And for some people—including me—it's easier to think in words than in graphics. Trying to think graphically and create slides the way Oulton recommends is awkward for us. It's like trying to play tennis left-handed if you're normally a rightie. However, there is one important difference. Playing tennis with the wrong hand is likely to be a losing proposition. But forcing ourselves to use more graphics and less text, even though it doesn't feel natural, will produce a lot of winners.

Presentation software can allow you to do "build sequences," where you add one point at a time, and can create strong transitions between slides. Doing a build sequence is a way of keeping the audience interested in your slide, but don't go overboard with these tools. Having a line of text swoop in, circle the screen twice, and land in the middle may be interesting . . . once. Do it for every point on every slide and your audience will want rip the mouse out of your hand and jam it down your throat.

Beware of using clip art and similar visual clichés in your orals. They will make your presentation look amateurish or uncreative. One good source of visual content is the graphics you've developed for the written proposal, but don't limit yourself to just those. Use your imagination. Graphs, charts, sketches, maps, diagrams, photographs, even text when displayed in an unusual way: these are all possibilities.

Video is a fertile means of supplementing your oral proposal. In most cases you will probably need to have clips created professionally and stored as digital media so you can integrate them into your overall presentation. Several short clips of 90 seconds or less each are usually more effective than one or two long ones.

If you're using a pointer—either laser or wooden—be careful not to play Zorro. People sometimes use laser pointers so ineptly that red dots are constantly bobbing around the screen, or they're circling words and phrases for no apparent reason. Keep these objects still, or lay them on a table, until you really want to add emphasis.

To create slides or overheads that deliver maximum impact, don't crowd them. Keep them simple and uncluttered. Use one distinct slide or overhead for each point. Develop a palette of two or three colors at the most for your basic design, then stick with it. Use consistent formatting when laying out each slide or overhead. And limit the amount of text. A useful rule of thumb is to limit each line of text to seven words and to limit the slide to no more than seven lines of text.

In general, for large rooms and big audiences, you are limited to using slides (the kind you generate with a presentation software program running on a computer) and/or video. The screens should be placed so everyone can see comfortably without wrenching their necks. Less formal presentations to smaller audiences can employ overhead transparencies, but in reality these have become old-fashioned. (However, some government RFPs still specify that you must use overhead transparencies as your only visual medium! Why? I have no idea.) Using flip charts or a whiteboard, either with content prepared in advance or dynamically as the presentation moves forward, can be very effective with small groups.

In the past, you had to turn the room lights down low for the image to be clear if you used slides or computer-generated presentations. Modern projection equipment generates such high lumens, that's no longer the case. In fact, turning the lights down is a bad idea unless you can put a spotlight on the speaker.

Finally, keep your slides or overheads legible. That means using san serif fonts (such as Helvetica or Arial) for the most part and using type that is large enough to read. How large your type needs to be depends on the medium you are using and the size of your room. The following are rough guidelines. Use your own judgment. But if you find yourself making the font a lot smaller than these guidelines suggest, it's highly probable you're crowding too much text into a single image. The guideline is no more than seven words per line, no more than seven lines per slide maximum.

> Overhead transparencies:
> > Main headings: 36 point type
> > Key points: 24 point type
> > Second-level points and text: 18 point type
>
> Presentation software and slides:
> > Main headings: 30 point type
> > Key points: 24 point type
> > Second-level points: 20 point type
>
> Posters and flip charts:
> > Main headings: 3 inches high
> > Key points: 2 inches high
> > Second-level points: 1½ inches high

Remember that you can supplement your proposal in nonvisual ways, too. A sound clip or a product sample that you pass around for people to handle can evoke a strong response from the audience. Models, miniatures, a piece of equipment, even human beings who are brought in for a brief part of the presentation can add visual interest to your talk.


## Rehearse

People who can deliver a presentation effectively without rehearsing are extremely rare. When I first began my career, I wrote a lot of speeches for top executives—the president of a major regional bank, the head of technology for one of the largest defense contractors, the head of international sales for a multinational consumer products company, and many others. All of them needed to rehearse. Even though they had given many, many presentations and speeches, they knew that the next one was different from all the others and they had a better chance of doing it well if they practiced.

Your primary goal is to become fluent in delivering your message, not to memorize it. If you will be using equipment, such as a laptop computer, a wireless microphone, a teleprompter, and so forth, you should practice with it. If you tend to speak in a monotone, work on adding some variation to your voice. Raise and lower the pitch a little more than usual. Speak louder and softer at various points to heighten the dramatic impact of what you're saying. Pause before or after key points. You may feel uncomfortable using these delivery techniques at first, but it's worth making the effort. Your audience will respond to the fact that you seem to be interested in and excited by your own message.

However, if you *sound* bored, they'll *feel* bored. Albert Mehrabian, a research psychologist at UCLA, studied the relative importance of words, tone of voice, and nonverbal behavior in face-to-face communications. He found that when the behavior does not match the meaning of the words, people tend to believe the behavior. In fact, according to his research, our feelings of liking someone are generated 55 percent by the person's body language, 38 percent by tone of voice, and only 7 percent by the words.

Now this does not mean your words don't matter. But it does mean that if you act nervous, uncomfortable, and edgy, you are not likely to convince the audience by telling them how delighted you are to be there speaking to them. Your body language is shouting down your words.

That kind of negative nonverbal behavior is far more likely to occur if you do not practice. Almost everyone gets nervous speaking in public, and if the presentation has millions of dollars of business riding on it, you'd be crazy not to be nervous. But the key is not to let your nerves show too much. And the best way to achieve that is to practice over and over so that you are completely confident in your message.

The best rehearsal tool is a video camera. Tape yourself as you deliver your presentation, then look at it as though you were watching a stranger. People often lapse into unconscious nervous mannerisms—twirling their pen like a baton, jingling the coins in their pocket, twisting a lock of hair around their finger, standing with their hands in the fig-leaf position as though they were afraid of being exposed. Some presenters rock back and forth, or go through a waltz step sequence, stepping forward, then to the side, then backward, over and over again. If you have any of these tics, a video camera will make them obvious.

People often worry needlessly about saying "uh" or "um" when they present. Forget about it! We use those space fillers all the time when we're engaged in ordinary conversation. Unless you are using them so frequently that they call attention to themselves, there's no reason to try to eliminate them. You're not auditioning for a job anchoring the evening news. You're an ordinary person delivering an important message as well as you can.

Finally, for complex or significant oral proposals, practice at least once in front of a live audience. Have them evaluate your presentation and make sure they ask you a lot of questions. The more you can simulate the real experience, the better prepared you will be.

## Control Your Nerves

It's perfectly natural to feel nervous before you give a major presentation. What you don't want to do is to allow nervousness to become so overwhelming that you feel paralyzed. For some people, speaking in front of group is one of life's most frightening experiences. Surveys show that fear of public speaking is the most common phobia of all, more frequent than fear of heights, snakes, insects, or financial problems. It's part of the "fight or flight" response that has helped our species survive life in the wild, and it'll help you now. Acknowledge the fact that you're nervous and try welcoming the feeling.

Maintain realistic expectations for your performance. You don't have to be perfect. You just need to be good. If you drop your notes, bend over and pick them up, take a deep breath, find your place, and start talking again. If your equipment conks out, smile and tell your audience you'll need to take a brief pause to figure out what needs to be done so you can continue. If you mispronounce a word, stumble over a phrase, or lose your train of thought, let it go. It doesn't have to be perfect, just good.

It's also a smart idea to avoid what I call the "fear impersonators." Eating a spicy lunch just before you give a presentation may leave your stomach feeling even queasier than it would normally. Consuming a lot of milk or cheese may leave your mouth feeling sticky. An excess of caffeine or nicotine can make you feel jumpy. So baby yourself a little and avoid doing things that will get your heart pounding, your stomach churning or produce other physiological reactions that feel like fear.

By the way, I strongly discourage you from using beta blockers, tranquilizers, or alcohol to calm yourself. They definitely work. The problem is that they work too well. Somebody who has a chemically induced sense of calm often comes across as a detached zombie, uninterested in his or her own presentation, disconnected from the audience, even a little bit spaced out. You don't need these crutches and they won't improve your performance.

How do you develop a positive frame of mind? By giving yourself frequent affirmations. What are you afraid of? That they won't like you?

That they don't want to hear you? That you don't have anything worth saying? That you don't have the necessary credibility? That's just fear whispering in your ear. Overcome it by repeating to yourself, "*I have a good message,*" "*the audience really wants to hear it,*" and "*I am the right person to deliver it.*"

Visualize a warm reception, faces smiling, heads nodding.

You will also find it helps to warm up before you start to speak. Just as an athlete would never start a game or enter a race without thoroughly warming up his or her muscles, you will benefit from spending a few minutes using your vocal cords. Make low sounds to relax your voice and take a few deep breaths, counting to five on the inhale and ten on the exhale. Roll your neck gently clockwise, then counterclockwise, and move your arms in large gestures to release some tension.

---

### To Control Your Nerves . . .

1. Rehearse.

2. Give yourself positive feedback.

3. Visualize success.

4. Warm up before you speak.

---

### Deliver Your Message with Maximum Impact

If you've prepared your message carefully and rehearsed it enough, you'll find that simply being yourself and delivering it to the best of your ability will be a success. Here are some things to keep in mind:

**Establish rapport first, then work on credibility.** One of the main reasons your customers are now using oral proposals is to find out if they want to work with you. According to research done by Leonard Zunin, senior psychiatric consultant for the California Department of Mental Health and an authority on attachment and loss, we can figure out in about four minutes if we want to listen to somebody. So how do we grab the customer's attention in the opening minutes? Not by going around the room and introducing everybody on your team. Not by providing a tedious summary of your company's experience, size, or qualifications. Instead, you grab attention by engaging them emotionally. Tell a story. Paint a verbal picture of what they have now and what they will have once you have delivered your solution. Cite startling statistics. Quote their CEO.

A strong introduction is critical for creating immediate rapport. If you spend the first ten minutes trying to impress them with how smart you are or how big and important your firm is, you're likely to do your cause some damage. If you focus instead on their business, their agency, their concerns, and offer specific, concrete insight into what they're trying to accomplish, you're more likely to win their interest.

***Stay relevant throughout your presentation.*** Sometimes nervousness can cause a presenter to lose focus. An unexpected question can cause you to spin off on a tangent. Use your outline of key points and the time you've allotted to each point as a way to keep yourself on track. You'll almost never feel like you have enough time in an oral proposal, and the situation will be even worse if you veer off into irrelevant content.

***Stress your differentiators and value-added components.*** Helping the customer understand why they should buy from you is just as important in an oral proposal as it is when you write. Make them obvious. For example, create a slide that lists the customer's key needs or objectives, what you offer in addressing that part of their requirements that they can't get anywhere else, and why it matters.

***Slow down and keep it simple.*** Simplicity is even more important in an oral presentation than it is in a written submission. People can't decode language as fast when they are listening as they can when they read. So slow it down, use simple language, and don't be afraid to repeat key points. Repetition improves clarity in oral presentations.

***Tell the truth.*** This one is so obvious that you may wonder why I even mention it, but people sometimes exaggerate or distort or lie when they are presenting. Maybe they're trying too hard. Maybe they're anxious about how strong an impression they're making. Maybe they think their presentation just isn't good enough without some embellishment. Whatever the reason may be, they end up misleading the audience. Don't do it.

## How to Handle Questions, Objections, Interruptions, and Disruptions

Sometimes an audience member tries to grab the spotlight for egotistical reasons. Squash that kind of behavior. A conversation that focuses on key points is useful; otherwise, respond concisely and firmly, then move on. If the person who asked the irrelevant question persists, tell him or her that because of time constraints you must defer any further discussion until the end of the meeting. Or you can offer to talk with that person individually at his or her convenience.

Here are some guidelines for handling questions, comments, interruptions, expressions of skepticism, and objections during your presentation:

***Differentiate between strategic and tactical issues.*** Answer questions that relate to the big picture—the strategic issues—right away. If you want, you can defer answers on minor points and technical details until the end of the presentation. To reassure the audience that you won't forget them, create a "docking station"—a sheet of chart paper or a blank overhead transparency—where you "park" the questions.

***Keep your answers brief.*** When you're nervous, you may say more than you need to, sometimes talking yourself into a problem. Answer as concisely as you can.

***Restate the question.*** This is particularly helpful if you're speaking to a large group, where your voice is amplified but the questioner's isn't. Other members of the audience may not be able to hear the question, so your answer won't make any sense. Also, restating the question in your own words gives you a chance to think about your answer and to confirm that you understand the question correctly.

***Don't answer too soon.*** Let the questioner state his or her question completely. Rephrase it to make sure you understand it. Sometimes the questioner is more interested in how you handle yourself than in what you actually say. Pause, take a breath, and think before you respond.

***Limit follow-up questions*** or comments to just one or two. Otherwise, you may end up in a dialogue with one person, ignoring the rest of the group. Of course, if the person who is asking all of the follow-up questions is the executive who has the buying authority, there is no reason to stop the flow.

***Don't bluff and don't lie.*** If you don't know an answer, or if the answer is one you'd rather not give, remember that anything other than honesty is an invitation to big trouble.

***Preempt criticism by stating the opposing point of view*** —and then indicating what you think is wrong with it. You'll take the wind out of the sails of anyone who might want to play the role of trouble-maker or naysayer.

**Defuse anger or hostility with humor.** However, resist using sarcasm. It alienates the audience.

Remember that **not all negative comments or questions are necessarily antagonistic.** People may be voicing concerns (buying objections) because they sincerely want you to deal with those concerns. They want to make a decision.

## Go Off on a High Note

After you have given your presentation and handled all the questions, take time to offer a formal conclusion. Don't just dwindle off with something vague (*"Well, that brings our presentation to a close, so I guess if there's nothing else . . ."*). By the same token, don't be long-winded. It's better to finish early than to try to fill up all the time allotted to you with extemporaneous comments.

When you've covered all the content, answered all the questions, or simply used up all the time available, take a deep breath and make a clear, formal close. Tell the audience that's what you're doing:

*"To summarize my presentation, I'd like to review the advantages of switching to Lambdon's MarketMaker retailing system."*

The conclusion is not the time to introduce new content or to try to squeeze in a couple of new points. Simply mention the key ideas very quickly and summarize your value proposition:

*"You'll find that the system is easy to access and use, that it enhances your company's professional image, and that it's based on proven technology. In short, it provides you with the best overall service."*

Then ask your audience to take specific action. Ask them to give you their business, to approve you as the vendor of choice, to extend your contract, or whatever it is you're seeking. The goal of an oral proposal is the same as the goal of one that's written: to win business. Make that your goal and make it obvious to your customer that you want their business.

# 23 Tracking Your Success

NOBODY CAN AFFORD TO WASTE EXPERIENCE. IT costs way too much to acquire it. So how do you learn from your proposal writing experience? And how do you convert those lessons into improvements that help everyone do a better job?

## Capturing the Lessons Learned

There are a number of activities you can engage in after you have submitted a proposal. Some of these are ongoing steps in the sales process. Others are intended to help you learn what works and what doesn't to improve your next proposal. Both kinds should be a regular part of your postsubmission regimen.

In the private sector, and even in some government bids, contacting the decision maker after you have submitted your proposal is a good idea. Maintaining open communication after submission may help win the deal, since it can be an opportunity to begin closing the deal and negotiating terms. (In some government bidding processes, however, you are expressly forbidden to contact the contracting officer, and doing so will result in your disqualification from the bid process, so make sure you understand what's allowed.)

### Talk to the Customer

The decision has been made. You won. You lost. The award was split between you and a competitor. Regardless of the outcome, there are still things you can do to learn and possibly to influence the future. Some of these activities include debriefings, win/loss analyses, and research to prepare you for the next opportunity.

**Debriefings.** If you were competing to win business from the federal government and have been notified that you did not win, you have the right to receive a debriefing after the decision has been announced. This is a legal right that you can exercise under FAR 15.506. Among state and local governments the rules vary, but often you can request such a meeting in these situations, too. And if you have been competing in the private sector, there's nothing to prohibit you from asking the prospective client to provide you with some insight into their process and how well your proposal stacked up. (Of course, there's nothing to prohibit them from telling you to get lost, either. In the private sector, they don't have to tell you anything.)

Focus on process, if you do go into a debriefing. You're not going to be able to turn a decision around but you can find out how the proposals were evaluated. You might ask how scores were assigned. If you think that the evaluators failed to understand or ignored important aspects of your proposal, try to think like a courtroom attorney. Ask a few innocent and nonthreatening questions that establish the assumptions, then start asking the tough ones. If you hear that some of your references were weak, ask which ones and what specifically they said that seemed lukewarm. You should also focus on specific content about your proposal and how it was reviewed. If you go in with a few prepared questions that address the actual content of your proposal, you're more likely to learn something you can use in the future to improve your work.

**Win/Loss Analyses.** Even if a particular client won't give you a formal debriefing, you can still learn a lot about how your proposals are doing. Start conducting regular win/loss analyses the same way that businesses conduct customer satisfaction surveys. That is, select a specific percentage of all the opportunities you propose and seek feedback. Conduct the analysis whether you win or lose. You can do it in the form of a questionnaire, a telephone interview, even a site visit if that's convenient. Be sure to make it clear that you are not trying to reopen the decision process, though. You only want to improve future proposals. Keep the analysis short, factual, and focused on the actual document—format, pricing, length, clarity, use of differentiators, and so on. If you have the resources, you might even consider hiring an outside firm to conduct these analyses for you. That makes the process more objective and also less threatening to your clients.

**Research.** Win or lose, maintain contact with the client organization and listen for opportunities that may lie ahead. Contact them regularly, sharing with them new ideas and developments, articles that you think will be of interest to them, and so forth. An ongoing campaign of regular communication can help establish strong recognition for you and your company and may help open channels of information that will be invaluable on the next bid.

### Talk to Your Colleagues

At the conclusion of each proposal project, after a suitable period of rest and healing for the proposal team, conduct an internal review for about an hour. The main goal is to review the process and the deliverable to find out how you can do a better job next time. What lessons did you learn from this experience? How can those lessons improve your performance or simplify the task in the future? The proposal manager can lead the discussion, but if the proposal manager is part of the problem or if there is conflict about which lessons need to be learned, you might want to bring in an outside facilitator.

# Lessons Lost

You often hear people saying that they want to capture the "lessons learned" from an important project, such as a major proposal. My question is, what do they do with those lessons after they capture them? Because they sure seem to disappear pretty quickly, given the number of proposals that repeat the same mistakes again and again.

A while back I worked with a company that was in a pretty desperate situation. They hadn't won a single bid for over a year. They had survived on some large projects that generated cash, but those were winding down. If they didn't win a major opportunity—and soon—they would be forced to lay off hundreds of employees. They had an opportunity to respond to an RFP for a huge engineering project, something that was perfect for them. Seeing it as a must-win situation, they asked me to help.

When I arrived on site, I led a series of workshops to create client-centered and persuasive responses to each of the twenty major "questions" or topical areas in the RFP. And when we got to the section on personnel, I asked them to throw out their traditional resumes, which were long and boring, and write them in a completely different way. For some contributors, the changes were invigorating. They enjoyed doing things in a new way. For others, it was more painful. Regardless, at the end of the process, they had a response to the RFP that was persuasive, value-oriented, and client centered. And a few months later, they learned that they had won.

Since then, however, I have learned that they have not incorporated a single thing we did into their standard processes. We found that doing things differently, following a different process, putting the emphasis on different areas of content, resulted in a win. You might even call those "lessons learned." But none of them were preserved. Instead, they have gone back to doing things the same old way—the way that had failed to win a single deal for over a year.

Sadly, in proposal operations, in spite of lip service to the contrary, lessons learned are quite often lessons lost. Most proposal organizations, and indeed most sales operations as a whole, have no institutionalized process for capturing those lessons. They believe that as soon as today's proposal has been delivered, they must rush off to work on tomorrow's.

Another difficulty for many companies is that there is no budget set aside for such analyses. As a support organization, the proposal operation must show that every minute of time and every dollar of budget is being directed toward winning business. An activity that's one step removed, like capturing lessons learned, could be criticized as frivolous, so proposal managers avoid doing it.

A third reason is that in many organizations the proposal effort is decentralized. In a decentralized organization, it's extremely difficult to gather any kind of information on what's working, and it's even more difficult to learn what doesn't work. After all, who wants to volunteer to be the example of how not to do it?

Finally, lessons learned are often lost because the proposal operation and the sales organization as a whole may not have any system in place for implementing change. In an engineering or project management environment, change management is a well-defined part of the process. There are documented steps for institutionalizing a better process when you discover one. That is seldom true in sales or proposal operations.

What's to be done? The first step, I think, is to acknowledge that doing things the same way, over and over, without being open to changes that may improve results, is a recipe for stagnation and eventual failure. Once you get your organization to make that cultural shift, you can apply these suggestions for incorporating gleaned knowledge into your standard procedures:

✦ ***Conduct regular lessons-learned meetings*** with the sales and proposal development team. At a minimum, this should happen right after a major bid has been completed. Ask these questions: *What worked? Where were the obstacles? What workarounds or solutions did we come up with?*

✦ For problems that come up repeatedly, ***create a task group to analyze the root causes***. What preventive measures can be implemented? What gaps in capabilities should be closed?

✦  What did you do differently? Did it work? Was there anything you did that was so effective you think it should become part of your standard approach in the future? If so, **document the change and figure out how to make sure everybody embraces it**. Training? Checklists? Tools? What's going to make this new way of working the standard way in the future?

✦  At least once a year, **stand back from your standard processes**—your unquestioned "best practices"—**and question them**. What's being done simply because it's always been done? What's no longer adding value to the final deliverable? Can these steps be eliminated? Can they be changed and made more effective?

✦  **Establish a formal process for institutionalizing change**. Document the changes. Incorporate them into internal training. Modify your proposal automation systems and databases to reinforce the changes. Begin including the use of these new methods into performance appraisals. Figure out what's going to work to convert lessons learned into accepted standard practices as quickly as possible, and then follow through.

## Get a Three-Dimensional View

To get a complete, three-dimensional view of the impact of any changes you make, measure results in terms of three goal areas—business performance, technical improvements, and customer satisfaction. This will give you a view of your success that is much more likely to be accurate and meaningful for you.

**Business performance** is typically measured in financial terms or in terms of productivity. In looking at your proposal processes, you might measure the gross revenues you win, or the total number of proposals prepared per proposal center employee, or the total dollar volume won by your proposal center on a per-employee basis. Any of those measures could be useful in showing general trends in terms of business performance.

Second, look at the impact of **technical improvements** to your proposal process. When you measure results attributable to technical improvements, your focus will primarily be on the impact of the tools you introduce or the degree to which existing tools are better utilized. Technical improvements usually produce process efficiencies that can be measured in terms of reduced time or effort. They might overlap with business results, but not always.

The third area where you should measure results is **customer satisfaction**. You obviously have one all-important customer—the one who signs the contract and sends you the check. But it's possible you have other customers, too. For example, if you're a proposal writer who supports salespeople, those folks out in the field are your customers. Are they satisfied with the work you do? Is it easy for them to get your help? Other potential customers include senior management and the marketing organization. Whether internal or external, a direct beneficiary of your work or someone who is indirectly affected by it, you can measure their satisfaction by conducting interviews, passing out surveys, or collecting anecdotal evidence. (You may find it's easier to quantify customer satisfaction among people outside the organization than it is to do it among your colleagues, by the way.)

Process improvements should have a measurable impact on the performance of your proposal operation. If you are an individual working alone, they should positively affect your ability to work efficiently and effectively, ideally helping you win more business while spending less energy in the effort. Let's take a look in more detail at ways you can obtain meaningful data in these three areas of potential results.

## Measuring Business Results

There are five ways to measure business results.

### 1. Win Ratio
The point of this sort of metric is pretty obvious. It's like glancing at the baseball standings—the team with the highest winning percentage is on top. For most sales executives, increasing the win ratio is exactly what they want to see. It's simple and straightforward.

*Last Year:*
500 proposals submitted, 200 deals won = 40 percent win ratio

*This Year:*
400 proposals submitted, 185 deals won = 46.25 percent win ratio

The interesting thing about these numbers is that even though fewer deals were won, the win ratio was higher. This could stem from putting in place a better bid/no bid analysis process, or from fewer opportunities in your industry due to economic conditions. But it could also mean the sales team was not doing as good a job of uncovering opportunities, even though you managed to win more of the deals they did find. Once again, you can see why measuring win ratio alone may not be adequate. But it is a starting point. And it's one measure that's obviously relevant.

### 2. Ratio of Opportunities Won / Total Opportunities

To address some of the inaccuracies inherent in measuring nothing but win ratios, you might consider tracking how you are doing compared to the total number of opportunities that were available. This may be a difficult number to know. If you're selling broadband access, the potential market is so large and diffuse that you could never know with any accuracy how many total opportunities there were in a given period. But if you are working in a focused market, such as local government, where all opportunities require an RFP as part of the formal procurement process, you may know exactly how many deals were on the table. For example, suppose the numbers look like this:

*Last Year:*
750 RFPs released, 200 deals won = 27 percent hit ratio

*This Year:*
600 RFPs released, 185 deals won = 31 percent hit ratio

Again, although there were 20 percent fewer opportunities available to bid on, the total number of deals you won declined only 7.5 percent. Your "hit ratio" went up. This measurement supplements a calculation of pure win ratio by taking into account opportunities that you did not choose to bid on and by adding the perspective of the size of the total market.

### 3. Win Ratio in Target Markets

A useful measurement is to segment your success by markets, particularly if you're trying to grow your business in a specific area. Suppose you have traditionally been a government supplier, but your firm has decided that it must expand into the commercial market. Tracking revenue by market will show whether or not you're making progress toward that goal, as these numbers indicate:

*Last Year:*
85 percent revenue won in government contracts
15 percent revenue won in commercial

*This Year:*
78 percent revenue won in government contracts
22 percent revenue won in commercial

Measuring performance by market segments helps separate out issues that might confuse or cloud the issue. If you won a huge government contract, your revenues might be way up, but as a company you might actually be losing ground in your goal of diversifying your market.

### 4. Ratio of the $ Won / Total $ in All Potential Bids

If you are winning a lot of deals, but those deals are all the small ones, and you're not winning any of the large opportunities, you may have a high win ratio and yet unexpectedly low revenues. By tracking the total value of all the contracts for which you compete and comparing that to the total amount you win, you can track your capture rate, like this:

*Last Year:*
$4 million revenue won / $24 million potential revenue =
17 percent capture rate

*This Year:*
$3.8 million revenue won / $20 million potential revenue =
19% capture rate

On a year-over-year basis, your revenues went down, but you captured a larger share of what was available, which means you actually did a better job in a declining market.

This kind of measurement can be further refined by tracking the total volume of revenue won in ratio to the total volume of revenue bid for all proposals in which the proposal center was involved. This will indicate whether or not the proposal team is having an impact on larger opportunities.

Another useful measurement based on revenue numbers is to track the ratio of the amount of new business won to the total opportunities won. This will help identify how much of your business is made up of contract extensions, work orders, and add-on business, and how much is made up of new customers. That may be an important measure for you. Capturing new business is notoriously more difficult than capturing add-ons and renewals, but many companies base their growth plans on winning new business, since it usually accounts for a larger revenue potential.

### 5. Ratio of the Cost to Win / Value of Wins

Finally, a measure of business performance that is relevant to those companies that have a dedicated proposal operation is how much it costs to run that operation compared to how much the proposal team has helped win. Everyone understands that winning contracts is the result of a multitude of efforts and skills, and that the proposal is only one part of that total package. However, a well-managed proposal operation should learn to operate more efficiently and effectively over time, so it should be able to handle more bids with the same headcount and/or increase the amount of revenue won through greater experience and insight. If this measurement is trending in the right direction, the ratio between the cost of running the proposal operation and the revenue won from proposals produced by that operation will grow larger:

*Last Year:*
Proposal center budget = $850,000
Revenue won = $38 million
Ratio of revenue to cost = 44.7:1

*This Year:*
Proposal center budget = $850,000
Revenue won = $64 million
Ratio of revenue to cost = 75.3:1

## Measuring Technical Improvements

Technical improvements to the infrastructure result in greater productivity, better utilization of resources, lower costs of operation, or similar measures related to time and effort. Here are some ways of measuring the impact of technical improvements:

### 1. Decreasing the Cost per Page
How much does it cost to produce a proposal? One way to measure the costs is to calculate how much you spend per page. For example, let's look at two years' operation in a large proposal organization:

*Last Year:*
Proposal center budget = $850,000
Total proposal pages produced = 50,000
Cost per page = $17

*This Year:*
Proposal center budget = $850,000
Total proposal pages produced = 60,000
Cost per page = $14.17

You can see that the cost has gone down considerably, primarily because the center was able to produce 20 percent greater volume of finished output with no increase in funding. This is an interesting measurement, but it ignores issues of quality and effectiveness. Producing 20 percent more garbage isn't necessarily an improvement. But if you couple this kind of metric with careful tracking of business results, you will have a useful insight into whether or not efficiency is improving without compromising effectiveness.

### 2. Decreasing the Cost per Outgoing Page / Incoming RFP Pages
This is an attempt to account for the complexity of the proposals being handled. Proposals are likely to cost more if they are written in response to RFPs that are much more complex. The assumption behind this is that responding to a 20-page RFP is probably less demanding than responding to one that's 200 pages.

### 3. Reducing Access Time to Existing Information
One of our clients established a rule: if you can't find the answer you need in 45 minutes, stop looking. We eliminated such wasteful effort by implementing automated search tools and a systematic database for them. Similarly, one of the major consulting firms had created such an enormous database of old proposals and specialized content, they found it was almost impossible to locate useful answers. So they decided to start over and create a subset of the database that would contain the best answers to frequently asked questions. In both cases, they might have had measurements that looked like this:

*Last Year:*
Finding an RFP answer among existing proposals: 42 minutes average

*This Year:*
Finding an RFP answer from redesigned database: 3 minutes average

### 4. Other Ways to Measure Technical Improvements
When you introduce new tools or technology, upgrade the skills of proposal writers, or provide other enhancements to the infrastructure designed to produce good proposals faster, you may find it helpful to track metrics such as these:

+ Hours per page
+ Hours per proposal
+ Number of process steps and loops

All of these measures should decrease if you're getting the right results from your technical improvements.

If you have implemented a proposal automation system or are using other technology to expedite information retrieval and document building, you might consider tracking the number of times the proposal database is accessed. Another way to measure improvement in the proposal "infrastructure" is to track how many times people outside the proposal staff access the database of information you have created. Although a crude measure, this statistic should tick upward if the database contains valuable information, if the tools you have provided are user friendly, and if the search strategies are carefully designed.

Finally, another way to determine if the tools and processes you introduce are having an impact on the practice is to measure the quantity of content in your proposal database. Although quantity is no substitute for quality, you can assume that without adequate quantity, the database or Web site will not be of much value, either.

### Measuring Customer Satisfaction: The Process

To use customer satisfaction as a metric, you first must define who is the "customer." The obvious choice, the final decision maker or the client evaluation team, may be only part of the answer. There may be consultants involved in the selection process. In fact, in some industries, such as employee benefits and health insurance, consultants and brokers often control the entire acquisition process. In addition, you may have internal customers whose satisfaction matters. The sales force is an obvious customer for your proposals—they are counting on the proposals to help move their opportunities toward closure. What about marketing? They might be customers, at least indirectly, since the work they have done in articulating value messages, understanding clients, and branding your company's products and services should help inform and guide your proposals. What about the legal department? Legal may play an important role in the review process to which your proposals are submitted.

After you've defined who is the customer, your next task is to gather quantifiable, objective measures of their satisfaction. Win/loss analyses, focus groups, interviews, surveys, and other research tools will help you get the data you need. One useful measure of internal satisfaction is to track Red Team scores. Are they going up? (Another interesting question is whether good Red Team scores correlate to winning proposals. If not, it's time to shake up the Red Team process!) If you are trying to track satisfaction scores from an internal customer, you might find it useful to conduct satisfaction surveys periodically.

Drawing a page from consumer marketing, the proposal operation can conduct focus groups to test win themes, graphics, document formats, and other proposal elements. The focus groups should include members of the sales force, marketing group, senior management, and respondents drawn from outside the company.

Even more powerful is to conduct conjoint analyses with actual customers, asking them whether they find this bit of evidence more compelling or that one, whether they prefer this product description or that one.

If your internal customers are not required to work with you in creating proposals, but rather have the option of doing it themselves, you might find it useful to track repeat customers. If members of the sales force come back repeatedly, they are voicing their approval of the work you are doing and its value in winning business.

## Implementing Metrics to Improve Your Proposal Processes

If you are producing a high volume of proposals that are not terribly complex, you will need to measure performance differently than does someone who produces only a few proposals a year that are extremely complex. If your firm has standard offerings, simply increasing the volume of proposals is a good thing. Your proposal operations can help achieve that kind of goal by creating reusable text and managing strategic themes for these offerings. Ultimately, more proposals should manifest in more wins just given the law of averages. Then you can look at the question of whether proposals for standard offerings issued with text and formats created by the proposal operation are winning at a higher rate than issued proposals that do not use the content and formats created by the proposal team. In companies where the proposal operation is a support organization and sales has the option of using it or not, this kind of metric can be invaluable in proving the proposal operation's value.

Finally, it's important to remember that external economic and business factors can make good numbers look bad and vice versa. Process improvements need to be measured over a long enough period to account for cyclical variations in business performance.

# 24  Creating a Proposal Center of Excellence

To CREATE A PROPOSAL OPERATION THAT IS A center of excellence we must identify the characteristics of the people we need in the operation, train them so they possess the right skills, and define the best practices and tools that will enable them to create outstanding proposals, as measured by revenue generation, win ratios, productivity, and customer satisfaction. (The metrics are important because a proposal center operation is not an end in itself. The center is justified only to the extent that it helps achieve the broader goals of business capture established by its parent organization.) In the previous chapter we looked at how to measure success. This chapter will cover the people, skills, methods, and tools necessary to achieve it.

## The Limitation of Traditional Models

The earliest proposal centers were developed in organizations focused on project engineering and government contracting. As a result, most analyses of how a proposal center should operate have focused on project management and workflow. This engineering-oriented approach made sure the document was completed on time and that it met the requirements laid down for it. The models were drawn primarily from U.S. firms handling complex Defense Department bids, and they assumed that what was being proposed was a one-of-a-kind project. Although the proposal might ultimately result in the sale of hundreds of tanks or avionic displays, the big proposal was typically focused on developing new systems or tools.

Unfortunately, proposal processes that work in a firm dedicated to large-scale engineering projects or government contracting are not likely to work well for companies in the private sector. In the business-to-business world, the range of products and services offered is staggering, but no matter what kind of product or service they are recommending, commercial proposals will have more in common with each other than they do with the kinds of proposals written for large government contracts.

## The Proposal Unit: Defining Its Mission

In any environment, a proposal center can define and implement best practices for proposal development, standardize the company's output, and raise the overall level of quality. It can create and maintain a pool of information and reusable content. It can become a repository of expertise in the intricacies of procurement rules and contracting policies. It can supply expert help to get major proposals done on time. And most important of all, a dedicated proposal team can be a valuable asset that helps the company win more business.

Typically, a proposal function that is well integrated into marketing and customer relationship activities will play a broader role in business development than simply writing proposals. Other roles and contributions for the proposal team may include:

+ Developing standard tools for customer assessments, such as an opportunity analysis worksheet, that focus on customer needs, issues, goals, etc.
+ Participating in account planning and competitive assessments prior to or at the outset of a bid opportunity
+ Participating in bid/no bid analysis
+ Assuring that proposal development resources are applied to those opportunities with the most strategic value to the organization
+ Maintaining a repository of current, persuasive, reusable content
+ Developing and maintaining win themes related to specific product and service offerings
+ Researching trends, issues, and themes, both on a customer-specific basis and in terms of the market in general
+ Acquiring expertise on the procurement rules that govern how contracts are awarded, particularly for government clients, so the account manager will know how much he or she can do before the release of the RFP to influence its content or even to circumvent it by moving the opportunity to sole source status
+ Implementing formal methods to assess the competition, both for specific opportunities and in general, and publishing competitive information to benefit the organization as a whole
+ Writing or assembling a large percentage of each proposal

+ Attending bidder's conferences
+ Attending customer debriefings, regardless of a win or loss

As the preceding list suggests, when defining the mission of your proposal center think beyond just proposal production. Although proposals will be the center's most important output, the proposal team can also support the rest of the firm, particularly the sales organization, by responding to their information needs. For example, your colleagues or customers might want a couple of answers, a case study, or product specs. Responding to these requests can make a valuable contribution to sales efficiency and effectiveness by defining processes to handle information requests, too. As a result, I recommend that you incorporate an element of information management into your proposal unit's mission and develop a workflow process that can handle requests that are not necessarily based on an RFP. For example, Figure 24-1 shows how a request might be processed differently depending on whether it's simply for information or for development of a proposal.

If your proposal operation is a support organization, you may find it necessary to establish a formal process by which you take on projects. Requiring your internal clients to enter into a "contract" with you enables you to clearly establish roles, responsibilities, and expectations on both sides. The contract should define the proposal project, timeline, charge rate (if any), scope of effort, and deliverables. It will prevent conflicts and missed expectations and may even enhance your role as a strategic resource within the firm.

## Integrating the Proposal Center into the Overall Organization

I have seen large companies spend big money recruiting quality people, setting up facilities, and otherwise creating an outstanding proposal center, only to find a year or two later that the center had become little more than a copy and production shop. What happened to the strategic vision? Where is the contribution to big wins and dramatic improvements in quality?

Usually those big results were never feasible in the first place because the proposal center was slotted into the wrong part of the organization and did not receive top management support. Both are necessary for a proposal operation to make the maximum contribution.

Where should the proposal operation fit into the organization? The best choice is to make it part of sales. Marketing is a reasonable alterna-

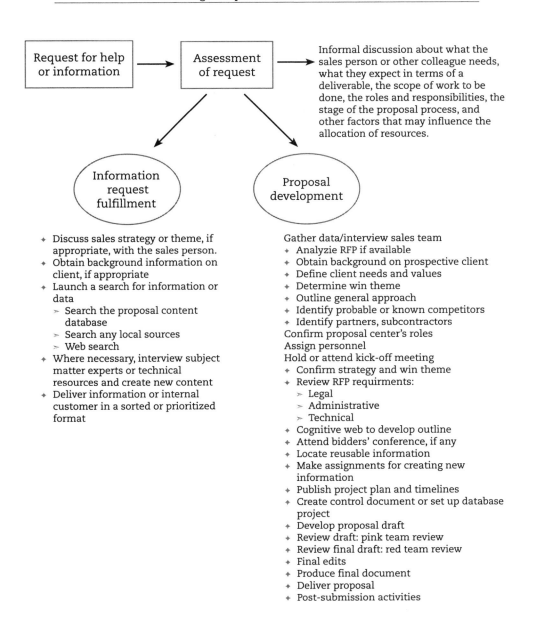

**Figure 24-1.** Workflow for Information Requests and Proposal Development.

tive to sales. The worst choices are to put it in engineering, operations, legal, or finance. After all, the proposal team is creating sales documents, not technical manuals. When the proposal unit reports to the head of sales, it is more likely to be seen as a critical element in the overall business capture process. If it's part of engineering or operations, it's likely to be seen as part of order entry, pricing, configuration, or contracts. Proposal team members need to understand and have access to the insights derived from the company's sales and marketing activities.

Once the proposal unit is properly slotted into the organization, it also needs to have the full commitment of top management. In fact, in a center-of-excellence proposal operation:

+ Executive management is committed to and supportive of the strategic role of the proposal center.
+ The management of the proposal center has communication paths to executive management for quick resolution of issues or problems.
+ Executive management and senior managers themselves participate in the development or review of significant proposals.
+ Proposal center personnel are expected to help develop win strategies on major bids.

## People: Putting the Right Staff in Place

One frequent problem that proposal writers encounter is that they are not seen as being on the same level as technical experts or account managers. Others may be reluctant to concede to them the authority to take charge of the process. As a result, they gradually get nudged into clerical or support roles. Proposal writing is not an administrative function. Someone with only clerical skills is not a person who can make big contributions to a company's success.

In top-notch proposal operations, everyone's roles and responsibilities are clearly defined in detail and everybody is focused by management directive on improving the organization's overall capabilities to bid successfully. To attract quality people the company creates an environment that is creative and challenging. In addition, the company develops a career path for people who work in the center so they can see a future for themselves.

At the minimum, an effective proposal team will have three key members. The roles can overlap somewhat, but it's a good idea to keep responsibilities as clearly defined as possible. The three essential members of any proposal team are the proposal manager, the writer, and the graphics expert. From time to time, you will also need to draw upon subject matter or technical experts.

***Proposal Manager.*** The proposal manager is responsible for bringing projects to on-time, successful completions. Just as important, the proposal manager facilitates development of the overall proposal strategy and makes sure that it is executed throughout the proposal. This manager will typically make assignments to other contributors, monitor their progress, and either edit their submissions or assign them for editing. In addition, the proposal manager will assure the technical accuracy of the proposal, gather and monitor pricing data, make sure the pricing is reviewed and approved, and monitor the overall effort to keep the cost of proposal development within budget.

***Writer.*** Proposals are communication vehicles. It goes without saying that you'll need people with strong communication skills, especially the ability to write clearly and quickly. In my opinion the best kind of background for proposal writing is not technical writing or marketing communications. It's journalism. If you can find someone who has made his or her living as a reporter, particularly if that person has a business background, you probably have someone who can crank out the text you need in a fast and dependable way.

Besides good writing skills, this person must be computer literate. Advanced knowledge of word processing techniques, particularly the use of templates, will make the writer more productive and will avoid rework during the final stages of editing. (It's extremely frustrating to discover that someone's contribution has lost all formatting because they didn't use the style sheet.) But computer literacy goes far beyond just word processing. The writer's job includes repurposing existing text and creating new text when it's required. For example, if a prospective client issues an RFP asking a number of new questions and you have nothing in your database that will answer them, the writer will need to do the research and writing necessary to create a new answer. Then, he or she must store the answer within your proposal automation system so that it's available for all future proposals. Creating and maintaining the database of reusable text and graphics is an essential part of the writer's role.

The writer typically writes the cover letter and executive summary, although sometimes those elements are handled by the salesperson. Finally, the writer's job includes editing drafts and finished documents, taking feedback from Red Team reviews and incorporating it into the final version, and sometimes overseeing production of the final document.

***Graphics Expert.*** This is the person most likely to be missing from a fully staffed proposal team. Often, proposal units draw on the marketing department for graphic support, or they contract with outside vendors on a one-off basis. From a budgetary standpoint that might make sense, but ideally you should have someone on the team who thinks visually and who can translate proposal-specific messages into crisp, interesting images. A good graphics person needs to be skilled in page design and layout issues, as well.

***Subject Matter or Technical Experts.*** Technical experts usually don't think proposal writing is part of their job and don't have a clue as to how to communicate in language that's appropriate to a customer. If you can find a technical resource with the ability to see things from the customer's perspective and to think creatively, you will have an enormous asset. Just be sure to store whatever contributions your technical experts make so that you don't have to go back and ask them to do it again. They hate that.

For many employees, particularly those in sales, marketing, and consulting functions, a rotation through the proposal center will be an extremely valuable part of their normal career development. Given the skills they will acquire, employees should see an assignment in the proposal operation as a welcome opportunity to grow.

# Skills:
## Assessing and Training for Outstanding Performance

According to a survey conducted by the Association of Proposal Management Professionals, best-in-class companies believe there is a correlation between win rates and their investment in proposal training. In fact, according to this study, well-trained companies achieve win rates of 50 percent or higher.

For maximum value and impact, any proposal-related training offered through the proposal operation must be consistent with the other training your company provides on sales and business development. If your salespeople have been trained in a particular sales methodology, your proposal team should go through an abbreviated form of the same training. That way the proposal specialists will understand and use the sales jargon and will know what kinds of information the salespeople will have obtained if they followed the sales process.

Center employees should receive specific, formal training in the best practices that govern successful proposal development, the techniques of managing a proposal project, and similar skills relevant to their job.

One important area of training that is often overlooked is preparing proposal team members to project credibility and to communicate their value clearly. If they are in a support role, and must work with the firm's high-powered account teams or senior executives, they can easily become intimidated. If they are prepared to deal with these personalities, the proposal team members will be more successful contributors.

Note that besides training the people who work full-time in the proposal operation, you can add value by providing proposal training for all employees who contribute to proposals. On specific proposal projects, you can provide formal training to those employees who are "borrowed" from other areas of the business for short-term stints. Likewise, you can develop and deliver brief training sessions to help mobilize a proposal team and to provide a common approach and vocabulary as they undertake a large project. Finally, the proposal team can create a tremendous resource for the company by creating self-study training, delivered via workbooks, cached on the Web, or stored on CD-ROMs. This training could be accessed and used by employees who may be working on proposals that the center can't help on, perhaps because the project is too small or because a more critical opportunity has used up all available resources. By providing training to your colleagues within the company, you will be helping them and yourself. When they see what is involved in creating a winning proposal, they'll do a better job of collaborating with you and they'll respect the proposal team as true knowledge workers and a source of intellectual capital.

# Methods:
## Incorporating Best Practices

If your proposal center has clearly defined processes that you consistently use to understand a customer's needs and requirements fully, your center will be seen as a professional unit focused on business development. If it has processes that primarily focus on how a proposal gets printed and bound, you will be seen primarily as a production shop. Obviously, both kinds of processes are important, but in my experience proposal teams usually ignore the importance of the first kind, those that are directed outward toward the deal.

As you develop and implement your processes for managing proposals, be sure to publicize the linkage between those processes and your company's overall sales or business development life cycle, so that others in the company will see that you are supporting their interests as well. Document and enforce the policies and procedures so that you handle opportunities in a consistent way, and establish a formal process for waiving or deviating from standard procedures.

This last point is important, because your proposal center will inevitably come under pressure to deviate from or abandon the defined processes. A senior sales executive may claim priority, may challenge your methods based on years of successful experience, may insist that you abandon certain steps because of the imperative of time, or may have some other reason for overruling the center's best practices as defined in its process handbook. Because your proposal center is a support organization, you can't just ignore these requests. You have to take them seriously, which means that one of the processes you need to develop is a way to handle exceptions and deviations from standard procedures. Develop your own processes, document them, train people on them, and use them. If you find ways to simplify or improve the proposal process, do it. But once you've established your processes, don't throw them out just because some big shot demands that you do things according to his or her rules. That's degrading to the value of your contribution and will sow seeds of chaos and confusion.

# Tools:
## The Right Resources and Facilities for Optimum Performance

The proposal operation must be designed for efficiency. This includes having the equipment necessary to do the job and the specialized tools to operate at peak effectiveness, including:

+ Proposal generation software
+ Individual workstations, fully networked and equipped with up-to-date office productivity software (given the realities of the marketplace, I recommend Microsoft Office for consistency across the enterprise and with the vast majority of clients)
+ Printers, phones, faxes, and high-bandwidth access to the Internet to facilitate collaboration within the center and with internal clients
+ Whiteboards, flip charts, libraries of resource material, and other materials for planning and managing proposal projects
+ Easy access to electronic stores of reusable content and other information

These tools are even more important if your proposal center is a virtual operation. If your team works this way, you'll need to add Web-based collaboration tools, messaging, and software to facilitate virtual meetings. Many of my clients have developed such proposal teams and have found that they are more productive and efficient than teams that are co-located, plus they dramatically reduce real estate requirements.

There are other kinds of tools a proposal operation can develop that will help it operate efficiently and help others in the company work more successfully. One example is a checklist or questionnaire that helps salespeople uncover the customer's requirements, business and technical needs, values, and desired outcomes. All of these considerations are important for qualifying an opportunity, understanding a customer's vision, and positioning a company as a potential partner in achieving success. If your company has a set of standard products or services, or if it has a sales initiative under way focused on a certain product line, your proposal team can help by creating prewritten draft proposals for the most frequently needed offerings. These can serve as the basic framework for building the firm's response to a specific opportunity. By incorporating common win themes, the most effective references and case studies, and other aspects of the proposal, the proposal center can save the field sales organization huge amounts of time, allowing proposal specialists to focus on strategic opportunities. The challenge, of course, will be creating an executive summary as part of these draft proposals that has enough specificity to sound appropriate and relevant to the recipient.

## Working in the Virtual World

As I mentioned, many companies have done away with the dedicated proposal center, co-located in centralized offices, and have instead moved to a virtual operation. This has produced some important benefits: they have reduced operating costs, in part from eliminating the need for corporate real estate, and they have reduced the company's carbon footprint by slashing the amount of commuting and travel formerly associated with creating a large-scale proposal.

But there is a hidden benefit from establishing Web-based workflow, infrastructure, and technology in support of virtual operations. The company is able to capture data in the background and to consolidate information quickly from multiple sources. Win/loss data can be collected as part of postproposal reviews and can be matched against account and opportunity data stored in the company's customer relationship management system. Quality data is also easier to collect because all work products are stored centrally. And work can be monitored efficiently because everyone is logging on to the Web-based systems, giving managers an opportunity to track team capacity and individual productivity.

For a virtual proposal team to achieve the levels of excellence that are possible with a team working in a single office, management must pay careful attention to the business culture. Erika Chandler, who led Cisco's Worldwide Proposal Experts team, believes that the manager of a virtual team must monitor the climate and attitude of team members regularly. That means having regular Web-based meetings, finding opportunities for informal socializing in the virtual world, and using social media techniques to build team spirit. Celebrating someone's birthday during a Web call can do as much to create team loyalty as having a cake in the office's coffee room. People tend to want to keep control of their own information, so it's vital to create a collaborative culture in which sharing is the norm. There are special challenges to managing in the virtual world, and failure to stay on top of them can lead to disillusioned or detached employees who are not contributing to their full potential.

Clear processes, including explicit definitions of roles and responsibilities and rules of engagement, will help members of the virtual proposal team in two ways. First, workers will know exactly what is expected of them and will know how to prioritize. Second, they will be able to resist scope creep and the imposition of people outside the team who request a deviation from established processes "just this once."

It is critical that all assignments be issued in clear, simple language and that the person receiving the assignment confirm it. This includes specific confirmation regarding deliverables, timing, formatting, and other elements of the finished product. Getting the assignment wrong in a virtual environment can easily mean that days of effort have to be flushed away. And due dates are made even trickier to handle when you are dealing with team members in multiple time zones.

The people who succeed in a virtual workplace must be highly disciplined, technically competent, and experienced in working on proposals. This environment is not a good choice for someone who is new to the role. In addition, you need people who are self-motivated and well organized.

Interestingly, one of the skills that the proposal manager and writer need when they are working in a virtual setting is outstanding telephone communication skills. Lacking the immediacy of facial expressions and body language, you must become adept at interpreting pauses during a phone conversation, asking confirming and clarifying questions, and practicing active listening.

The impact of setting up a virtual proposal center and focusing on excellence can be tremendous. According to Chandler, Cisco has seen dramatic cost savings in real estate, energy, and travel, while seeing win rates climb. The use of virtual proposal teams is a trend that is only likely to grow in the coming years.

## Surviving and Prospering

In tough economic times, support organizations often feel the sharp edge of the budgetary paring knife. To keep your proposal operation from falling victim to cost-cutting measures, there are a couple of things you should do.

First, publicize the proposal unit's contributions and successes regularly. Make sure senior management is aware of the group's value. Seek and publicize testimonials from influential internal clients who have been helped by your expertise. Issue quarterly summaries of accomplishments, and relentlessly advertise your own return on investment—the amount of business you have won compared to the cost of operating the proposal unit. You'll need to tread a fine line here, since you can't take all the credit for wins. If you do, you're likely to infuriate the sales organization. However, you can't retreat blushingly into silence, either. Give yourself some credit.

Second, expand the value you provide. One area you should think about seriously is providing generalized information management for the company, or at least for the sales and marketing organization. Chances are your proposal operation is the best-organized repository of facts and insights in the company. If you have created a library of reusable content, with effective search and retrieval tools to support it, you are closer to providing effective information management than are organizations that have spent millions on dedicated systems for that purpose. Look for opportunities to open access to your knowledge stores, publicize the importance of maintaining the information so that it is current and accurate, and make yourself indispensable to other areas of the company. Even if your firm considers having the sales force write most of the proposals, eliminating the need for a dedicated proposal center, they will have second and third thoughts about eliminating a useful information resource.

# 25 Special Challenges

Suppose you or someone you love needed a brain surgeon. No, really—try to imagine that situation. Or maybe treatment for cancer. Something extremely serious.

How would you go about choosing a doctor?

Here's what you wouldn't do. You wouldn't put a spreadsheet on the Web and invite submissions from doctors and medical groups who might be interested in providing brain surgery services to your family. And you wouldn't then take all of the spreadsheets and add up the various checkboxes and pricing information to decide which physician you're going to choose.

And yet all kinds of businesses and government agencies make buying decisions that way. Admittedly, they're not hiring a brain surgeon, but they are making choices that are nearly as important for their survival as an organization. They issue RFPs that are little more than Web-based forms or spreadsheets and then tell interested vendors to fill them out. No other information is required. Or welcome.

Requiring vendors to fill out reams of data and complete spreadsheets on pricing is a lousy way to buy anything. I've always believed that this kind of granular RFI or RFP actually gets in the way of making an intelligent buying decision. Here's why:

***The process is mindlessly reductive.*** It assumes that every product and service is a commodity. Most of us have enough sense to realize that for anything significant or important, price is not the only criterion that should guide our decision process. Go back to the example of choosing a physician to operate on your loved one—would your selection be based only on cost? Or would you want to know about the doctor's prior experience, how many surgeries of this type he or she has performed, whether the doctor is board certified, what others in the medical community think of this doctor's skills, whether the doctor has published results or demonstrated leadership in other ways? Most of all, you'd want to know if you can trust this doctor to do what's best for the patient and to communicate with you clearly, honestly, and empathetically. Buyers who depend on spreadsheets implicitly deny the relevance or importance of any value-added components, any differentiators, any distinctions in service delivery models, any special experience or personnel or tools. For these buyers, value has no value and relationships don't matter, either.

*It encourages consultants and brokers to create overly complex forms and complicated processes.* Unfortunately, it's in the consultant's self-interest to make the buying process as complex as possible and to minimize the meaningful differences among vendors. The consultants prefer to keep vendors at arm's length from the actual customer and to focus the customer's attention mainly on the consultant's ability to manipulate a huge amount of data. That's part of the reason the RFPs they issue are so complex, why they give you so little room to respond, and why they focus on technical details for the most part.

*It puts foolish limits on content.* Suppose I have a radically new way of handling your document storage requirements. It'll save you money, it's ecologically sensitive, and there's been nothing like it before. But you—or your consultant—have never heard of it, so you're requiring me to fill out an online form that was designed for the old-fashioned kind of document storage, the kind that involves putting paper in boxes and hauling it away in trucks and stacking it up in big warehouses. Who's really the loser here? Me? Or your business, which continues to buy the same old thing in the same old way because you (or your purchasing agents or your consultants) don't have the knowledge or imagination to ask the kinds of questions that let me make my case effectively? It makes more sense to provide an open-ended bid process that gives vendors more room to tell their story than a cell in a spreadsheet does.

*It virtually eliminates formatting.* Most online bid processes don't allow you to use even the simplest formatting tools—boldface type, bullet points, color, tables, or graphics. Basically, the prospect wants you to pour all of your content into their online blender so they can hit "puree" and see what pours out.

I urge all proposals writers to think carefully about responding to these kinds of RFPs. You must recognize that you may be dealing with someone who doesn't understand (or maybe doesn't believe in) differentiators or value. Is that going to work to your advantage? Perhaps this is the time to politely decline to bid.

But let's suppose you have to respond for whatever reason. Is there any way to make your proposal stand out?

First of all, if there are any areas of the RFP where you are allowed to enter free-form text, make sure you write as persuasively as possible. Second, write a well-structured, persuasive executive summary and use it as the covering e-mail when you submit your completed RFP online. Maybe nobody will read it, but it's not that much extra work and it might help. Third, if you make it past the first stage of reviews, make sure you seek a face-to-face meeting with the client and then develop an absolute killer proposal presentation, one that emphasizes your understanding of the client's needs, the value you can deliver, and the differentiators that set you apart.

## Dealing with Brokers, Consultants, and Other Necessary Evils

In today's complex business environment, many companies turn to consultants, brokers, or other outside resources to handle the bidding process.

As proposal writers, we tend to dread these situations. The broker or consultant is likely to manage the process tightly, keeping you at a distance from the actual client. That makes it hard to know if the Request for Proposal to which you're responding reflects the client's interests accurately or is more a product of the broker's convenience.

What do you do if the prospective client has already hired a consultant or a broker? Well, it's not an easy situation. Here are a few thoughts about how to deal with these situations:

✦ Most of these brokers will reuse the same RFP (or parts of it) over and over again. That gives you an opportunity to save time, because you can have an "ABC Broker" response already stored in your database. Or you can skew answers you use to commonly asked questions to address their particular orientation or bias.

✦ If the client has appointed a broker or consultant, request a joint meeting including both the broker and the client. Make it clear that you're not trying to get between them or usurp the broker's role, only that you want to understand how to offer the best possible solution. If the broker refuses to provide any access whatever, consider this a pretty big caution flag.

✦ If the broker's role is primarily to be an arm of purchasing, with the intent of driving costs down, or if the broker is using an e-procurement tool that makes it almost impossible to differentiate yourself, think carefully about responding. Do you really have a realistic chance of winning on price alone? You also need to consider whether you would be willing to agree to a split award, since it's not unusual for brokers or consultants to break up the award among several vendors. (Sometimes this leads to the best possible solution, but admittedly it also creates more complexity and further enhances the role of the broker.) Also, test to determine whether the broker intends to use some kind of reverse auction strategy to get you and a competitor or two locked in a pricing death spiral. If that's the plan, walk away.

✦ Sometimes what the client needs and what the broker asks for are at variance. Because the broker is a gatekeeper, you must respond to the RFP as written, even though you think it may not be addressing the most important issues. Pointing out that the RFP is wrong or misguided isn't going to win you any points. Chances are the client will never see your objections, because the broker will simply throw your bid out as being nonresponsive. Instead, respond to the RFP according to the rules so that you can make it past the first hurdle. You might consider including an optional approach, but make sure your primary recommendations are compliant with the RFP.

✦ If the RFP is too far off the mark, it's better to "no bid" the opportunity. If you win and the project fails, you know that the consultant won't admit that it was their poor analysis or badly written RFP that's at fault. As a result, it's absolutely vital that you have a robust and comprehensive bid/no bid process in place. Use it consistently. Don't second-guess yourself.

✦ Most gatekeepers have a narrow range of issues that they consistently emphasize. Track the issues that each major broker or consultant uses in making decisions and emphasize them in your proposals to those brokers.

✦ Keep track of your success rate with various consultants. Request a debriefing and find out what the decision criteria were. We can often learn a lot if we're willing to listen.

✦ If there are some brokers or consultants who never give you any work, no matter what, stop bidding on their projects. Why waste the time and resources? Write a letter to both the broker and the client and explain why you have chosen not to bid.

✦ On the other hand, it makes sense to launch a "sales" effort focused on the key brokers and consultants. Meet with them, find out what they're looking for, discuss with them what it will take to win, and figure out how you can make those brokers successful in their job as well as providing a good solution to the ultimate client.

## Writing in the Midst of a Storm— Dealing with Bad News and Negative Publicity

Every business relationship will hit a rough spot from time to time. The customer may be disappointed in our execution on a given contract. Negative press coverage may raise some concerns. As long as the experiences and the reportage aren't so bad that they become toxic to the relationship, we can usually recover. We regain trust through honesty, accuracy, and effective communication.

But what do you do if you're trying to write a proposal in the middle of churning seas of bad news? The kinds of negative publicity are legion—product defects, product recalls, lawsuits, accidents, regulatory violations, malicious tampering with your products in the marketplace, defections of key personnel, loss of a major client. All of these may cause eyebrows to go up and frowns to turn down.

Or what if you are trying to win business from a client who is currently unhappy with your firm? They have refused to sign off on the most recent phase of a project. They are invoking service-level agreements and demanding refunds. They are claiming that your product does not perform in full compliance with the specifications contained in their original RFP. They are unhappy because of personnel changes your company has made that affect their project.

What do you do during an oral proposal when you are ambushed by hostile questioning and negative attitudes from within the customer's decision team?

Figure 25-1 shows the range of options available to you in dealing with these situations, assuming that the accusations or bad news are basically correct. Lying, denying, and ignoring are negative approaches that are predicated on the notion that your customers (or the public in general) are stupid, that they have short memories and even shorter attention spans. History is full of examples of businesses that decided to use one of these approaches, only to have it blow up in their faces like a land mine. Sometimes ignoring bad news or negative publicity is probably the safest of the three bad choices, but as one vice president of sales memorably put it, "Bad news does not get better with age."

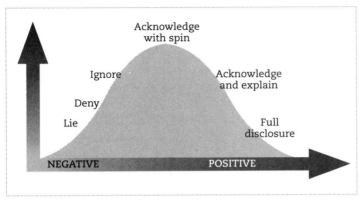

**Figure 25-1.** Ways to Handle Bad News.

That means you're better off confronting the situation directly. One option is to acknowledge that the situation is essentially true, but to put a spin on the way the facts are interpreted to minimize the damage. Thus, if your CEO was indicted on charges of embezzlement and tax fraud, you may want to indicate that although charges have been filed, not all the facts are yet known in the case. It would be unfair and contrary to the justice system to pronounce someone guilty before they have had a full and fair trial. In the meantime, the company is moving ahead with an acting CEO.

It's not great, but it may relieve some of the heat. A slightly more courageous approach is to acknowledge the facts as they are known and explain how this sad situation came to pass. In the case of a felonious CEO, your response might be that the indictment has been handed down and that although there is still much evidence and information that must be disclosed, at this time the company is changing the way sales are recorded and the way cash accounts are handled. The situation has brought to light weaknesses in the internal controls that are being fixed.

Finally, full disclosure is a rare and somewhat risky approach. Basically, you grab the advantage by telling the public everything and taking fast action to rectify the situation. The most famous example of this approach to dealing with bad news, the one that appears in textbooks, is the way Johnson & Johnson responded to the deadly product tampering associated with their pain reliever Tylenol. Rapid action, full disclosure, and aggressive change managed to preserve an extremely valuable brand name.

If you are writing a proposal, the "acknowledge and explain" approach is usually your best choice. It gives you the opportunity to be forthright without necessarily conceding that the situation is completely bad. Warren Buffett's advice on communicating during a crisis applies to the proposal writer or salesperson who is trying to close a deal during one, too:

+ Admit that not all of the facts are known.
+ State the facts that you do know.
+ Make sure you get them right. At this point, you start reestablishing trust by communicating accurately.
+ Quickly shift to a discussion of what you are doing to solve the problem, to minimize its impact, to correct any damage done, and to prevent similar problems from occurring in the future.

If you are a salesperson who is dealing directly with customers, candor is your best option. When the negative situation is based on the customer's unhappiness or dissatisfaction with your firm's performance, avoid blaming the customer for the problem. That's just not going to get you anywhere. It is reasonable, however, to point out that situations are never black and white, that there are a number of variables that have contributed to the current situation.

In your proposal and in your presentations, stick to your core message. In a proposal, that message is based on the assumption that the client has a need, that you can meet that need, and that you can deliver superior value in the process. The negative news or unpleasant experience is undercutting the issues of credibility, but if you have the problem right and if you have a compelling value proposition, all is not lost. Focus on total value and work hard to find external champions—members of the profession, industry experts, even attorneys, accountants, or other professional advisers—who will speak on your behalf.

One approach to take if the customer's unhappiness is based on poor execution of contract terms by your team is to acknowledge that there have been problems. Explain that in the process of defining those problems and developing a corrective action plan, you and your colleagues have gained knowledge about the client environment that a new vendor simply would not possess. As a result, no one is better positioned to solve the problems than you are and no one is better able to avoid them in the future. This is a tightrope and you may be greeted by skepticism, but you need to say, "Yes, there have been problems, we may have underestimated the challenge at the outset, but we fully understand it now and we are the best choice to manage the project to a successful conclusion."

When dealing with bad news in either your written or your oral proposal, you may want to reframe the issue. By reframing, you change the nature of the questions being directed at you in the RFP or during the question-and-answer period following your presentation. Here are typical reframing statements:

+ This is an important issue, of course, but we believe the most important issue is . . .
+ You're right to be concerned, and what we have done is . . .
+ In the past that was a problem, but let's focus on what we have done about it because those changes will help guarantee a successful project for you . . .
+ It's important to look at what the facts are, all of the facts, and to separate the facts from rumors . . .
+ This is a complex issue. We are continuing to gather information and opinions from experts and a variety of sources, both within our company and from outside, including . . .

What if the bad news that has been reported about your company is actually false? In a way your task is more difficult. In public opinion, as in logic, you can't prove a negative. I can't prove beyond doubt that I never cheated on my taxes, that I never short-shipped a load, that I never mishandled radioactive materials in my lab. In a situation where you are trying to refute something that is false, your best options are to draw upon third-party evidence to establish a strong record of performance. Also, focus on the policies and procedures in place that were designed to prevent exactly the kind of problem your firm is accused of. If possible, provide documentation that the processes, policies, and procedures were monitored and followed. You might be able to use traditional forms of credibility-building content, such as references and case studies, to counterbalance false accusations. Finally, if you know that what is being claimed is not true, you might consider offering guarantees, service-level commitments, or other tactics designed to minimize the customer's perception of risk.

Sometimes the bad situation arises from the client having had a negative experience with you, either during earlier phases of the same project on which you're bidding or in conjunction with completely different contracts. Maybe there was a cost overrun. Maybe you missed a critical deadline. Perhaps your firm's work was judged to be substandard. You might have failed to meet your service-level commitments, or you might have had an unacceptably high level of turnover during the course of the project. Whatever the specifics of the negative experience might be, you're now in a very difficult position. It's tough to climb back. If we hark back to our discussion of the primacy principle in Chapter 6, you can see that the same concept applies here. People assume that what they have experienced already in working with you will be normative of future experiences. Research suggests that it may take as many as seven positive experiences to overcome the negative one.

To recover lost ground, acknowledge the problems. Don't blame the customer for them, even if you believe that they were largely caused by failings on the customer's part. In your proposal, aggressively reposition your firm. Accept ownership and responsibility for making things right. In your proposal content, focus on the lessons learned and the changes made to your management philosophy, product design, service delivery model, or whatever needs to be improved.

For example, if you are bidding for a services contract, one that you have had for a while and done poorly on, you should try to restore the customer's trust by indicating that you will provide, among other things:

+ A new, better-trained staff
+ Better management controls and greater accountability
+ Improved methodology
+ Enhanced resources or equipment
+ Explicit commitment to success from your top management
+ Value-added components that exceed the customer's expectations
+ Financial options that provide for penalties if key deliverables are missed

The only completely unacceptable approach is to suggest in your proposal that the client will be getting more of the same. Why on earth would they want that?

When hostile questions are being fired at you—whether it's during a sales presentation or an oral proposal—take a deep breath and remind yourself that you're not on trial here. You have the right to decline answering hostile, antagonistic, or adversarial questions. However, you're better off answering if you can.

You will find that you get better results if you structure your answers to the difficult questions in the three-part format we discussed in Chapter 15 for significant RFP answers. First, restate the question, acknowledge that it's a good question, and clarify any aspects of it that might be misleading, unclear, or inflammatory. Next, validate that the customer's concern is relevant and appropriate. Finally, provide the details that answer or address the question, focusing on any value-added components of your answer, if possible. For example, suppose you are proposing to provide healthcare insurance to a company and one of the decision team attacks your company for its refusal to pay claims from chiropractors, massage therapists, acupuncturists, and similar practitioners. You might say:

*Your question focuses on determining eligibility for various forms of what are sometimes called nontraditional treatments. This is a very relevant question, given the rise of noninvasive and holistic medical treatments, Eastern methods, and approaches to wellness. The entire medical industry has been challenged in this regard, and often the patient population has been ahead of the industry in general. Part of the problem is that we must take a conservative approach to approving new treatment modalities based on questions of efficacy, liability, and standards of care. However, we have changed our coverage options to recognize the growth of alternative therapies and to provide plan members with greater flexibility in establishing a treatment regimen that works for them and that they believe in. For example, we now provide . . .*

When you're faced with the challenge of writing a proposal or presenting a solution during a period of negative coverage or during a crisis, ask yourself what part of the trust relationship is broken. Is it your firm's credibility? Is it the sense of rapport and shared values? Is it the client's perception that working with you is relatively risk free? Keep your content as accurate as possible and strive to overcome negative news with superior value.

Above all, don't bluff and don't lie. Just like your momma told you, honesty is the best policy. Even if you lose this particular battle and don't win the business, your candor and directness may go a long way toward healing the wounds and helping the client start to trust your firm in the future.

Then the business cycle can begin again.

# Index